METAPHYSICS OF POWER

JULIUS EVOLA

METAPHYSICS OF POWER

ARKTOS
LONDON 2021

ISBN	978-1-914208-09-6 (Paperback)
	978-1-914208-10-2 (Hardback)
	978-1-914208-11-9 (Ebook)
TRANSLATION	John Bruce Leonard
COVER & LAYOUT	Tor Westman

 Arktos.com fb.com/Arktos @arktosmedia

CONTENTS

NOTE FROM THE TRANSLATOR

THE FOLLOWING BOOK contains a selection from the manifold articles which Julius Evola published over the course of his life on a variety of subjects. Most are translated here for the first time. They have been chosen especially for their bearing on the question of political philosophy and political regimes, topics which Evola naturally addresses throughout the corpus of his books, but to which topic he himself never dedicated a single major work, save perhaps his very early *Pagan Imperialism*. Yet his cornucopic article writing, published over the course of many decades and in a variety of Italian journals, contains a great many insightful and illuminating jewels regarding his views on political things, and given the growing interest in Traditionalism broadly and Evola in particular, it has seemed to me timely to produce a volume that might address and rectify some of the confusions that have lately emerged regarding Evola's thought on these matters, as well as furnishing further intellectual and spiritual arms for all those who would stand against the encroaching chaos of our fast-declining day. The reader will find herein, among a great many other things, clarification on Evola's ideas regarding such central topics to our own day as democracy and liberalism, freedom and authoritarianism, activism, family, education, and the possibility (and possible means) of rejuvenating Tradition in our rudderless times.

As ever in my translations of Julius Evola, I have attempted as much as possible to preserve the tone and spirit of Evola's original — a tone of high culture and high contemplation, an excellence of language which is scornful of the democratic facility and cloying banality of our day's general parlance. Where Evola has introduced an Italian neologism, I have not hesitated to do the same in English, and where Evola has prefered an abstruse word to a common, I have sought an equally rare English cognate. The use of abundant foreign terms and phrases, especially from Latin, Greek and French, which characterises all of Evola's work, has been duplicated in this translation. Where it has seemed useful, I have provided elucidating footnotes. It has been necessary in many places to truncate Evola's elaborate Italianate structures, particularly where they prove so complex and unwieldy in English as to obscure the sense; but I have not shied from lengthy renderings of Evola's longer formulations, nor have I attempted in any way to smoothe out the often fine contours of his subtle thought. I have moreover retained his use of the halfway impersonal 'we', in preference to the much more common 'I'; I am aware of the unusual, and perhaps excessively formal, sound of this in English, but I am convinced that it reflects something of the spirit of the Baron's work and the nature of his message. I also suspect that the use of the first-person singular would often add a personalistic colouration to his words that I sense he would implicitly shun.

It is difficult to maintain such fidelity in the transference from a Romance language to an Anglo-Saxon one, yet I reckon that our tongue is resilient enough to bend even round such tight corners as these, and I hope to have done some service, through my English rendering, to Evola's finely crafted, lofty and razor-sharp Italian.

JBL

THE STATE

1. ON THE DECLINE OF THE IDEA OF THE STATE

I F WE ARE TO STUDY the process of decline which the idea of the State has suffered in recent times, and if we are to study this process, not in its exterior and consequential aspects, but rather in its deep causes and in its entire bearing, then we must take as our point of reference a general vision of history centred on the perception of a fundamental phenomenon: the phenomenon, that is, of the *regression of the castes*. This vision is important for its double characteristic of being at one and the same time *current* and *traditional*.

It is current insofar as it corresponds to a more or less precise sensation which is today heralded in a variety of almost contemporaneous ways in the writers of various nations. The doctrine of Pareto regarding the 'circulation of the elites' already contains this conception *in ovo*.[1] And while we ourselves alluded to it through specific reference to the ancient caste system in our book *Pagan Imperialism*,

---

1   Vilfredo Pareto (1848–1923) was an Italian political scientist and sociologist, but also an engineer. He was responsible for a number of very interesting theories, among which that cited by Evola here, according to which every society, no matter its governmental form, will always have a ruling elite, and that when it appears that this elite has been dissolved or overthrown, it is merely substituted with another. Julius Evola mentions Pareto often in his work, and devotes a laudatory essay to him in Chapter 30 of *Recognitions* (Arktos: 2018). — Trans.

which was at once our battle cry,[2] it has been expounded in a more
definitive and systematic form in France by René Guénon[3] and in
Germany (albeit with a number of extremistic exaggerations) by Berl.[4]
Finally, and most significantly, a similar conception has appeared today in a work animated by the '*squadrista*' spirit, and has in that work
furnished the premises necessary to denounce the 'cowardice of the
twentieth century'.[5]

But our argument has a second and more generic claim to currency, owing to the spiritual 'climate' which has come both philo-
sophically and culturally to replace the ponderous positivistic myths
of yesterday. As can easily be intuited, the notion of a regression of the
castes has presuppositions strictly antithetical to those of the progres-
sivistic and evolutionistic ideologies which the rationalistic-Jacobin
mindset has introduced even into the sphere of science and historical
methodology. This mindset has elevated to the level of an absolute
truth that which is suitable, at bottom, at most to the situation of a
parvenu: the idea that the higher derives from the lower, civilisation
from barbarisms, man from beast, and so forth; until it issues finally
in the myths of Marxist economy and the Sovietic evangelicals of
'technological messianism'. In part under the impetus of certain

---

2   Italian: *libro di battaglia*, literally, a 'battle book'. This follows the Italian idiom
    cavallo di battaglia, meaning literally a 'warhorse', but metaphorically indicat-
    ing a flagship enterprise or a signature song or piece in the case of a musician or
    artist. — Trans.

3   René Guénon, *Autorité spirituelle et pouvoir temporel* (translated *Spiritual
    Authority and Temporal Power*), 1929.

4   Heinrich Berl, *Die Heraufkunft des fünften Standes* (*The Advent of the Fifth
    Estate*), 1931. [Trans. note: Evola discusses this book at greater length in his in
    Chapter 3 'The Advent of the 'Fifth Estate'' of his last book, *Recognitions*, avail-
    able from Arktos Media Ltd.]

5   Reference to the eponymous book (*Vigliaccheria del XX secolo*, published in
    1933) by Giuseppe Attilio Fanelli, not to be confused with the revolutionary
    anarchist of the previous century of the same name. The former Fanelli was
    an early Fascist, but was expelled from the party in 1923. He remained a firm
    supporter of corporatism and of the monarchy. — Trans.

tragic experiences, which have dispelled the mirages of an ingenuous optimism, in part on account of a true interior upheaval, such evolutionalistic superstitions, at least in their most one-sided and pretentious aspect, have been banished today from the most conscious and revolutionary forces. The possibility therefore arises of recognising a different, contrary conception of history, one which is new, but at the same time remote and 'traditional'. The doctrine of the regression of the castes in its relationship with the idea of the decline of the State is surely one of the fundamental expressions of this conception of history.

The fact of the matter is that, in the place of the recent materialistic and 'democratic' myth of evolution, the greatest civilisations of the past uniformly recognised the right and the truth of the opposite conception, which we may analogically call 'aristocratic'. This conception affirms the nobility of the origins, and it perceives in the course of recent times, rather than any kind of acquisition of truly superior values, an erosion, a corruption and a decline. But here, so as not to give the impression that we are passing from one kind of superficial partiality to another, we must also observe that in the traditional conceptions which we have mentioned the concept of involution almost always figures as an element in a much vaster 'cyclical' conception; and this conception, though in a rather amateurish form, and constrained by narrower and more hypothetical horizons, has today made its reappearance in the theories regarding the ascending auroral phases and the descending twilight phases of the 'cycle' of the various civilisations, as can be seen in the work of Spengler, Frobenius or Ligeti.

This observation is not without its importance for the intention of the present writing. Indeed, we do not at all intend here to tendentiously emphasise viewpoints which accidentally align with those of 'sinister prophets': we intend rather to objectively specify certain of the aspects of the history of politics, which become visible the moment one takes a higher point of view. And if by this route we will have occasion to note negative phenomena in the society and in the political formation of recent times, we do not intend to recognise in this fact a kind of destiny, so much as to identify the traits of that alternative which we must before all realistically and manfully recognise if we are to proceed to a possible and true reconstruction. Thus, our study will be divided into three parts.

First, we will consider the 'traditional' antecedents to the doctrine in question, which consist essentially in the 'doctrine of the four ages'. We will then pass over to examine the schema from which the idea of the regression of the castes draws its specific sense, so as to identify this idea historically and to consider in all of its degrees and aspects the progressive fall of the idea of the State. Finally, we will offer considerations regarding the elements which the clarified conception offers us, both for generally comprehending the most characteristic politico-social phenomena of our times, and for determining the paths which are apt to carry us toward a better European future — toward the reconstruction of the idea of the State.

1. — The traditional sensation of an involutionary process realising itself in recent times — a process for which the most characteristic term is the Eddic epithet of Ragnarökkr (the obfuscation of the divine) — far from remaining vague and incorporeal, once constituted an organically articulated doctrine, which can be found a little in every part of the world with a wide and striking degree of uniformity: *the doctrine of the four ages*. A process of gradual spiritual decadence through four cycles or 'generations' — *this* was how the sense of history was traditionally conceived. The best-known form of this doctrine is that of the Greco-Roman tradition.

Hesiod speaks of the four ages which are characterised symbolically by four metals, gold, silver, bronze and iron, through which, from a life 'similar to that of the gods', humanity passed to social forms that were ever more dominated by impiety, by violence and by injustice.[6] The Indo-Aryan tradition posits the same doctrine in the terms of four cycles, the last of which has the significant name of 'dark age' — *kali yuga*. These cycles were accompanied with the image of the gradual failure, in each of them, of the four 'feet' or supports of the Bull, which symbolises *dharma*, or the traditional law of non-human origin, by which each being is allocated its right place in the social hierarchy defined by the castes.[7] The Iranic conception is similar to the Indo-Aryan and Hellenic, and the same can be said for the Chaldaic conception. The same idea finds some echo in the Jewish tradition, albeit in a peculiar transposition, in the prophetism which speaks of a splendid statue, whose head is gold, whose chest and arms are silver, whose abdomen is copper and whose feet are iron and clay: a statue which in its different parts (and as we will see this division has a singular correspondence with that which determined, according to Vedic tradition, the four principal castes of primordial man) represents four 'kingdoms', one following upon another, beginning from the 'gold' of the 'the king of kings, to whom the God of heaven has given sovereignty, power, strength, and glory'.[8]

This motif is not only reproduced in Egypt (with certain variants that it is needless to examine and explain here) but even across the ocean, in the ancient imperial Aztec traditions. The relation between the doctrine of the four ages — which to a certain extent is projected in myth or within the penumbras of the highest prehistory — and the doctrine of the regression of the castes and the related decline of the idea of the State can be established in two ways. First of all, by means of traditional man's very conception of time and of the unfolding of events in time. For traditional man, time does not flow uniformly and indefinitely, but rather fragments into cycles or periods, each point of which has its own individuality, and all of which together constitute the organic completion of a whole. The specific chronological

---

6 Hesiod, *Works and Days*, 109 et seq.

7 *Mânava-dharmasâstra*, I, 81 et seq.

8 Daniel 2:37–38.

duration of a cycle might vary. Quantitatively unequal periods could
be grouped together, given only that each of them had reproduced
all the moments typical of a given cycle. On this basis, an analogical
correspondence traditionally held between the greater cycles and the
lesser, which permitted one to consider one and the same tempo, so to
speak, on octaves of varying size.[9] Effective correspondences thus hold
between the rhythm 'four' as a figure in universal key for the doctrine
of the four ages on the one hand, and the rhythm 'four' as a figure in a
narrower, more concrete and historical sphere on the other, in relation
to the progressive descent of political authority from one to the other
of the four ancient castes. And the characteristic points in the first
doctrine, which are presented as myths — which is to say superhistori-
cally — can for this very reason introduce themselves into the sense of
concrete and analogically corresponding historical upheavals.

The second justification for our bringing the two doctrines into
relation lies in this: that in the hierarchy of the four principal castes, as
it was traditionally conceived, we find fixed, so to speak, in immobile
coexistence, as superimposed strata of the social whole, those values
and forces which would gradually come to dominate in each of the
four great periods, through the dynamics of a historical becoming,
albeit a regressive one. We cannot venture here into an investigation
which we have already undertaken in all due breadth elsewhere.[10] We
limit ourselves to observing that with respect to the highest caste, that
of the stock of divine kings, and in the very concept of the function
which these incarnated, there can be found recurrent expressions,
symbols and figurations wheresoever this caste manifests, which
always and uniformly correspond to those the myths refer to as the
generations of the first cycle, of the golden age.

While we have already seen that in the Jewish tradition the first
golden epoch stands in direct relation with the supreme concept of

9 Cf. Hubert-Mauss, *Mélanges de Histoire des Religions* (*Miscellanea on the
History of Religion*, not translated into English), Paris, 1929, pp. 189 et seq.
10 Cf. J. Evola, *Revolt Against the Modern World*, Trans. 2007, Part II.

regality, there is a legendary relation between the god of that era and Janus in the classical; this is significant, because the latter stood symbolically for a function which was simultaneously regal and pontifical. In the Indo-Aryan tradition the golden age is that in which the regal function, wholly awakened, operates through truth and justice, while the dark age is that in which this function 'sleeps';[11] in the Egyptian tradition the first dynasty has the attributes of the solar and Osirified kings, 'the lords of the two crowns', conceived of as transcendent beings; and even in the traditions of Iranified Hellenism the sovereigns not rarely took on the symbolic insignia of Apollo-Mithras, understood as the solar king of 'those in the golden age'. On the other hand, it would be easy to demonstrate that the last epochs, the dark age, or the iron age, or the age of the 'wolf', is represented directly or indirectly by the dominion of the 'nether' forces — the promiscuous forces tied to material and to work as to a dark destiny — *ponos*.[12] The lowest caste corresponded to this in the traditional hierarchy ('the dark age', it is explicitly said,[13] is that age characterised by the advent of the power of the servant caste, which is to say, of the pure *demos*). Meanwhile, with regard to the intermediary epoch, whether it be the epoch of the 'demigods' as 'heroes' (Hellas) or that in which the king is characterised only by 'energetic action' (India), or in which Titanic forces appear in a state of rebellion (the *Eddas*, the Bible), we are referred more or less directly to the principle proper to the 'warrior' caste. Let this suffice so far as concerns the 'traditional' framework for that view of history which we will now proceed to consider in its essential traits.

2. — As our premise, we must of course clarify and justify that which we have called 'traditional hierarchy', as well as the very notion of caste itself. The fundamental idea is that of a State, not merely as an

---

11 *Mânava-dharmasâstra*, IX, 302.

12 The reference is to the Ancient Greek πόνος, meaning primarily pain or suffering, and hence work, task, business or toil. — Trans.

13 *Vishnu-purâna*, VI, I.

organism, but as a spiritualised organism, such as might by degrees
lift the individual from a pre-personal naturalistic life into a supernatural and super-personal life, through a system of 'participation' and
of subordinations such as might constantly guide every single class
of beings and every form of activity back to a single central axis. We
are dealing here with a politico-social hierarchy with an essentially
spiritual foundation, in which each caste or class corresponds to a
determinate *typical* form of activity and a clearly determined function
in the whole.

This meaning took on peculiar relief in the Indo-Aryan conception, which, beyond the four principal castes, conceived of the higher
castes rather than the servile as the 'divine' element of 'those who are
reborn' — *dvija* — culminating in 'those who are like to the sun', as
against the 'demonic' element — *asurya* — of the 'dark' beings — *krsh-
na*.[14] In this way, one of the modern authors we have already cited,
Berl,[15] takes his premise from a dynamic-antagonistic conception of
traditional hierarchy, almost a battle between *cosmos* and *chaos*: the
sacred aristocracy would incorporate the 'divine' into its function of
Olympic order, and the mass would incorporate the 'demonic' (not
in the moral Christian sense, but in the sense of its being a pure
naturalistic element). Each tends to drag the other along with it, and
each of the intermediate forms corresponds to a given mixture of the
opposite elements. So far as the reason behind the quadripartition
goes — with *four* principal castes — it proceeds from analogy with the
human organism itself. Thus, for example, the four castes in the Vedic
tradition[16] are brought to correspond to four fundamental parts of
the 'body' of primordial man — and everyone knows the use made of
such analogies for the organic justification of the State, which can be

---

14 Cf. Albrecht Weber, *Indische Studien* (*Indian Studies*, not translated into
    English), v. X (Leipzig, 1868), pp. 4–8; E. Sénart, *Les castes dans l'Inde* (*The
    Castes in India*. Paris, 1896), p. 67.

15 H. Berl, *Die Heraufkunft des fünften Standes*, cit., pp. 18, 27.

16 *Rig-Veda*, X, 90, 11–12.

found both in Greece (Plato)[17] and in Rome. In reality, every higher organism presents four distinct but mutually supportive functions in a hierarchical connection: at the lower limit are the undifferentiated pre-personal energies of pure vitality. These however are dominated by the system of vital exchanges and the general organic economy (the system of vegetative life).

Next, the *will* is superordinated to this system, as that which moves and directs the body as a whole in space and time. Finally, at the summit, a power of liberty and intellect, the spirit as the supernatural principle of the human personality. Transposed in terms of social hierarchy, it is precisely this which forms the analogical reason for the four ancient Indo-Aryan castes: in respective correspondence to the subpersonal vitality, organic economy, will and spirituality, therefore stood the four distinct castes of the serfs, or *çudra* (the affluent, agricultural, commercial); the industrial bourgeois (within ancient limits), or *vaiçya*; the warrior aristocracy, or *kshatriya*; and finally a purely spiritual aristocracy that furnished the 'divine kings', or the virile priestly natures, the 'solar initiates' who, conceived of as 'more than men', appeared to the eyes of all, unimpugnably and above all other men, as those who had the legitimate right to command, and who possessed the dignity of Lords: and it was in a certain sense the *brâhmana* (we will later explain why it was only 'in a certain sense') who represented this latter caste in ancient Aryan India.

We call this quadripartion 'traditional', and not simply Hindu, because it can effectively be found in a more or less complete form in various other civilisations: the Egyptian, the Persian, the Hellenic (to some extent), the Mexican,[18] even reaching so far as our Medieval Period, which demonstrates the social super-national quadripartition

---

17   Probably a reference to Plato's *Republic*, though the primary comparison of that dialogue is not the state to the organic body, but the state to the soul. See in particular Book IV, beginning from 436a. — Trans.

18   By which Evola certainly means to indicate the civilisations that existed before the arrival of the Spaniards in the territory now belonging to Mexico. — Trans.

into the servant class, the bourgeois (the Third Estate), the nobility and the priesthood.

Here we are dealing with more or less complete applications, now in the form of classes, now in the form of authentic castes, of one and the same principle, whose value stands independent from its historical realisations and which, in any case, presents us with an ideal scheme capable of bringing us to comprehend the true sense of the historico-political development of the thresholds of these so-called historical periods, all the way up to our own days. Given the overall meaning of the hierarchical system, it would be inexact to qualify it as 'theocratic', and would lead to confusions, given the present acceptation of that word. While one sees 'theocracy' in the type of a State governed by a priestly class, as it appears in the most recent forms of Western religion, this is not the case for the constitutions in question. At the apex of the hierarchy, in its truly originating political forms, we find rather an indissoluble synthesis between the two powers, the royal and the priestly, the temporal and the spiritual, in a single person, who is conceived almost as the incarnation of a transcendent force.

The *rex* was simultaneously *deus et pontifex*,[19] and here, this last word is to be taken in the anological transposition of its etymological sense of 'maker of bridges' (Festus, St. Bernard): the king, as *pontifex*, was the maker of bridges between the natural and the supernatural, and in him was eminently recognised the presence of that force from on high, capable of animating rites and sacrifices, which in turn were conceived as objective transcendent actions capable of invisibly supporting the State and propitiating the 'fortune' and 'victory' of a race.[20] If we turn our gaze from Ancient China and Ancient Japan to Ancient Egypt, the earliest royal Hellenic-Achaean and then Roman forms, the primordial Nordic lineages, the dynasties of the Incas and so forth, we see this concept represented everywhere. We do not find at the zenith

---

19 All Latin phrases. *Rex* is 'king'; *deus et pontifex* means 'god and bridge-builder'. — Trans.

20 Cf. again J. Evola, *Revolt Against the Modern World*, I, §1 et seq.

a priestly caste or church; we see that the 'divine regality' did not receive its dignity and authority from any exterior source (as occurred when the rite of investiture arose). As was said in Ancient China, and as was repeated in the Ghibelline ideology of the Holy Roman Empire, it had its 'mandate from Heaven' directly, and presented itself as a kind of *'superhumanity'*, both virile and spiritual at the same time.

It is essential that we clearly establish this point, so that we can identify where, *ideally* speaking, the regressive process began within the traditionally higher political ideal. In this ideal, the hierarchy of the four classes or castes (we cannot distinguish between class and caste here, nor indicate the metaphysical premises by which an endogamic closure was justified)[21] therefore made sensible the progressive degrees of an elevation of the personality in correspondence with interests and forms of activity which grew ever freer from the bonds of immediate and natural living. For, as compared to the anonymity of the masses intent on merely living, the organisers of work, the patriarchal possessors of land, already represented the sketch of a 'type', of a 'person'.

But in the heroic ethos of the warrior, the active overcoming of human limits is already clear enough, the force of a 'more than life', enthroned as the calm domination of the lord, *lex animata in terris*.[22] The ideal of fidelity — *bhakti*, the Indo-Aryans called it, *fides* as the Romans knew it, *fides*, *Treue* and *trust* as it was repeated in the Medieval Period — in the double form of fidelity to one's own nature and fidelity to the higher castes, produced the solidity of the hierarchy and formed the path toward a dignifying participation of the lower in the higher through service, dedication, and obedience before a principle of eminently spiritual authority. And it is precisely where the regime of the castes — as in India — had its greatest rigour that we see the highest castes imposing themselves, not through violence, nor

---

21 Cf. Ibid., I, §15.

22 Latin: 'the law given life on earth'. — Trans.

through wealth, but rather through the profound dignity of the function that corresponded to their nature.

With this, we have all the elements necessary to comprehend the course of the latest times as a gradual decline of the power, of the authority and of the idea of the State — as indeed of the values and predominate values thereof — from one to the other of the levels corresponding to the four ancient castes.

3. — Indeed, the epoch of the power of the 'divine regality' recedes so deeply into the penumbra of prehistory that today it is extremely difficult for most men, if it is not impossible for them, to reconstruct its right sense. Either one believes that one is dealing with myths and superstitions, or else one reduces everything to the aforementioned little hasty scholastic formula: 'theocracy'. And whenever anyone still remembers what up until yesterday subsisted of the vestiges of this primordial and sacral conception — namely, the doctrine of the divine right of Kings — still he wholly ignores the effective premises of this doctrine, nor is he able in any case to reintegrate it into the whole vision of life and of the *sacrum*, from which it originally drew its power and its 'legitimacy' in the higher and objective sense of the word.

Of course, it would be presumptuous of us to wish to identify, historically speaking, the causes of the decline of the idea of the State from that supreme level, so far does this phenomenon recede into the unsteady terrain of prehistory. Nonetheless, in the ideal sphere, something can be said with a sufficient margin of likelihood, following the concordant testimonies that the oral and written traditions of all peoples furnish us: we find the signs of frequent opposition among the representatives of the two powers, the one spiritual and the other temporal, whatever special forms the one power or the other might take on to adapt to the variety of circumstances.

This phenomenon of opposition could not possibly be original, and indeed in ideal terms signals the beginning of decadence. We can say that the primordial synthesis, expressed by the notion of the Divine Regality, was replaced by the separation of and then the antithesis between spiritual power and temporal power; these are to be understood in the terms of a spirituality which is no longer regal but only priestly, and a regality which is no longer spiritual and sacred but simply and materially 'political' and laical. The hierarchical tension slackens, the apex collapses, and something like a fracture is produced, which must fatally persist, until it comes to erode the fundamental integrity of the traditional whole.

In this respect, the coming to power of a simply priestly caste expresses either a renunciation from on high, a usurpation from below, or both of these things together, and marks the initial trait of a descending arc. It would be useless to say that we find ourselves here before a relatively recent phenomenon. The same primacy that the priestly *brâhmana* caste won for itself in India is probably to be considered as the effect of the importance that was ever more assumed by the *purohita*, the priests originally at the service of the king, who was himself once conceived of as 'a great god in human form';[23] and this change occurred when the original unity of the Aryan races underwent its dispersion.[24]

In Egypt, up until about the XXI dynasty, the solar king delegated a priest for the performance of rites only in exceptional cases, and the priestly authority remained ever a reflection of the regal; only later was the priestly dynasty of Thebes constituted, to the detriment of the royal dynasty.[25] This is an upheaval which, moreover, appeared also in Iran, but was repressed with the ousting of the priest Gaumata, who had sought to usurp the royal dignity.

---

23 *Mânava-dharmasâstra*, VII, 8.

24 Cf. H.F.K. Gûnther, *Die nordische Rasse bei den Indogermanen Asiens* (The Nordic Race in Indo-Germanic Asia, not translated in English; Munich, 1934), pp. 46 et seq.

25 Cf. A. Moret, *Le caractère religieux de la royautée pharaonique* (The Religious Character of Pharaonic Royalty, not translated in English. Paris, 1902), pp. 314 et seq.

In Rome, according to the tradition, the *rex sacrorum*[26] could not be constituted save by the delegation of a power which, from the founding of Rome up to the times of Numa, the king conserved for himself, and which the sovereign took once again for himself in the imperial period — and phenomena of this kind can certainly be observed elsewhere. In any case, the affirmation of Pope Gelasius I, that 'after Christ, no man can be at the same time king and priest', which stigmatised the aspiration of the kings to assume a sacred dignity as diabolical temptation and the hubris of mere creatures,[27] will be sufficiently conclusive so far as the development of the aforementioned phenomenon is concerned: in the same way that we must recognise behind the Ghibelline demands of the medieval emperors and the very character itself of the great Knightly Crusader Orders an attempt at times manifest and at times occult, and unfortunately for the most part anachronistic and uncertain, to rebuild the synthesis of the two powers, of the regal and the sacral, of the heroic and the ascetic — and, recognising this background to those orders, we must see the struggle between Empire and Church as the final episode of an affair which takes its origins in the very beginnings of the process of decline we have just examined.

And it is surely a process of decline which we are here describing, for this reason: that, from the separation of these two powers, a dualism commenced which was doubly destructive — the dualism of a spirituality which is rendered ever more abstract, 'ideal', incorporeal, supermundane in the bad and renunciatory sense, on the one hand, and on the other, of a political reality which is made ever more material, secularised, laical, agnostic, dominated by interests and by forces that not only belong to the merely 'human', but finally also to the sub-human, to the pre-personal element of the pure collective.

---

26 Latin: 'king of the sacred'. — Trans.

27 *De anathematis vinculo*, 18. Cf. A. Dempf, *Sacrum imperium* (trans. It. Messina, 1933), pp. 73–74 of the Italian translation. [This book has not been translated into English. — Trans.]

Once the apex has collapsed, the first decisive phenomenon in this decline, with which the centre passes from the *first* to the *second* of the four castes, can be defined as the 'revolt of the warriors'. This phenomenon too has approximately universal traits, and is expressed not only in real or legendary history, but also in myths: almost all peoples, often in relation to the doctrine of the four ages (above all in the bronze age or the age of the 'wolf' or the 'axe' or of the 'heroes' in a limited sense) bear the memory of more or less 'Luciferian' revolts, of races of 'giants' — the biblical *nephelim* — or of titans, or of non-gods — the Indo-Aryan *raksasa* and the *asura* — which rise against figures symbolising a divine spirituality, often just to affirm the principle of war or of mere violence — which is to say, a distortion of the principle proper to the warrior caste — or to usurp a symbolical fire, which however transforms into a motif of Promethean torment. And when it is not a question precisely of usurpation (which means, in concrete terms: of the attempt on the part of a simply temporal power to subordinate and reduce the spiritual authority, albeit an authority which has become merely 'priestly', to the status of *instrumentum regni*),[28] we perceive in any case a revolt which is synonymous with simple abdication and mutilation. Guénon very justly observes[29] that each caste, putting itself into revolt and aspiring to constitute itself as an automaton, degrades itself in some way, insofar as it loses with this very act the participation and the faculty of recognition of a higher principle — loses its own character, which it possessed in the hierarchical whole, in order to assume that of the caste immediately inferior. To refer to historical horizons which are nearer to us, this descent occurred upon the advent of the epoch of the 'warrior kings', which is visible above all in Europe.

No longer a manfully spiritual aristocracy, but only a secularised *military* comes to stand at the heads of States: this is true even of the

---

28 Latin: 'instruments of rule', in the sense of mere means toward the end of governing. — Trans.

29 René Guénon, *Autorité spirituelle et pouvoir temporel*, op. cit., p. 111.

last great European monarchies. Qualities which are above all *ethical* in nature define this aristocracy: a certain intimate nobility, a certain greatness and heroic superiority connected to the heredity of a selected *blood* and also physical prowess and natural prestige, which are the common marks of the most recent and already secularised type of the aristocrat.

Guénon justly observes that it becomes more appropriate at this point to speak of 'power' rather than 'authority',[30] as the former almost inevitably evokes the idea of potency or force, and above all a material force, a potency with a visible external manifestation and which is affirmed by employing external means, while spiritual authority, interior by its very essence, is affirmed by nothing save itself, independently of any sensible support, and is exercised, in a certain sense, invisibly: inasmuch as one can still speak here of authority, it is only through an analogous transposition.

Let us proceed now to consider the second collapse, by force of which the centre of the warrior caste is brought yet lower, down to the caste of the *merchants*. If we take our bearings by the history of Europe, this second collapse announces itself with the twilight of the Holy Roman Empire — indeed, already with the work begun by Philip the Fair. Spiritual authority, transforming itself into temporal power, has as its characteristic a materialistic and devastating hypertrophy of the principle of state *centralisation*. The sovereign fears to lose his prestige over those who are, at bottom, by now his equals, which is to say the various feudal Princes; and to consolidate this prestige, he does not scruple to oppose the nobility itself, allying himself with the Third Estate and not hesitating to support the demands of this Estate against the nobility.

Thus, in order to centralise itself and to absorb within itself the powers that belong collectively to the whole nobility, we see regality enter into conflict with this nobility, working toward the destruction

---

30 Ibid., p. 30.

of feudalism, though it itself arose from the same: and it cannot attain this destruction without relying on the support of the Third Estate, which corresponds to the *vaiçya* [the Hindu caste of the merchants]. It is for this reason that we also see the kings of France, beginning with Philip the Fair, surrounding themselves almost constantly with the bourgeoisie, above all those who, like Louis XI and Louis XIV, pushed the work of 'centralisation' the farthest — that centralisation, moreover, from which the bourgeois was later to derive the benefit, when it took possession of power through the revolution.[31]

At this point the process of the substitution of the *national* system for the feudal system commences. It is in the fourteenth century that the nationalities begin to constitute themselves through the afore-mentioned work of centralisation. It would be right to say that the formation of the 'French nation' in particular was the work of the kings — who thus prepared, without willing it, their own ruin. And if France was the first European country in which the royalty was overturned, this happened because it was precisely in France that 'nationalisation' had its point of departure. On the other hand, it is well to recall how virulently the French Revolution was 'nationalist' and 'centralising', and also the revolutionary and subversive use which was made of the so-called 'principle of nationalities'[32] during the entire course of the nineteenth century, right up to the First World War.

Thus, already in the constitution of the mercantile republics and of the free cities, in the revolt of the Commons against the imperial authority and then in the wars of the peasants, we have the harbingers of the swelling subversive wave from below. The centralising absolut-ism of the warrior kings, in the act of constituting 'public powers' in materialistic substitution of the purely spiritual cement given by the previous ideal of *fides*, with the abolition of every privilege and of the

---

31 Ibid., p. 112.

32 Ibid.

very notion of the *jus singulare*[33] in which there was yet conserved something of the ancient principle of the castes — this absolutism clears the path, from above, for this wave from below, this demagogy, and even goes out to meet it: and, once the monarchy had been unseated or reduced to an empty symbol with constitutions and with the famous formula of Thiers to the effect that '*Le roi règne, mais il ne gouverne pas*,'[34] the public powers were to become the organ in which the mere collective, the nation was to be incarnated, from the first under the guise of the Third Estate.

Modern capitalism takes form through the liberalistic Jacobin illusion, which abased the idea of the justification of the State to the *mercantile* and utilitarian idea of a 'social contract', and finally the capitalistic oligarchy, the plutocracy, ends up controlling and dominating the political reality. Power descends, that is, to that level which in traditional terms corresponded to the level of the third caste, the ancient caste of the *merchants*. With the advent of the bourgeoisie, the economy comes to dominate all things, and its supremacy is openly proclaimed with respect to every subsistent remnant of those, we do not say spiritual, but simply ethical principles which yet survive in the Western political world. This is the Paretian theory of 'residues' and the Marxist theory of 'superstructures'. By the force of a highly significant logic, the royal denomination passes over to the 'kings of the dollar', to the 'kings of carbon', the 'kings of steel' and so forth.

4. — *But just as usurpation brings usurpation, now after the bourgeois come the serfs who, in their turn, aspire to dominion.* The pseudoliberalism of the bourgeoisie was destined to fatally summon 'socialism' in the form of a mass regime, just as this was destined to summon up

---

33 Latin for 'singular law', to be understood in contrast to common law, or *ius commune*. The *ius singulare* was a law granted in exception to the general law for special groups or situations. — Trans.

34 French: 'The king rules, but no longer governs'. — Trans.

still lower elements, the pure 'demonry' of the collective.[35] Fomented by internationalistic, antitraditionalistic, illuministic and democratic destructions, all inevitably connected to the 'modern' type of civilisation and culture, with Marxism, the 'Third Internationale', the 'Communist Manifesto', the revolt of the proletariat against the capitalistic bourgeois, and, finally, with the Russian Revolution and the new collectivistic Bolshevic ideal, we stand before the final collapse, the advent of the *fourth* caste: power passes to the hands of the mere faceless mass, which comes to instaurate a new universal epoch of humanity under the crude insignia of the sickle and the hammer. And here Berl paints the image for us: for him, with the advent of the Fourth Estate we stand at the vestibule of the subhuman world.

The Fourth Estate is disanimate and its aim is the disanimation of life, of society, of human interiority itself: and these, after standardisation and American Taylorism, are the ends pursued by the so-called 'proletariat purification' of the remnants of the 'bourgeois ego' and of the Soviet's so-called 'technological messianism'.[36]

On the other hand, if we extract the real content from the mythical form, upheavals of this kind were foreseen by more than one traditional teaching. The *Eddas* prophesy 'bitter days' in which the beings of the earth — the *Elementarwesen* — will debouch to trample the divine forces, and the 'sons of Muspell' will break Bifröst's bow, which joins heaven to earth (let us recall the aforementioned symbolism of the pontifical symbol of sovereignty as 'maker of bridges').[37] An analogous theme is found for example in a legend which arrived at the Medieval Period from remote times and constituted a kind of medieval *lietmotif*: the legend of the 'demonic' peoples of Gog and Magog who, smashing the symbolical iron wall with which the imperial figure had shut the way (symbol of the traditional boundaries and

35   H. Berl, *Die Heraufkunft des fünften Standes*, op. cit., p. 18.

36   Ibid., p. 36.

37   One of the likeliest etymologies for the word 'pontifex' (and the etymology that Evola himself prefers) is 'maker of bridges'. — Trans.

the idea of the State as *cosmos* victorious over *chaos*), will burst in to
attempt to win the last battle, to become the masters of all the powers
of the earth. On the other hand, we have already made allusion to the
fact that, according to the Indo-Aryan tradition, the *kâlî-yuga*, or dark
age, is characterised by the predominance of the servant caste, by the
emergence of a race of faithless barbarians, 'infatuated with the world
only for the treasures that it contains'.[38]

Subtracting from all of this the choreographic-apocolyptic element, it would be difficult here not to recognise the correspondence
of the new Soviet 'civilisation' of the 'faceless beast' — faceless because
it is composed of an innumerable multitude — in the act of ration-
ally building the most modern instruments of mechanical power. Our
contemporary Julien Benda prophesies the epilogue of the phenomenon (which he identified) of the *trahison des clercs*:

> Humanity, and certainly not just a fraction of it, will take itself to be the
> object of religion. Thus we will arrive at a universal brotherhood which,
> far from abolishing the spirit of the nation with its appetites and its prides,
> will be their supreme form: the nation calling itself Man, and God the
> enemy. And from that moment, unified in an immense host and an im-
> mense workshop, no longer knowing aught but disciplines and inventions,
> disparaging every free and disinterested activity and taking as God nothing
> but itself and its whims, humanity will come to great things, which is to
> say, a truly grandiose control of the material that surrounds it.

Here in Benda's manner of writing we see precisely a kind of updated
tradition of the terms of the ancient traditional prophecy. In reality, if
we have come to believe that not only the idea of the caste, but even
that of 'classes' has been overcome, and if the conviction has arisen
that the family itself and even the personality are but so many 'bourgeois prejudices', and, finally, that the Traditional idea of the nation
no longer has a future, but is to be replaced by the highest ideal of
a homogeneous, proletarised international conglomeration, with

---

38 *Vishnu-purâna*, IV, 24; VI, I.

work as its only glue — if all of this is believed today, then it is easy
to recognise that here the way is being prepared for a social concept
which conforms, not to one or another of the castes, but in truth to
the casteless itself, to the *pariah*: that group whose members were
considered precisely to be those without personality or cult: in short,
the 'free man'.

So it is that first the individualistic and Enlightenment disunity,
and then the barbaric ferment arising from the Slavic soul in marriage with the historical materialism of the Jew Karl Marx, presage the
glorification of the pariah and of its constitution as a universal model
through the mirage of a purely Arimanic power, which seems to produce the vaunted 'progress' of the West. And thus it is evident that as
a general sense of this process of the regression of the castes and of
the fall of the idea of the State, we find the involutive transformation
of the spiritual personality into the prepersonal collective which was
symbolised, in mystical form, by the totem of the primitive societies.
In reality, only by adhering to a free activity can man be both free and
himself. Thus in the two symbols of pure action (heroism, the assumption of life to 'rite') and of pure consciousness (contemplation, ascesis)
sustained by a regime of just inequality (*suum cuique*), the two higher
castes opened paths of participation to man in that supermundane order, in which alone he can belong to himself and can grasp the integral
and universal sense of personality. By destroying every interest in that
order, by concentrating on the passional and naturalistic part of his
being, on practical and utilitarian ends, on economic realisations and
on every other one of the objects which were originally proper only to
the lower castes, man abdicates, he uncentres himself, he disintegrates,
he opens himself once more to those irrational and prepersonal forms
of collective life, when it was precisely elevation over these things
which constituted the effort of every culture truly worthy of the name.
And so it is that, now that this disunity and the individualistic revolt

have come, the collective in the social forms of recent times[39] acquires ever greater power, up to the point of reawakening, in new but still more fearsome form (more fearsome because it has been mechanised, rationalised, centralised and translated into the terms of social, economic and statal determinism) the totemism of the primitive tribes.

The nation conceived in Jacobin terms, 'race', society or 'humanity' rise now to a mystical personality and demand of the individuals who form a part of them unconditional dedication and subordination, while hatred is demagogically fomented in the name of 'freedom' — hatred for those higher and dominating individualities, before whom alone the principle of subordination and the obedience of individual human beings was ever sacred and justified. And this tyranny of the mass does not limit itself to affirming itself in the 'political' or 'social' aspects of the life of the individual: it arrogates to itself a moral and a spiritual right. It demands that culture and spirit cease to be disinterested forms of activity, paths for the elevation and the dignifying of the personality and thus for the realisation of the very presuppositions of every true and virile hierarchy; it demands that they become the servile organs of the collective temporal body; it ostracises every 'movement which is supernatural or in any case alien to the interests of the class' (Lenin), and in this way it discovers 'in every intellectual an enemy to Soviet power' (Zinoviev); and finally it proclaims the morality of precisely that man who affirms that mind and will have value only when they are reduced to servile instruments of the body.

Moreover, the quadripartite regression does not have a politico-social and psychological character alone, but also brings the regression of morality to an inferior morality, a given conception of life to an inferior conception of life. Indeed, while the 'solar' epoch took for

---

39 Italian: *i tempi ultimi*, one of Evola's favourite phrases. The Italian is ambiguous, as it can mean both 'the end times' and 'the most recent times'; Evola generally intends this expression, in the translator's opinion, in both senses simultaneously, but this is difficult to clearly capture in the English, which has therefore been uniformly rendered 'recent times' throughout. The reader is invited to recall this double meaning wherever this expression occurs. — Trans.

its own the ideal of pure spirituality and the ethics of active liberation from human caducity, and while the 'warrior' epoch took for its own the ideal of heroism, of victory and of lordship and the aristocratic morality of honour, of fidelity and of knighthood, in the 'merchant' epoch the ideal is wealth (*prosperity*),[40] the pure economy, profit conceived — according to a Puritan deviation derived from the Protestant heresy — as the sign of divine favour, the 'ascesis of capitalism', science as an instrument for technico-industrial exploitation leading to production and new profit and the degrading rationalisation of life. And at last, with the advent of the 'servants', the ideal of 'service' arises, anodyne to the socialised collective body and the universal proletariat work ethic ('whoever does not work does not eat'), leading to the degradation of every higher form of activity into assumption under the category of 'work' and 'service' — which is to say, to that which was only the 'duty' and the '*modus essendi*'[41] of the last of the castes.

Analogous considerations — observations of a quadripartite rhythm within the decline of many other spheres — could be easily set down here: in family, in art, in war, in property, etc.[42] The doctrine of the regression of the castes here truly manifests its fecundity: it gives us the possibility to grasp the comprehensive sense of a variety of phenomena which are usually considered in isolation, heedless of the intelligence to which they are all subjected. These phenomena are confusedly opposed by many, without any sense of the true enemy lines nor of the positions through which alone a true defence and a radical reconstructive reaction would be possible. This precisely must be the point that draws our attention: the reconstructive problem, the restoration of the true idea of the State. Guénon rightly observes[43] that to the degree to which one sinks into materialism, instability grows, and change comes ever more rapidly.

---

40 Evola uses the English here. — Trans.

41 Latin: 'way of being'. — Trans.

42 Cf. Evola, *Revolt Against the Modern World*.

43 René Guénon, *Autorité spirituelle et pouvoir temporel*, op. cit., p. 121.

Thus the reign of the bourgeois cannot have but a relatively brief duration in comparison to the regime which it succeeds, and if still lower elements attain to power in one way or another — in the varieties taken by the advent of the mere collective — we can predict that their rule will be in all likelihood the briefest of all, and will mark the last phase of a certain historical cycle, since it is impossible to descend any lower.

2. ON PHILIP THE FAIR

I T IS A CURIOUS FACT, but not for that without its significance, that the figure of Philip the Fair today has been evoked on various occasions, sometimes in relation to the anti-Jewish campaign, sometimes in treating of the origins of the modern State. It has even happened that some have called Philip the Fair a 'pre-Fascist king', by which they mean to say that he was Fascist *avant la lettre*, a precursor to certain aspects of Fascism. In our opinion, however, there is in all of this only to be found demonstration of that lack of principles which characterises certain circles, and of the confusions that derive from the bad habit of taking up sporadic motifs for contingent ends, neglecting to procure for oneself serious knowledge of the matter at hand and of investigating the true meaning of the epochs or the men to which it refers. We do not believe it would be without interest if we were to examine here the case of Philip the Fair with precision, an effort which will prove very useful in clarifying such confusions and letting us comprehend a rather tragic and sad turning point in European history, the consequences of which are even now far from being exhausted.

Toward this end, we will employ a work published on this subject in these very days in Italian translation: we speak of a section of the great *History of France* by Jules Michelet, the noted historian of the so-called French 'Romantic school' of the last century.[1] We are entirely in agreement with the translator of this book when he asserts that Michelet's historical constructions of that period, far from being 'overcome', often present us with brilliant intuitions and daring syntheses, for which one would seek in vain in more recent historiography, as the latter often becomes, on the pretext of scientific rigour, flat, arid, two-dimensional. Even with respect to the subject which we intend to discuss here, 'in its most essential lines the more recent historiography not only has not far surpassed Michelet's vision, but in certain ways has flattened it and has muted its significance'.

In Philip the Fair, those forces first took definite form which would subsequently provoke the disintegration of medieval civilisation and propitiate the birth of 'modern' civilisation — 'modern' in the inferior sense of the term, as synonymous with the anti-Traditional civilisation and with desacralised and materialised man. Through Philip the Fair, the debauched grandson of St. Louis of France, these forces triumphed for the first time over feudalism, over knighthood, over the papacy: 'by means of a shyster, a bankrupt and a counterfeiter', as Michelet says in the very first pages.

The first important act performed by this King was to secularise the State, which is to say, to transform the previous spiritual type of the State into a secular and laical type. Thus already in 1287 he excluded the religious element from the administration of justice, not only in his Parliament and in his direct domains, but also in the nobility. The ironic and hypocritical justification which Philip the Fair produced for this act of his is wholly characteristic: in bringing it about that no clergyman might have a place in Parliament, he declared that he had 'had the scruple of reserving such men to the government of spiritual things'. Moreover, Philip the Fair would later align himself against the Papacy itself, which he finally succeeded in bending to his will and making into the instrument of his ends.

---

1   J. Michelet, *Dal vespro allo sterminio dei Templari*, trans. It. E.Omodeo-Zona, (Laterza, Bari: 1941), XIX.

Pope Boniface VIII (1294–1303) pursued a decided reaffirmation of the privileges and the power of the pontificate, thus entering into conflict with the powerful feudal families of Rome (above all the Colonna) and with the European monarchs, in particular with Philip the Fair, who, to subjugate the papacy to his own interests, succeeded under the papacy of Clement V in transferring the papal court to France, in Avignon.

There are some who will find all of this 'modern' and even agree-able: it is the emancipation of a 'strong' State from the clerical tyranny, it is a manifestation of force and political consciousness. In reality, we are speaking of a fall in level. Suffice it in this regard to compare the meaning of the battle conducted against the Church by Philip the Fair and by the House of France with that which was undertaken by the previous Germanic Ghibelline emperors. These opposed the Church because they conceived of the Empire as an altogether spiritual and 'supernatural' reality, one having therefore its own 'divine right' which in no way meant remaining subject *sic et simpliciter*[2] to the hegem-onic pretence of the Roman Curia. In Philip the Fair and, in general, in the House of France, the question was altogether another: we are speaking here of a mere temporal power that rejects every spiritual authority, refuses to recognise it in every domain, and affirms itself against the Church. We could be said to stand at the beginning of modern anticlericalism of the Enlightenment and Masonic kind. One might, from the current point of view, approve of the exclusion of the clergy from the ranks of State and from the administration of justice. But this is only a detail, the exterior aspect of the situation. It is the sense of the thing which really counts and which must be understood on the basis of the ideal world, not of today, but of that time. Whether or not it is a question of the role of the clergy, what is realised for the first time with Philip the Fair is the banishment from the State of those who ought to exclusively occupy themselves with 'spiritual

---

2   Latin: 'as such' (lit. 'so and simply'). — Trans.

things'; in other words, the spiritual element, confined to a domain of its own, was to cease to have any influence whatever on the life of a State that materialises ever more, and that — under the banner of absolutism — becomes the enemy of the aristocracy itself. Nothing is substituted for that which is denied, that which is excluded. We can well speak then of a degradation and a fall in level, rather than the presumed gesture of a 'strong State'.

In parallel to the secularisation of the State, Philip the Fair also brought about its centralisation. He therefore gave himself to creating an administrative superstructure aimed at suffocating the feudal system, even while it mechanised and bureaucratised the statal infrastructure: thus he came almost to revive the statist model of the late Empire, with more than a single absolutist accent, in clear contrast to the virile and strongly personalised hierarchical ideal proper to the Medieval Period, and to the strictly ethical and spiritual premises thereof. Thus the royal power, its ambition set on full tyranny, was to ally itself against the feudal nobility and to seek every means of undermining its prestige and crippling its power. Toward that end, Philip the Fair, just as the irresponsible Kings of France who carried on his work, had to seek recourse in the aid of lower elements. He rested indeed on the plebs themselves, flattering them with promises of liberty, so as to make of them a powerful instrument against the aristocracy, which was supposed to be the guarantor and the strongest foundation of regality.

As Guénon justly observes in this regard, it was no accident that France was the first country to have a revolution. The French Revolution was prepared by the anti-aristocratic and centralising action which was commenced by none other than Philip the Fair, and continued by his successors. Once the nation had been deprived of its very skeleton in the elimination of the feudal nobility and by the growing degradation of what remained of the aristocracy in a mere 'court nobility', and once the laical public powers had been created which centralised a power which had once been organically distributed in a series of partial sovereignties, these 'public' powers were to become the very organ through which the plebs, supplanting the kings themselves, who adored that class and tactically used it against the most ancient and truest nobility, were then to incarnate and affirm themselves. In this we see the consequences of a clear logic, not to speak of a kind of immanent justice. In every epoch, absolutism has always prepared the way for demagoguery.

Indeed it is precisely for the centralising work that he carried out that Philip the Fair might appear, in the eyes of some, 'modern' and agreeable — once more, on account of a fundamental ambiguity. As indeed we ourselves have had occasion to observe, those who think in this fashion forget to examine the very different meanings that centralism and totalitarianism might have, depending on their historical antecedents. Today a kind of centralisation and totalitarianisation of the State has been imposed for the simple reason that we have as our own historical antecedent the chaos of the liberalistic and democratic chaos, for it was necessary, some way or other, to neutralise the centrifugal tendency of a general dissolution which would have in the end swept away every institution, every political authority, every tradition. Things took on quite a different aspect in the time of Philip the Fair: the antecedent, in those days, was constituted precisely by the feudal system, to whose liberties it would have been enough to apply a small brake, if one were to find in it the solidest and most vital basis of a true order. It is precisely centralism which, as compared to the articulation proper to the hierarchical-feudal system, had the meaning of a dissolution, a levelling, a destruction of all that which was yet qualitative and differentiated. It is therefore absolutely absurd to draw parallels between the work of Philip the Fair and the totalitarian statist idea of today, as the latter represents the overcoming of the individualistic and 'liberator' dissolution of the latest period.

Moreover, Michelet has clearly brought into the light the lethal consequences that followed from the initiative of the irresponsible King of France in that period, even on the material plain. Given that the bureaucracy of the King's men had need, for its maintenance, of a hefty taxation, the State was slowly forced to transform its economy, and more precisely to adopt the primacy of liquid capital, represented by gold, over landed property. 'The Medieval Lord', writes Michelet, 'paid his servants with letters patent and the fruits of the land; the great and the small all had a place a his table; their payment was in their daily meal. As for the immense machine of the royal government, which substitutes, for the thousand natural and simple movements of the feudal regime, its own complex movement, nothing but money could give this machine its impetus'. But the ever more important role that gold comes to play in this system was destined to slowly turn to the advantage of those who in those days made of it above all a commerce of their own — that is to say the Jews — which subverted the fiscal situation and fomented deep hatreds. Philip the Fair thus ended up intervening directly, through two master strokes.

The statist Moloch having ever greater need of its golden food, Philip the Fair saw fit to furnish it with what it needed by the shortest way possible — namely, by taking gold from those to whom his own system had made it most massively flow. We are speaking once more of the Jews; and this is why in 1288 the King interdicted every power which the Church possessed over the Jews: they were to become his own thing, his special reserved quarry. At precisely the right moment, he issued a decree of expropriation. 'The operation was undertaken that very day with a secrecy and a deftness that do honour to the agents of the King', writes Michelet. 'It seems that not a single Jew escaped. Not resting content with the sale of their goods, the King gave himself over to persecuting those indebted to the Jews, declaring that the records these latter had kept were sufficient as a title of credit and that for him the writing of a Jew would suffice'. Here we have then the true sense of that anti-Judaism which some today would like to ascribe to the glory of Philip the Fair, in total ignorance of the true circumstances which surrounded it. The theft which the Jew had perpetrated through usury is supplanted here by the pure and simple

spoliation of the royal decree, with this as an aggravating factor: that
the goods of the Jews had been accumulated essentially by cause of
a subversion provoked by the King himself. And the severity the
King's agents showed the Jews was no greater than that shown to the
Christians indebted to them, from whom these agents were able to
extort even that money and those goods which the Jews themselves
had not been able to obtain. God protect us, then, from taking anti-
Judaism of this sort as our model...

But the Jews did not give enough. Philip the Fair thus studied another move, this time directed against the Christians. His new glorious and innovative action was the falsification of the currency. Philip
the Fair raised the value of the currency and diminished its weight:
thus with two liras he could purchase eight. But when it came to receiving rather than paying, he would not accept his own currency save
at a third of its nominal value. 'Thus he made two bankruptcies in
an inverted sense', observes Michelet. Here one can in truth recognise
in Philip the Fair something 'exquisitely modern': it can indeed be
said that Philip the Fair inaugurated in history, through a conscious
intention, that nefarious system of inflation, which would play such
a great role in our times, and in which the Jews were to demonstrate
themselves masters.

And yet a crisis arose even in that time, because the fraud was too
visible. The King could not insist on this method beyond a certain
point, and so it was necessary to seek other ways of making money.
The new victim, after the despoiled Jews and the exsanguinated populace, could not be the nobility as a bloc (which still had hands capable
of taking up arms), nor the Church with its authentic monastic orders
(which yet enjoyed too much prestige). And so Philip the Fair discov-
ered in the Templars the fit subject for a new *coup de main*.

It was necessary to seize the riches accumulated by this ascetic-
warrior Order, which had rendered so many services to Christianity:
and that, by means of a decent pretext, such as might impose itself
on the Church itself. This pretext or expedient — one can call it what

one likes — was heresy. Philip the Fair, a brutally laical sovereign for whom problems of a transcendent type were the last of all concerns, suddenly discovers the 'heresy' of the Templars and denounces the scandal that this 'heresy' represents for Christianity as a whole. The Pope did not at first hide his disdain for the accusation levelled against the Order: but in the end, he could not resist the pressures of the King nor ignore certain enigmatic aspects of Templarism itself — enigmatic aspects upon which the required emphasis was lain, naturally, through an intentionally tendentious interpretation. And so the Templars were brought to trial. This trial, which was particularly complex and tragic, concluded with the destruction of the Order and the transference of all the riches it held in French territory to the hands of the King. And Philip the Fair, the very day that the Templars were arrested, went personally to establish himself in their central headquarters in Paris, called the Temple, so as to inventory his loot. 'This nice sequestration made him rich in a single blow', Michelet comments.

Another characteristic proof of the aforementioned lack of principles in those who today would recall the figure of Philip the Fair, is to be found in their supposition that this despicable figure of a counterfeiting and perjurous King (it was by means of a perjury that as a young man he obtained his liberty from Charles of Anjou) had, with the trial against the Templars, anticipated the battle against Masonry, the Templars having been — it is supposed — a kind of Masonry of their day, strongly Judaised, the practicants of mysterious and sacrilegious rites. The blunder that one makes in this regard is no less than that committed by those who valorise Philip the Fair's anti-Judaism, his totalitarianism and his laical idea of the State. Only that to clarify the problem of the Templars it would be necessary to engage in a series of considerations which would be rather out of place here.

Here it must suffice to observe that in the Order of the Templars, more than in any similar organisation of that time, the highest ideal of Ghibelline civilisation had been realised: that is, of a close solidarity between the warrior element and the ascetic element. To this was added the exigency that the best members of this Order should participate in higher forms of wisdom, light and strength by means of special rites, which were not to be revealed to the profane. Generally speaking, there lived, in the Templar Order, the idea of the Crusade as symbol and interior reality. 'It was a Crusade made fixed and permanent,' Michelet says in this regard, 'the noble representation of the spiritual Crusade that every Christian wages against the internal enemy until his death'. In an elite, however, there was also something more; there was a kind of 'initiation', which is to say the transformation thanks to which a man no longer aspires to something superhuman, but effectively possesses it already whilst living.

Here however arises the fundamental problem: namely, if this deeper vein of Templar spirituality, whose existence is demonstrated by various witnesses and which was tied to symbols and special rites, had an altogether Christian and orthodox character. We believe that this query can be answered in the negative: nonetheless, our point of view should not be confounded with that of individuals who hold that wherever certain forms of spirituality are no longer purely Christian, one must speak of superstition, of degeneration, and of — Masonry. Nor must what is no longer simply Christian perforce be considered anti-Christian; it might also be, for instance, super-Christian. Michelet himself, though he does not have any clear competency in this field, writes, 'The candidate [of Templar initiation] could believe that beyond the vulgar Christianity the Order would reveal to him a higher religion, would open to him a sanctuary behind the sanctuary. The name Temple was not sacred only to the Christians. ... The idea of the Temple, higher and more general even than the idea of a Church, soared in a certain way above all the religions. The Church had a date; the Temple had none, but was contemporaneous with all ages. It was as a symbol of the perpetuity of religion itself'. Only that the word 'religion' here seems little apropos, and might generate confusion. Religions are something positive; they are tied to specific times and to races, and their frontiers cannot be overcome in the name of a

misunderstanding or a truly Masonic or Enlightenment universalism
without running afoul of deviations and destructions. But on a plane
yet higher than that of the religions, there can exist a truly transcendent reality, a unity, so to speak, a zenith of unique and essential content, existing beyond its many various and conditioned expressions.
Now, there is good reason to suppose that the high Templar hierarchies had connections precisely with this higher tradition.

And the fact that there were sometimes symbols here which appeared also in Jewish currents signifies just as little as the frequent use
made in the Christian writings of that time of images and parables
drawn from the Old Testament, which is to say from the Hebrew
tradition. It would rather be much more interesting and conclusive
to examine the relations (to which Michelet himself alludes, if only
fleetingly) which existed between Templarism — a chivalry which was
more than Ecclesiastic and more than simply Christian — and the
Grail cycle. We note for example that in one of the most important
texts (Wolfram von Eschenbach) the knights of the Grail are called
Templeise, which is to say, Templars, since there is no talk of a 'temple'
in that work. Moreover, the present author himself has treated of this
subject in one of his books, in which he sought to clarify the sense
which the Templars had in that historical period: they were, in the
highest sense of the word, the 'Order' of Ghibelline civilisation, just as
the centre of that civilisation, the *Sacrum Imperium*, was to a certain
degree the incarnation of the ideal of the 'Kingdom of the Grail'.

In that work we recognise, as Michelet does, the continued existence of the Temple, at least as as a tradition, in the teachings of many
secret organisations after the tragedy of the Templars: but in that
book the present author also furnishes the elements necessary to
distinguish the cases in which one can speak of a legitimate spiritual
inheritance or, at least, of the manifestation of akin influences, from
other cases in which we perceive counterfeits or the usurpation of
names and of symbols on the part of sects which have an altogether
different nature: this is the case for instance with Masonry, in which,

among other things, the elements which were proper to that ancient Ghibelline tradition are used abusively.

Returning to Philip the Fair, it is precisely in relation to the Templars that one becomes clearly aware of that destructive end pursued by the dark forces that acted through him. Indeed, the attack on the Templars must not be thought of as a mere expedient, as we have already noted, to procure money for the King, after the spoliation of the Jews and the falsification of the currency. From a higher point of view — a point of view about which Philip the Fair was the first to know nothing whatever — the attack was levelled rather against men who incarnated the highest tradition of the Medieval Period, who bore in themselves, as has been said, an idea which, apart from its transcendent and super-Christian aspects, was founded on a synthesis of the virile and warrior element with the spiritual and ascetic one. The highest vocation of Ghibellinism fell into its sunset together with this idea. As a consequence, we find the dualism which was to grow ever sharper in centuries to come, and which has lasted up to our own days — that is, the dualism of, on the one hand, an abstractly religious spirit, at most mystical and contemplative in the pallid sense of these words, and on the other a deconsacrated political reality, a laical State, and purely material forms of virility and of warrior affirmation. In the Templar ideal, as in that of the chivalry of the Grail, both of these limitations are overcome. Beyond the material, vulgar motives of Philip the Fair, which are tied to the individual and his situation, there exists a deep logic in his various actions: he, who gave the first serious blow to the feudal system and who initiated the laicisation of the centralised and anti-aristocratic state, was certain to strike out as well against the inheritors of the best tradition of the Middle Ages which preceded him.

These then are the terms in which the true significance of Philip the Fair is to be understood in medieval history. Philip the Fair was effectively an original antecedent of the modern world: but of that modern world against which we fight, since, appearances notwithstanding, this entire world has no meaning if not as a subversion, as a fall and a renunciation. It is in an altogether different direction that we should seek figures to represent us, and symbols that can confirm our will to rebuild and to develop the forces which are yet intact in our kind.

3. DUMÉZIL AND THE STRUCTURE OF THE STATE

T HE PORTRAIT WHICH cultivated persons generally paint of the religion of Ancient Rome is, more or less, that it was an isolated complex. Adhering to the schema followed by the current teaching — and, moreover, to the method adopted by more than one specialist of Roman things — they proceed, after a hasty nod to the pre-Roman Italic civilisations and the Etruscans, to consider Roman cults and institutions in detachment, save as they might note the Greek and Oriental influences which these cults and institutions subsequently underwent. As this is how things presently stand, the publisher Einaudi has done well to publish, in Italian translation, the work of a well-known French scholar, G. Dumézil: *Iupiter, Mars, Quirinus* (Torino, 1955),[1] which offers an example of the application of a different method — the comparative method, on an 'Indo-European' basis — in the study and the interpretation of the Roman world.

This method is certainly not new. The discovery that civilisations, such as the Hindu, the Iranic, the Greek, the Roman, the Celtic, the Germanic and various others still all share a common root dates back to the second half of the last century.

---

1 This book by Georges Dumézil (1898–1986) has yet to be translated into English from the French *Jupiter Mars Quirinus* (1944–1948). His 1940 work *Mitra-Varuna*, which has been (New York: Zone Books, 1988), treats of similar questions. — Trans.

The thesis was demonstrated first of all in the philological sphere, with respect to the inheritance of the elements of a single original language. From this area, the thesis passed on to the racial, seeking to reconstruct prehistoric migrations of groups of peoples all from a single stock — the Indo-Europeans — who, speaking this original language, gave to the aforementioned civilisations their essential fingerprint. Finally came confrontation with the problem of cults, of divinities, of institutions and of juridical forms, with the intent of establishing other parallels and points of comparison.

As was natural, the initial enthusiasm gave way to prejudices, errors and fantasies. Only recently has the comparative method been refined, and the Indo-European thesis been formulated in a scientifically satisfying way. Dumézil is among those who have made the best use of it, and for some years now he has applied it to the study of the Roman civilisation. The book noted above includes the major essays which he published along these lines from 1941 to 1948.

Written with extreme clarity and vivacity despite its erudite appurtenances, this book is interesting in the first place for its method. New horizons are opened here, for Roman things are considered in light of that wider cycle of civilisation, of the Indo-European heritage. This heritage, to be sure, might have received a particular and original formation in Rome, but without ever wholly losing its features. Indeed, it is only in this framework that not a few Roman motifs reveal to us their deeper and more original meaning.

In the second place, this book is interesting because Dumézil felicitously takes up once more the idea, already advanced by Vico and de Coulanges,[2] of an internal, organic unity of the cults, the social

2   References to Giambattista Vico and Numa Denis Fustel de Coulanges. Vico (1668–1744) was an Italian philosopher and historian, best known for his 1725 work *The New Science* which is considered one of the first works of philosophy of history. It attempted a systematic understanding of historical cycles in the form of *corsi e ricorsi*, or 'occurrences and recurrences,' and the movement between civilisation and barbarism. De Coulanges (1830–1889) was a French historian, whose best known work, also his first, is that mentioned here by

bodies, the vocations, the functions and the institutions of ancient civilisations. In Rome, no less than in every traditional civilisation, all of this was originally organised around a single axis.

Then there comes the specific aspects of Dumézil's research. He holds that all civilisations proposed a partition of 'functional divinities', which reflects an analogous social partition. These would be, in the first place, divinities that incarnate the idea of sovereignty in both its mystical and almost magical aspect (sacred power which affirms itself directly, which triumphs without fighting), as well as legal; then, warrior divinities; and finally, the divinities of fecundity, of riches, of productivity. The three types of gods have their correspondence in three functional castes or classes: the lords or priest-lords, the warriors, and the bourgeoisie or proprietors and farmers or animal breeders. Through complex and tenacious research, Dumézil demonstrates that this tripartite structure, well-attested in the East, was not alien even to Rome — though here, the principle of a somewhat uniform social unity, based on the civic sense, eventually prevailed over the principle of hierarchico-functional articulation. The triad of gods in Rome according to Dumézil was Jove, Mars and Quirinus. The tripartition of the major Roman priesthood, the Flamines, corresponded to these. The social counterpart was constituted by the three ancient tribes of the Ramnes, the Luceres and the Titienses. These traces of a common legacy survived in Rome up to that time in which they became simple archaic hold-overs, no longer accessible[3] to the animating idea which had constituted their basis.

So far as the special aspect of his research goes, however, Dumézil sometimes lets his theses lead him by the nose; he seeks to reduce too

Evola. It has been translated into English as *The Ancient City*, and it treats of the centrality of religion as a binding factor in the ancient Greek and Roman civilisations, so much so that the decline of the old cults led to a corresponding decline of society as such. — Trans.

3   Literally, 'no longer *transparent* to the animating idea which had constituted their basis.'

many things to his schema. This is not the place to enter into critical considerations, so we will mention only two points. In the first place, rather than a social tripartition, the fact of the matter is that we often encounter a quadripartition: sovereignty, warrior force, bourgeoisie, and workers. It matters little that, as Dumézil observes, the fourth caste was not composed of Indo-Europeans in the East, but of subjected peoples, because he admits that the Romans and the Nordics came to their tripartition through association with ethnic groups originally heterogeneous and even inimical to them.

The second point is this: Is the social tripartition or quadripartition truly a characteristic of the Indo-Europeans, almost a mark by which they can be recognised? Or is it a schema having an intrinsic value, an internal necessity and even an analogy in the articulation of the human being? Whatever Dumézil might think of this, we believe that the second alternative is the correct one, and that one may say at most that the Indo-Europeans were the peoples who, more than any others, succeeded in recognising and applying the ideal to an organico-functional hierarchy. This ideal however maintains its objective and normative value, and is not to be considered as the casual creation of a given human group.

The importance of this last point will not escape the reader, supposing only that he, laying aside everything which Dumézil's book might compellingly reveal regarding a Romanness as studied through a new and wider view, is brought by all of this to intuit the lasting and concordant meaning of a group of great civilisations — civilisations understood as a true order of social functions all referred to a State which, as Plato said, exists as idea, beyond the bounds of history and prior to any particular more or less imperfect realisation.

4. THE TWO FACES OF NATIONALISM

I T IS A MATTER of fact that the world war, rather than exhausting the process of demarcation of the European and extra-European nationalisms, has led this process to its acute phase. There is thus good reason today to submit some considerations aimed at clarifying this fact.

What is the sense of nationalism in the framework of a philosophy and a culture? We pose this as problem, to which we believe we can offer the following solution: *the nationalistic direction admits of two ideally distinct and antithetical possibilities, though these are often confounded with one another in practice. The one has the sense of degeneration and regression, the other rather of the path to higher values — as the prelude to resurrection.* Let us see how such an idea, so apparently rich in consequences even in its enunciation, can be made comprehensible.

One cannot understand a phenomenon like nationalism without framing it in a view of the whole of history, which rests on the solid basis of worthy criteria. Now, to such a view, the progressive fall of political power from one level to another appears as a positive fact. The levels in question marked in ancient civilisations the qualitative differentiation of human possibilities. The process proceeds from the very limits of 'historical' times up to our days, with particular regard to Western political history.[1]

It is known which remote tradition held to the analogy between the political organism and the human organism. In every higher form of corporeal organisation, there is however a hierarchical connection of four distinct functions: at the lower limit, there are the undifferentiated energies of pure vitality — but over these rule the functions of organic exchanges and the general organic economy — which in their turn find in *will* the moving and directing force of the body in space. Finally, at the summit, a power of intellect and liberty, as the centre and light of the entire organism.

There once existed traditions which willed a division and a hierarchisation of rigorously corresponding classes and castes for the greater part of the States, to which these same classes and castes became almost spiritualised corps. The four distinct classes of the servants (workers), merchants, Warriors and finally the bearers of a simultaneously regal and priestly authority corresponded to vitality, the organic economy, the will and the spirit. The castes were arranged hierarchically one over another: the masses, under the control and the government of the experts of the traffic and use of natural and economic resources; these, under the authority of the warrior aristocracies — which in their turn were gathered around that individual who, in a complete and dominating type, almost bore witness to something in man which goes beyond man.

The ancient East (India) and the Far East knew a similar type of social organisation, which Ancient Greece and Ancient Rome also partially showed, reemerging in the political doctrine of Plato and

---

1   We first formulated the idea of the regression of the castes in our *Pagan Imperialism*; we have found it as well better defined in the ideas of V. Vezzani, which however has not yet received a written exposition. Finally, R. Guénon has presented it in a systematic form in his work *Autorité spirituelle et pouvoir temporel* (Paris, 1929).

Aristotle, to then have a final social resurgence in the Catholic-feudal Middle Ages.

It is important to observe that such an organisation corresponded to the type of a *qualitative* hierarchy, and marked the differentiation of higher forms of interest and of individuality. In the ancient East, the two higher castes were called the 'regenerators', and were the expression of a spiritual elite; in this vision, the Warrior and the Aristocrat had more a 'sacred' than a 'political' meaning. Every hierarchy based on economy, work, industry and collective administration was enclosed in the two lower castes, equivalent to that which is in the human organism the corporeal-vital part.

For this reason, the hierarchy of the four castes represented even perceptibly the progressive degrees of an elevation of individuality through the adhesion to forms higher than those proper to immediate life. With respect to the anonymous mass, which is intent on nothing but 'living', the organisers of work and of wealth — the second caste — represented already the outline of a type, of a 'person'. But in the heroism of the warrior, and in the ethos of the aristocrat — the third caste — the form of a 'more than life' can already be felt with greater clarity, of a being which gives itself a law of its own, surpassing thereby the natural, instinctive, collective and utilitarian element. If finally in the primordial notion of the Lords, the Ascetic, the King and the Pontifex were confounded into a single being, this already indicates a universal and almost supernatural achievement of personality, the complete expression of that which, on the other hand, does not have in the common man the strength to liberate itself from the contingent, to be itself and itself alone. To the extent to which such dominators, consummate individuals, formed the axis of the entire social organism, this organism was a body upheld by the spirit; temporal power and spiritual authority coincided and the hierarch was *legitimate*, in the absolute sense of the term.

Having established this schema — whose ideal model, the basis of its value, is independent from the degree to which and the forms in which any given society of the past might have realised it — one can ascertain, from crude evidences, the whole process of a progressive 'fall' of power in historical times. The era of the 'Sacred Kings' — whose nature was simultaneously imperial and priestly — already stands on the threshold of 'mythical' times. The apex disappears, power passes to the immediately inferior grade — to the caste of the Warriors: there remain Monarchs of the laical kind, military leaders or lords of temporal justice.

The second collapse: the great European monarchies decline, the aristocracies fall into decadence through revolutions (England and France), and the very Constitutions become but inane surviving remnants as compared to the 'will of the Nation'. Through parliamentary, republican and bourgeois democracies, the constitution of capitalistic oligarchies thus expresses the fatal passage of political power from the second to the modern equivalent of the third caste — the merchant caste.

Finally the crisis of bourgeois society, the proletarian revolt, the despotism of the masses which have constituted themselves as purely collective, economic and international entities — all of this portends the final collapse, by which power will pass to the last of the castes, nameless and faceless, with the consequent reduction of every *standard of living*[2] to the plane of material and number. That is to say: it will be precisely like that man who can no longer tolerate the tension of the spirit, and then that of the will, and then that of the force which moves the body — and he abandons himself — and he rises again magnetically almost as a body without soul, under the impulse of another force, emerging from the margins of pure vitality.

The time has come that we recognise the illusion of all myths of 'progress', that we open our eyes to reality. The time has come to recognise the hard destiny of spiritual destruction which has weighed down the West and which today is maturing its latest fruits.

---

2   Evola gives this expression in the English. — Trans.

To reach our specific problem, it would be well to emphasise that at the centre of the involutive progress just now described there stands the displacement of the individual to the collective, a displacement which comes about in strict dependency with the aforementioned reduction of the interests from which the two higher castes drew their legitimate hierarchical authority, to the interests proper rather to the lower castes.

In reality, it is only by adhering to a free activity that a man might be free in himself. Thus in the two symbols of pure Action (heroism) and pure Consciousness (contemplation, ascesis) maintained by an aristocratic regime, the two higher castes opened to man paths of participation in that 'supermundane' order, in which alone a man might belong to himself and might gather the integral and universal sense of personality. By destroying every interest in that order, by concentrating itself on practical and utilitarian aims, on economic realisations and every other of the objects peculiar to the lower castes, man disintegrates, decentralises, opens himself to stronger forces that tear him from himself and consign him to the irrational and prepersonal energies of the collective life, elevation over which constitutes the effort of every truly superior culture.

So it is that in the social forms of the latest times the collective acquires ever greater overbearing power, up to the point of almost giving life once more to the totemism of primitive communities. The nation, the race, society, humanity rise to the level of a mystical personality, and demand of the individuals who form a part of them unconditional dedication and subordination, while at the same time in the name of 'liberty' hatred is fomented for those higher and dominating individualities in which alone the principle of individual subordination and obedience was sacred and justified. And this tyranny of the majority does not stop at affirming itself in that which has political and social character in the life of the individual: it arrogates to itself a moral and a spiritual right, and, by demanding that culture and spirit cease to be disinterested forms of activity, paths for the elevation of

the individuality, and that they become organs dependent on the col
lective temporal entity, it declares the morality of those who affirm
that the mind has sense and value only as an instrument in the service
of the body. Man, before feeling himself as a personality, as an *I*, must
feel himself as a social group, a faction or a nation — this is one of the
specific commandments of the latest subversive ideologies, through
which the relationship according to which primitive man felt he stood
with regard to the totem of his own tribe or *clan* returns with extreme
exactitude.

In the reawakening of the Russian race, in its claiming for itself,
in the form of Sovietism, a universal prophetic mission, we find
confirmation of this meaning of regression in primitive social stages,
present in many modern forms. This is precisely the opinion of those
who in the new Russia see the definitive revolt of the barbaric Asiatic
race, which rejects the attempt at European civilisation, undertaken
for two centuries by the Tsar, and tends to ally itself with the forms
of social decomposition of the European world. Bolshevism is the
establishment in modern form of the ancient spirit of the Slavic race:
race without tradition, that in its social mysticism, in its amalgama-
tion of sensuality and of spirituality, in the predominance of pathos
over ethos, of instinctivity over rationality, brings us back to the forms
of prepersonal undifferentiation and promiscuity proper precisely to
primitives.

The great upheaval of the war has returned this element to its free
state, and provided a fearful ferment of decomposition for it within
the yet-healthy parts of Europe. 'Soviet civilisation', in announcing the
advent of the 'proletarian era', openly consecrates itself to the destruction of the 'leprosy' of the personality and of liberty, these 'poisons
of bourgeois society', principles of every evil; to the abolition, not
only of private property, but of every independent thought and every
'supernatural movement, which to that same extent is alien to class
interest' (Lenin); to the advent of the 'all-powerful mass-man' who,
all by himself, must live and give form to every mode of individual

life and thought. The modern side of Bolshevism is to be found only in its 'method': mechanisation and rationalisation are but pre-chosen methods for the realisation of that universal and purely economic 'mass-man' social regime which already dwelt mystically within the Slavic soul. And thus Soviet civilisation runs up against another race, as it well knows — a race which likewise arrogates to itself a universal mission of regeneration, and the presumption to represent the last word on civilisation: America.

In America the process, rather than expressing the efficiency of a people which has remained in the pre-civilised state, follows the inflexible determinism which desires that man, in the act of closing himself off to every form of pure spiritualism, so as to give himself over to the will of temporal things, ceases *ipso facto* to belong to himself, and becomes instead a dependent part of an irrational collective entity which he can no longer dominate. America, along the path of that sanctification of the temporal and that laicisation of the sacred which the Protestant heresy prepares, has thus come precisely to this end. Taking the ideals of the material conquest of the world which Europe proposed for itself to their final conclusion, it entered — almost without realising it — into the pragmaticising and the physicalisation of every sense of power, of sanity, of activity and of personality, so as to build a still more fearful form of barbarities. Here the Ascetic is considered a wastrel, an anachronistic parasite, 'useless to society'; the Warrior, a dangerous hothead whom timely preventative humanitarian-pacifistic measures must eliminate so as to set in his place, perhaps, the *boxeur.*

The perfect type, on the other hand, the spiritual champion, is rather the 'man who works, who produces', and every form of activity, even spiritual, is not appreciated save as a species of 'work', of a 'productive work', of a 'social service': which fact could not be a more characteristic demonstration of who at the apex of such a society there stands precisely the type which represents the last of the ancient classes, that of the slaves relegated to toil. Here, too, having renounced his spiritual personality, man ceases to have any value beyond the conditions imposed by the collective organisation, seized as it is by the fever to produce, to 'achieve', to move: conditions which, moreover, usurp a moral and even religious value, and tend to standardise these same souls in a collective levelled *forma mentis*, so far as to extinguish even the capacity to perceive the degree of degeneration constituted by all of this.

These are forms through which the cycle comes to its conclusion and the collapse is fulfilled. Russia and America are two indices and two convergent faces of one and the same thing. The body regresses from being a human organism, as it was when it was ruled by the light and by the authority of the upper castes, to the type of a sub-human mindless organism. The advent of the faceless beast is come.

And now, we have all the elements necessary to seriously confront the problem: *What is the sense of nationalism in the modern world?*

One type of nationalism appears with a clear physiognomy already from what has been said above: it is the degree immediately antecedent to the international forms of economico-proletarian collectivism. In this nationalism, what counts is not the arising of one distinct national consciousness against others, but rather the fact that the 'nation' becomes a person, an entity unto itself; and the incapacity to overcome that right of the earth and of the blood, which regards only the natural and infra-intellectual aspect of man — the impossibility that the individual might possess any value other than in the terms of a given collectivity and a given tradition[3] — all of this is elevated to the status of an ethical value. The mere fact that a thing is 'national' here confers on it an authentic mystical aura which protects its inviolability and demands respect.

---

3   When — as here — we speak of tradition in the negative sense, we wish to refer to that concept of tradition which does not implicate any truly intellectual, and thus superethnic, element, and which — to speak with Chesterton — represents an extension in time of that right accorded to majorities with respect to space: the right of the dead over the living, resting on the condition that the dead are of one and the same race.

This ethnic infra-intellectual element not only fails to recognise the authority of higher principles, but also reduces these principles to its own service: the 'nation' demands the first tribute — only secondarily, and in subordinate fashion, is there a place for reality, truth and spirit. But in certain nationalistic forms, even this is outdone: every disinterested and objective criterion is accused of abstractism; even so far as reality, truth and culture are concerned, it is claimed that one cannot do without national tradition and political interest. Hence one speaks of our scientific tradition, our philosophical tradition and even our religious tradition, and one approaches everything which is not 'ours', and which does not 'respect the nation', out of the prejudice that it has no value. At the least, one bears toward it suspicious disinterest.

And just as higher activities are not tolerated to manifest themselves freely so as to create a reality superior to the ethnically conditioned reality, so in the framework of such a nationalism there is no respect for the higher personality save insofar as such is an 'exponent' of the nation. This nationalism, born in the revolutions which have overturned the remnants of the aristocratico-feudal regime, expresses therefore a pure 'crowd spirit': it is a variety of democratic intolerance for every leader who is not a mere organ of the 'popular will', and is utterly and in all things dependent on the sanction of this will. Thus we easily see that between nationalism and anonymity in the Soviet or American style, there is at bottom only a difference of degree: in the first, the individual is dissolved once more into his original ethnico-national bloodlines, in the second even the differentiation proper to these ethnic bloodlines is passed over, and a wider collectivisation and disintegration within the mass element is produced.

For the one degree to pass over to the other, it suffices that the mysticism of race give way to a structure of purely economico-mechanical type. In this structure, on account of its impersonal nature, the last remnants of qualitative difference are torn out by the roots, and with the rationalisation and the mechanicalisation of social life, the way stands virtually open to the advent of the mass-man without fatherland. Now, given that civilisation today stands precisely on the plane of economico-mechanical power, and that every criterion of value and of greatness is brought back more or less directly to this same plane, it is perhaps only a matter of time before this passage takes place.

But we are permitted to ask: can nationalism have another meaning? We hold that this question can be answered in the affirmative. It is said that nationalism appears as a kind of passage at the boundaries of that political domain which has fallen into the hands of the third caste, but before the rule of the last. Now, this very nature renders it susceptible to a double significance, because, while we might encounter this form of passage in the direction of the fall, we can equally well encounter it anew in the direction of a rise, of a possible reintegration. Supposing that the bottom has been reached, those who find the strength to lift themselves up once more would encounter nationalism once again — but another kind of nationalism altogether. Just as for the amplitudes which are called 'vectors' in physics, this phenomenon cannot be defined save on the basis of its directionality.

For the first kind of nationalism, the direction is toward collectivisation, realised on the level of the 'nation'; for the second, it proceeds rather from collectivisation toward the reconstruction of a new *aristocratic* hierarchy.

To express the presuppositions of this second nationalism, the words of Paul de Lagarde, the well-known exponent of German nationalism, are emphatically worth consideration:[4] the 'human' being is lesser than the 'national' being, the 'national' being is lesser than the 'personal' being. In other words: as compared to the quality 'humanity', the differentiating element 'nation' adds an incremental value X, and the element of the single personality adds to this X a further incremental value Y. The idea of a hierarchy thus emerges, a hierarchy which proceeds from the abstract toward the concrete. The abstract

---

4   P. de Lagarde, *Deutsche Schriften*, vol. I, p. 164.

here is the collective, the general; the concrete on the other hand is the different, the individual. As compared to the formless mass 'humanity', the rise toward differentiated national consciousness might constitute an initial progress: but the national consciousness, the ethnic trunk, must in its turn represent a formless material as compared to the individualities which, in their fulfilment, in their becoming what they are, in their actuation in forms of life which are higher than those conditioned either by the blood or by collective exigencies, carry it from the state of chaos to that of cosmos, from potentiality to act. And then the relations are inverted: rather than the nation being the end of the individual, it is now the individual, as aristocratic and spiritual personality, who is the aim of the nation, however much it remains a kind of mother to him, in that material condition the earth might represent with respect to a tree, which nonetheless detaches itself from this earth in its upper parts and rises toward the free heights.

Thus the fundamental point of difference is given. To clarify it definitively, it is enough to return to the qualitative sense of the ancient hierarchy of the castes. A nationalism that is the prelude to resurrection, nationalism not as the movement to, but the overcoming of, the mechanico-collectivistic state is not possible, save as the basic exigency is posited to restore an order of irreducible values to the whole of praxis, both 'social' and economical, so as to confer to those values a primacy and a direct authority over the rest. Without this, there exists no hierarchy, and without hierarchy the return to a higher, spiritualised type of State is not possible. Indeed, hierarchy does not signify merely subordination, but it means the subordination of that which has an inferior nature to that which has a superior nature — and whatever can be measured in terms of utility, interest, worldliness is inferior. Everything which expresses a pure and disinterested form of activity is superior; every other criterion is illusory or perverting.

We may speak of the 'illusory' whenever we find a hierarchy in the framework of mere economy, based therefore on differences of monetary, political, career or class rank in the Marxist sense, and so forth. Only with the rise of interests superior to the economic taken as a whole, can the principle of a true hierarchy be born: we must depart from the idea that we do not live to develop an economy, but that the economy is a means toward an end: but this end is inner elevation, the unfolding of the personality in an integral and 'overworldly' sense. Hierarchy becomes even 'perversion' when it expresses the servitude of the non-practical to the practical, as with the spirit which makes it- self an organ of the body; and, unfortunately, this is to be observed in the great majority of cases, given the dominant 'pragmatism' acting on all planes, even on that of science, alongside the petty Machiavellism and general social-climbing of our times. There is nothing more anti- hierarchical, and indeed nothing more anarchical, than such fictitious types of hierarchy.

In the framework of a restorative nationalism, it is a question of giving before anything order to everything which in the social whole corresponds to the vital-corporeal or animal part of a human organism and that which was the domain of the lower classes: work, economy, political organisation in the strict sense, up to the point of an 'economic peace' which, by 'releasing' them, will permit energies of a higher type to free themselves and to act on a higher plane. Then we can begin to aid in the reconstruction of the second caste, that of the warrior aristocracy, with the first of the aristocrats, the Monarch.

Immediate aristocracy is that in which the ideal of the higher for- mation of the personality can be realised. Do not look to the corrupted and degenerate lineages, against which a facile demagogic critique can be levelled: look rather to the original type of the Lord as that being in whom self-mastery, refinement, disinterest, culture, honour, fidelity and above all the quality of the leaders have become a consolidated conquest standing upon the solid basis of *blood*. The aristocracy is the necessary prolongation of positive nationalism, because while this nationalism delineates the borders of blood, a kind of ethnic trunk, aristocracy within these confines operates a selection and a further differentiation, carrying the process to a higher level, from the general and from the collective toward the individual, which is the sense of all true progress.

Having arrived at the reconstruction of an aristocratic tradition, the first gleam of spirit in the body of the State will be newly lit, and nationalism, having attained its proper task, can give place to higher forms, corresponding to types of State that were upheld by the second caste. This will be characterised by an absolute personalisation of all relations — by the passage from the mechanical to the organic, from constriction to liberty. For example, in other times, there were no soldiers, but only *warriors*, and these did not fight for the 'nation' or for 'right', but for their King; they did not 'obey' the 'social law' but were 'faithful' to their Lord. He who obeyed, who knew how to obey, did so almost with pride. The responsibility was directly assumed by the Lords, by the Monarchs, and not passed on to faceless entities or ideological taboos. Authority rested on the greatness of the personality and on dedication to that which could not be sold nor bought, nor measured in terms of 'use' — that which is no longer of 'life', but already participates in 'more than life'.

In its turn, this will be the basis for a type of State of a yet higher form, which is however so far from us that here we can make but the merest mention of it. However, it might be observed how many men might remain free and distinct as bodies, while being one in a single idea, just as, when the elites of various bloodlines will be able to elevate themselves to a plane of true spiritual superiority, the roads will be virtually open for a new *universal* culture. This does not mean 'internationalism', and still less a levelling humanitarianism, both of these being the creatures of a materialistic mentality: since the reality and the political distinction of the States stands on the same level as those of bodies, it is not of the unity of bodies that we are speaking, but rather the unity of culture, of meetings in a superindividual reality. The Catholic Middle Ages, the Roman Empire, and India all show examples of this universality: they show us the possibility of a profound unity of culture and of spirit within the plurality, even the mutually combative plurality, of States or ethnically distinct races. If one can speak of a future *European* consciousness, it is only in this sense that one must speak of it.

But this already exceeds the task we have proposed for ourselves, of delineating the two contrary meanings of nationalism. We hold that these meanings are now quite clear. As for examining to what extent the varieties of those nationalisms today which are present and struggling within the various States, this is a problem of empirical character, which falls entirely outside of our consideration.

5. THE RECONSTRUCTION OF THE IDEA OF THE STATE

I N OUR LAST ESSAY we examined the decline that the idea of State has suffered through historical times, which is to say, in the development of history upon which alone the gaze of the many usually falls. In order to identify this decline, not in its exterior, recent and consequential aspects, but in its entire extension and, essentially, in relation to quality, we took as our basis the doctrine of the *regression of the castes*, a doctrine whose traditional prefigurations we have indicated in a variety of peoples. This doctrine demonstrates to us how power and political authority declined gradually from one to the other of the planes and values, which originally defined the quadripartition of the social whole in a 'royal superhumanity', warrior nobility, merchants and servants. The idea of the State therefore fell from one to the other of these planes, proceeding finally from the organic to the mechanical, from the superpersonal to the materialised collectivistic subpersonal — the Sovietised and standardised.

The current times present themselves effectively — if we may be permitted to use this forbidden expression — as a turning point, inasmuch as with Bolshevism, 'socialism', all the varieties of collectivism, however they might be masked by dictatorships, national systems or racist ideologies, the process of regression seems to have reached its limit, from which any further development cannot long tarry in taking another direction, given that we cannot go any further down than

we have already. Here however it falls to us to consider the constructive counterpart of our previous exposition. We proceed then to the
examination of the possibility of reconstructing the idea of State, of
the conditions to which it is subject, of the relations that it — on the
basis we have already explicated — can have with the ideals of those
revolutionary, anti-bourgeois and anti-proletariat forces that are still
standing today.

If the process of regression is quadripartite, there is reason to suppose that the reconstructive process too must proceed through four
successive stages of integration, not only so far as a system of order is
concerned (even Bolshevism has the value of an orderly system), but
also and above all with regard to the affirmation of ever higher values,
values which are ever more liberated from what is today meant,
through the materialistic contamination of the concept, by the word
'politics'.

The first point to bring into relief is that, for one thing, the
European peoples have arrived at such a point that we are forced to
consider dangerous extremes. Francesco Coppola, in his time, found
a rather felicitous expression for this; he spoke of the *bad conscience
of Europe* with respect to the crisis that menaces it in its relation to
non-European peoples.[1] In reality, Europe itself, with the perverting
ideologies which have blossomed in its decadence, has created a kind
of Nemesis, which it to say that it has itself propitiated the formation
and the development of extra-European forces which have engulfed
it. America itself emerged by carrying to their utmost consequences
the capitalistico-industrial and 'atavistic' ideals which were initially
glorified by a liberalistico-Enlightenment Europe as comprising true
'civilisation'.

The ideology of Karl Marx served as a point of reference for the
formation and the constitution of an entity of modern power from the
ancient promiscuous and barbarous substance of the Slav *demos*. The

---

1   Francesco Coppola (1878–1957) was a politician, journalist, writer and teacher
     in international subjects. — Trans.

notorious principle of 'popular sovereignty', together with the equally notorious principle of 'nationality' which had already devastated our great medieval ecumenical civilisation, was premised on the revolt of the peoples of colour, or at least on their autonomy, which would put an end to the supremacist dreams of the 'white race, master of the world'. And we could go on. For Europe, *in primis et ante omnia*,[2] the most pressing thing is to open our eyes to this lesson of recent history, which is full of profound meaning. It is a question of comprehending that the first task is that of an *internal purification*, which is to say of an elimination of those anti-traditional, rationalistic, materialistic, mechanistic, anti-hierarchical ideologies with which Europe is infected. Europe must first of all offer the example of *detoxification*, that is of the rejection of those ideologies of which Europe knew nothing whatsoever before the latest forms of the decline of the idea of State, before the advent of the 'third estate' and subsequently of socialist internationalism and of the glorification of the collective in the various forms of gold-hungry and mechanistic civilisation.

The second step is to recognise that modern civilisation and society represent a deviation essentially for this reason: for that character of *teratological hypertrophy* of certain values with respect to others. This is certainly not the first time in history that one witnesses the manifestation of anomalies, in the sense of one-sided developments of the lowest, most 'human', most materialistic possibilities at the expense of those that in a normal and spiritual type of State defined the higher and ruling social strata. But hitherto these were always sporadic manifestations, whose negative character was altogether clear. Modern society is rather characterised by a *rationalisation* and a *naturalness* of the *abnormal*. That everything today should be measured in terms of those values which were in ancient times proper only to the inferior castes, that no one is any longer able to think save in terms of 'economy', of 'work', or of 'politics' (in the materialistic and

---

2   Latin: 'in the first place and before anything'. — Trans.

secularised sense), or of 'payment', or of 'service', or of 'collectivity' and
so forth, even when one is dealing with questions of an entirely different order — up until yesterday this seemed altogether normal, and
it seemed natural that everything else was nothing but 'abstraction',
'utopia', 'inane idealism', 'antihistoricism', all fit for wastrels.

The reconstructive problem is for this reason above all a problem
of *limits*, which is to say of *circumscription*: then it is a problem of
integration, of *compensation*, of *hierarchy*. It is a question, so to speak,
of restraining a force which is devastating to the extent that it is unleashed, to the extent that, believing itself to be a reason unto itself, it
bears everything else along with it: it is a question of yoking this force
to valid laws which derive, not from it, but from higher interests and
principles. To this end, it is necessary to clear the road of all those political formations and all those social myths which, proceeding from
below, delude themselves that they are capable of creating order — an
order which is merely momentary, contingent, violent, producing
those last forms of the fall of the idea of State. This represents effectively the emergence of the irrational, deprived of the light of any true
principle.

In this respect, an ambiguity can be seen in many contemporary
political phenomena, an ambiguity which makes them into both
potential forms belonging to a downward direction, and potential
supports for reconstruction. The first among these phenomena is
nationalism. We have already stated in what sense the affirmation of
the nationalistic phenomenon constitutes a fall: to the extent in which
it signifies the advent of the democratically self-organising collective,
meant to supplant the aristocratico-spiritual form of unity with a
thoroughly laical and secularised one, positing as supreme values that
can be defined only by race, or blood, or soil, or history in the inferior
sense of these words, and in all of this almost resuscitating *totemism*:
since just as for totemism, so too for this kind of demagogic nationalism, the precept is that the individual, before feeling himself in the
dignity of a person, must feel himself as a group, a collective, a faction.

Moreover, even laying aside the racistic kind of nationalism, every *statisation* too enters this downward path; and this is true whether it proceeds from the centre, absolutistically (as was the case already with the forms of nationalism favoured by the kings of France) or whether it proceeds from the periphery, as the 'social' ladder of the State. For which, however paradoxical it might seem, once we have considered the essential thing, we perceive that there is at bottom nothing but a difference in degree standing between collectivistic nationalism, internationalism and Soviet-style or American-style anonymity. And the essence of the question is this: the type of relations which hold between the individual and the group. In the first case the individual is dissolved once more into ethnico-national stocks which become almost mystical entities; in the second case the very difference proper to these stocks is left behind, and there is a tendency toward a more massive collectivisation and disintegration of the person into the element of the mass, so that the fatherland comes to call itself 'humanity' or 'international'.

We are speaking of the two phases of the process of collectivisation, and to move from the one to the other it suffices for the 'race' or the 'nation' to give way to a rationalised structure of a purely economic and mechanical kind. Indeed, this structure, by its very nature, is impersonal, since the last remnants of qualitative difference have been extirpated and all borders have become pure concepts, or else artificial limits set between powers which, 'modernised' as they are, differ from one another in almost no qualitative way. And thus the roads are virtually open to the rise of the mass-man, without fatherland, unified by that law which was once only the law of the lowest of the traditional castes: *work* and *service* without light. Taken in this aspect, nationalism finds its place, in the process of the quadripartite fall which we have clarified, between the epoch of the dominion of the *third caste* (the epoch of the 'merchants', capitalism, liberalism, plutocracy) and the epoch of the dominion of the last caste (Bolshevism).

But precisely by way of this placement, it is possible to conceive of a different kind of nationalism which, in a like intermediate position, can be encountered, *not by descending, but by reascending.* This is a nationalism which has value not for its internal 'collectivising', but for its external differentiation; which is to say, as a force which withdraws from the collectivistic-internationalistic collapse, reacts against it, establishes new and firm divisions within which an organising function in the higher sense must manifest, a differentiating force which already belongs to a higher kind of force — a *spiritual* force.[3]

In this direction, it is essential to overcome the arguments of that demagogic and socialite polemic which, while leading one to believe that one battles *individualism* — that product of natural-right dissolution — in reality turns essentially against that which is the basis and the presupposition for every civilisation worthy of the name: *the dignity of the person.* In reality, if one is to speak of *organisation,* one must first speak of *differentiation,* that is, the affirmation of the principle of the personality. And the distinctive character of the true State is precisely this: that it is a virile State, a personalised State, a State which smashes apart every myth of collectivism and of 'socialism'.

---

3   This conception of the nation was, in certain aspects, found in the best kind of Fascism. When Mussolini declared that the democratic myth of the nation had been liquidated — that myth 'which aggregates the people in the greatest number, lowering the level of the many' — and when he maintained that the nation was 'neither race nor geographically individuated region, but a historically perpetuating lineage, a multitude unified by an *idea*'; when he conceived of the State almost as an 'entelechy' which forms the nation from within, as a force, but a spiritual force; when he stated that it was not 'simply a mechanism to limit the spheres of presumed individual liberties', but was rather almost 'the deepest soul of every soul', 'the interior form and norm, which disciplines the whole of the person'; when, on this basis, he rejected the socialist myth, and affirmed the subordination of the economy to the transcendent idea which constitutes the nation, as the body to the soul, and added to this the supreme conception according to which service is justified essentially by way of participation in a 'higher life, free from the limits of space and time' — in all of this, we were given the fundamental elements for a positive nationalism, for an anti-Jacobin, anti-collectivistic, spiritual reconstruction and reorganisation.

Its premises can be clearly constated in these felicitous words of Paul de Lagarde: 'Being 'human' means less than being 'national', and being 'national' means in turn less than being a person. In other words: as compared to the quality 'humanity', the differentiating element of 'nation' adds the value x, and the element of 'personality' adds to this x a further increment of value y.'[4] This very well expresses the concept of a progressive differentiation, from the formless toward form, from the general toward the concrete, from the collective toward the personality.

With respect to the amorphous mass of the democratico-humanitarian or Sovietico-proletariat myth, the renewal of national limits constitutes therefore a first movement forward (albeit an elementary one), in the sense however of delimiting a zone, within which a further differentiation can be effected: that of the *personalities* which become themselves, elevating themselves to higher forms with respect to anything common, elementary, simply ethical, instinctive or materialistic which might associate them.

To this higher differentiation there will correspond an order which is itself higher. When single personalities have arrived at the point that they have become *types*, with each of them having *its own* meaning, *its own* countenance, then the material will exist for a qualitative hierarchy, based on effective, virile differences, created not by exterior constraints but by the very adherence to activities and to interests which are ever more of a superpersonal character, which is to say, free both from the individualistic limit and from naturalistic promiscuity.

The first reconstructive application of such principles is to be found in the *corporative idea*: the ethical, traditional, qualitative aspect of corporativism would hold in the terms of a reconstruction on the plane of the economy. This aspect would be presented by corporatism as *deproletarising differentiation*, as the creation of qualitatively distinct organisms, formed and internally supported by the ethical

---

4   P. De Lagarde, *Deutsche Schriften*, v. I, p. 164.

principle of solidarity, almost by a spirit of the body in the positive sense, in relation to the tradition of the various arts—in place of the two squalid, procrastinatedly uniformistic fronts of the Marxist ideology.

By this route a return can be prepared to the very spirituality of ancient traditional corporatism—first Roman, then Romano-Germanic, not to speak of the analogous forms existing also in other extra-European peoples: there could be *a personalisation and a spiritualisation of the economic sphere.* Corporatism would suffice to differentiate, articulate and hierarchise that which in the social whole corresponds to the corporeo-vital part of a higher organism and which formed that domain in which the two lower castes could affirm the dignity of personality, through joy in work, pride in one's own art, the identification of a vocation to profess, the honour of one's corporation and the harvest of one's production.

But in this reconstructive work the further aim must not be forgotten, which is that of *decongesting the State of the economy,* to promote a self-discipline of the economy which, through the wise directives of 'economic peace' and the cessation of the convulsions of a ridiculous economic hegemony, would allow the superior energies to release and to give form to a higher plane, the task of the next integrative moment.

For this higher plane, since it would already exist beyond the 'masses', beyond the 'economy', and since here the world that was proper to the two superior castes would reopen, the difficult problem would arise of clarifying what future form might correspond precisely to these castes, that is to the 'warriors' (the warrior nobility) and to the 'spiritual lords'; for it is only in these elements that the new hierarchy can persist and justify itself. With respect to this problem we can offer here but the most summary considerations.

Certainly, a warrior aristocracy would have to be conceived as the higher plane for the realisation of the ideal of the personality—nay, for a realisation which might prolong, through the self-mastery of the one part and the heroic readiness of the other, that which is personal in the superpersonal. It is needless to say that the ideal of war ought to hold as the presupposition for any work of restoration, war not as a 'useless slaughter' or tragic, inevitable 'necessity', but rather as a path to overcoming, to transfiguration, to the heroic trial of a people before the tribunal of history; just as the terror at war, pacifism and humanitarianism are to be considered as the inseparable parts of the demoliberal world and the utopia of the 'technological messianism' of the late European decadence.[5]

Yet the problem which is imposed on us Traditionally, but which the times render arduous, is to see how war might be withdrawn from the great levelling, how it might hold as a specific function of a specific class which finds it vocation in it — a caste, not of 'soldiers', but of *warriors*. But this problem might be resolved, if not entirely, at least partially, in the sense of a *privilege* to *command*, reserved to a certain elite and connected as much as possible to a tradition.

Leaving aside the warrior aspect, that is, the ideal of a formation and higher differentiation in the terms of a warlike personality, the problem of the aristocracy in general must do without those often degenerate and corrupt lineages of that patriciate which is, today, thanks only to a tradition of titles, practically divested of its authority and on the other hand ready for the worst kind of concessions. For save as this is lain aside, the demagogic critique will have free reign, which, through the arraignment of specific persons — in many cases justified — it would arraign as well a principle and an ideal — which is in no wise justified.

We can indeed always conceive of the aristocratic type as that of a personality in which mastery of self, superiority over mere living, a kind of ascesis of power, refinement, united to a sense of fidelity and honour, have become a conquest that, recorded in the blood, manifests

---

5   Italian: *ultima decadenza europea*. This can mean simply the 'latest European decadence', but it is also quite to Evola's broader point that we have reached the bottom, that it also could mean the 'last' or 'final' European decadence — that decadence, beyond which it is impossible to sink any lower. — Trans.

bit by bit in the generations as a naturalness of a higher order. Such
an ideal could not fail to present still a degree of prestige — and the
fundamental problem, in the last analysis, would be to provide a corresponding education aimed toward permitting such a prestige to
slowly gain ground in those strata which, finally liberated from the
'morbid suggestion of despots', have gone on so gloriously to extol the
boxeur and the cowboy,[6] the movie actor and — at most — the popular demagogue.

However, even were we to arrive at this point — even were we to
arrive, that is to say, at the point of reconstructing in one or another
form the reality and the authority of a new 'aristocracy' — it would
still remain to be seen how this aristocracy might refer itself to a yet
higher principle and to acquire a higher meaning by participating in
this principle. Indeed, it is this which is required for the highest integration of the idea of State. Whatever their greatness, the aristocrati-
co-warrior political forms do not and cannot represent the final limit.

At the highest point, spirit and power must become one thing
only, and the purely aristocratic forms have always represented a secularisation, and thus an involution, of this higher synthesis. Thus, in
the context of the present Western civilisation, this point would be the
hardest to resolve concretely. The reason is twofold:

1) On the one hand, Western man has a religious tradition which
   today more than ever seems incapable, not only of surpassing
   the sectarian limitations proper to it to attain to something truly
   catholic, meaning universal, not promiscuously but in a virile way,
   by referring to a super-rational and supersentimental metaphysical reality higher than mere 'belief', but even of simply penetrating
   and comprehending the very foundation of that which it itself
   presents under the mere form of dogma and of 'revelation'. If it
   seems to many 'enlightened' spirits today anachronistic to speak
   of religion, how can they be made to understand that politics must

---

6   Evola gives the first word here in the French, and the second in English. — Trans.

not only be religion, but even super-religion? That the State, to be 'traditional' in the higher sense, must incarnate to a still higher degree than the Church a transcendent spirituality, a force which is effectively from on high, not as empty rhetoric, but as living reality? Nazi Germany, with certain of its transformations of religious politics, has shown to us into what aberrations one might fall when echoes of similar ideas fall upon an unprepared soil — when, in the first place, a fundamental transformation of mentality has not first been effected.

2) On the other hand, what the common man considers most familiar, that is his cultural, scientific, speculative patrimony, has a purely laical, anti-traditional, 'humanistic' character: at bottom, it is naught but the ideological derivation of the era of the advent of the bourgeois and of the plebs, an appendix or a superstructure to a civilisation which is built essentially on the basis of values which are not only not spiritual, but are not even aristocratic — of 'socialistic' values which more or less converge in the realisation of a power not too dissimilar to that which an omnipotent beast might consider its own ideal.[7]

This alternative is excessively paralysing. It has worked to *uniformise* the modern world, but not to *unify* it. The very problem of the form in which a higher unity of the people might be realised remains indeed entirely indeterminate to it, given that to arrive at such a unity, there must be the capacity to posit at the centre of each single State an element which, in its absolute spirituality, is utterly identified with analogous elements realised by other States — and all of this while, in the material, meaning political, respect, the greatest possible autonomy remains to every individual people. First Enlightenment democracy with its rationalistic ideal, then Bolshevism with its technico-proletarian ideal have attempted the technique of such unification in the

7   To better understand this, cf. the second part of J. Evola *Revolt Against the Modern World*.

terms of a degrading materialism, of levelling, of the mechanistic or intellectual uniformity of humanity, leading to their final consequences the premises inherent in the very development of laical Western civilisation.

We hold rather new life must be given to the other form of unity, to a spiritual, super-rational and non-international unity, made possible precisely by an integration of the various national hierarchies in a transcendent element. Let us recall the example of this which stands nearest to us: the *Holy Roman Empire*, the ecumenical unity of the Western nations on an anti-secular front, under the insignia of one who posited himself, not as one laical Prince before another, but as *lex animata in terris*,[8] the bringer of transcendent authority. Save that even in this example a limit is still present, which history itself shows us, recalling us to the perennial antithesis between Church and Empire, between Guelphism and Ghibellinism.

For this very reason, the true breakpoint recedes still further, to be found in those forms in which the dualism of the Christian belief was not yet constituted, for which Servius offers testimony: *Majorum haec consuetudo ut rex esset etiam sacerdos et pontifex*,[9] in those forms of 'solar' regality', before which every separation between spirit and power cannot help but appear as a deviation and the inevitable principle of decline for the supreme ideal of the hierarchy. However this may be, it can be said that such a problem — of the form which might be assumed in a non-anachronistic fashion by a purely spiritual authority as the supreme integration of renewed, fortified and reorganised political bodies, and as the basis for a new supernational European reality — is preceded by a series of other problems which

8   Latin: 'law brought to life on earth'. — Trans.

9   The full sentence is as follows (Servio, *Ad Aen.* 3.80): *maiorum enim haec erat consuetudo, ut rex esset etiam sacerdos et (vel) pontifex, unde hodieque imperatores pontifices dicimus*, meaning, 'indeed it was consuetude among [the ancients] that the king was at once priest and pontifex, for which reason even today the emperors are called pontifex'. — Trans.

are still more concrete and urgent. This is not to say that the former problem is less important than the latter, or that, to farsighted gazes, it does not appear as the lynchpin for the complete overcoming of the cycle of the 'dark' or 'iron age', and the definitive destruction of the various usurpations operated by the inferior castes, which the ancients called *asurya*, meaning the 'non-divine ones'. Not for nothing does the traditional myth recount that it will be the holy emperor himself who, awakening from a symbolic slumber, must summon together those who are still faithful, in order to wage the final war upon the debouching of forces which symbolise that element which every Traditional hierarchy always yoked, conquered and transfigured.

It is just such a myth which must be to us as a fount of strength. Hesiod, gazing upon the spectacle of the iron age, exclaimed, 'That I had never been born!'.[10] Against this, other traditions teach that those who endure, against all odds, in the 'dark age' will be supremely rich with supernatural fruits. The forces which still remain standing, despite everything, will find congenial this truth of the ancient heroic vocation of Western Man, of the man who already knew the prayer, 'Lord, for our enemies, give us the strong!'

---

10 This is somewhat inaccurate. Hesiod 's exact words are, 'I would that I were no part of the fifth generation [the iron age] of men, but had died before or been born afterwards'. Translation mine; see *The Works and Days*, 175 et seq. — Trans.

6. TOWARDS A NEW SCIENCE OF THE STATE

I. IN HIGHER MATHEMATICS, a special order of magnitudes are studied, which are called *vector quantities*. These magnitudes are not defined by their quantity, or their place, or by any other of the usual factors, but essentially by a *direction*. If it be allowed, we would like to take our cue from this for a 'vectoral' consideration, which is today required in the critique of the various views and ideologies regarding the doctrine of the state, the philosophy of law and the philosophy of morality. *We mean to say that it interests us far less to know what a doctrine is — in and of itself, abstractly, academically — than to identify with precision what it actually seeks, its tendencies, that toward which it aims, sometimes unbeknownst even to its own advocates.*

The present situation is such that one must take into account precisely this aspect, in every theory. We hasten to add that with this we by no means intend to align ourselves with pragmatism, insofar as such a term is taken to mean the attitude of those who measure the truth in the light of utility alone, the idea in the light of action alone. The method to which we have alluded rather seeks to discover the 'truth' from out of the variety of truths; which is to say, in a certain sense, the final and, as we were saying, sometimes unconfessed needs that are hidden behind the apparent 'objectivity of the various doctrines, that condition their form and their varying persuasive force and that, overriding every abstract and 'philosophical' formulation that might be made of them, are the true cause of the real influence that certain ideas exercise in a given historical period.

In our exposition of the *preliminaries for a new science of the state*, we have in our previous writings already specified which of these must form its fundamental spiritual premises: personality, an organic-hierarchical conception of the state, an instrumental assumption and a 'transfiguration' of the 'telluric' and irrational aspect of the forces which are at the bottom of the various atavistic anti-bourgeois and anti-proletarian currents of our time. Beyond this, it is a question of seeing what system might best harmonise with and satisfy those premises which, as we have said, are most necessary for a general framing of the new science of the State. But before anything, we proposed to ourselves to undertake an examination of the best-known attitudes in this regard, to ascertain whether in any one of these there is anything valid in light of the ends we have enunciated above. We now wish to commence with a disquisition of the kind, and for this we have indicated the 'vectoral' method: this is not the place to entertain abstract critiques of the various moral and juridico-political theories, so much as to measure the same in the light of their 'sense', of their latent 'intention'.

II. We will commence with the so-called 'positivist school', so as to immediately liquidate it and to eliminate it from our considerations. Whatever forms this school adopts, its basic assumption is that the notions of law, of political order and of duty can be explained and justified, departing from philosophical premises that negate the very essence of the personality. For some of the positivists, the person is the mere product of his social environment; for others, of tendencies and naturalistic appetites, or else of a psychological determinism; for others still, of a 'contract'; and for the rest, finally, it is the product of the mixture of all of these things. In short, it is the common characteristic of the entirety of 'positivism' to consider as effectively real and primary only 'objective' factors, which means extrapersonal factors, even when they are 'psychological'; and then to require of these factors, in a more or less automatic game, a self-styled 'positive' justification for basic moral and social ideas and of the science of the State.

We can consider Marxism and Bolshevism as characteristic expressions of such doctrinal deviation; indeed, they represent its instinctive reduction to the absurd. Bolshevism commences from the radical denegation of the reality and the spiritual value of the person and believes itself capable of conducting humanity to a better state and to happiness itself through collective and 'objective' procedures, thus bringing every residual legitimation of authority and of the law down to the same level. But every other form of 'positivism' also presents the same absurdity, even if, so to speak, in a less intense and more diluted form: the disanimation, mechanisation and 'socialisation' of man is the true sense, the true *terminus ad quem*,[1] of the entire current. We therefore have no truck with all of this. It is not our world. It lies beyond the scope of our problem.

We might also mention that the very theory of the so-called 'rule of law' either exhausts itself in merest description, or else it reflects the same error. The process is ever insipid and impersonal which, according to this theory, leads from the stage of naturalistic will of the individual to forms in which power and right identify with one another or presuppose one another in the form of a kind of superindividual 'objective person'. Thus we remain more or less within the orbit of the Hobbesian *Leviathan*; the individual is located in that which, beneath this presumed 'rule of law', cannot in truth be imposed save as a pure *fact*. Moreover, by its very nature and incompetency, this theory is incapable of indicating anything that, as the meaning of a true moral and spiritual adhesion, can consecrate and confirm the connection of the person with such a State, even when such a state really exists and stands 'objectively' before him.

---

1   Latin: endpoint or goal (lit. 'limit to which'). — Trans.

So as to anticipate a facile reply at this point, we must recall that in our previous writings we have already denounced the confusion surrounding the utilitarian-sociological variant of the school in question. There are some confused individuals who believe they can refer the character of spirituality and of a 'moral end' to certain material needs, so long as these are no longer individual, but rather collective and general. Thus, one might for instance connect the notion of right to the ends of a well-being communal and social rather than individual, and thereby believe one has furnished an ethical basis and a superior justification to these needs, when we are actually dealing simply with a shift of level. If we wish to discover the final 'direction' of theories of this kind, we will find either a confused collectivistic mysticism, which we will shortly speak on, or else a kind of domestication of the individual, which terminates in recognition of how, in general, the common weal, the end of super-individual institutions, also produces clear advantages — in terms of well-being, safety and other materialistic factors — for him as individual. But this thoroughly bourgeois 'logic' has today been overcome: not only the nature of the new atavistic currents, but also the consideration of every historically decisive phenomenon rules out that any given variety of the equation 'well-being = happiness', be it individualistic, socialistic or even nationalistic, can serve as the solution to that problem which we have posed for ourselves, and justify both duty and right in the framework of the new State.

III. By alluding to a confused collectivistic mysticism, we have already passed over into the sphere of a second current, the so-called historical-sociological school, which, in the end, leads to consequences none too different. In this ideology, neither the personality nor a truly spiritual principle find adequate place. One discourses here, in a tone somewhere between the romantic and the revolutionary, on the 'conscience of the people', the 'spirit of the nation', the 'immanent life of history', 'humanity' and so forth, and from such abstractions one believes one can draw something capable of justifying the law on the one hand, and the loyalty of the individual, which is at once *conscientious* and free of second thoughts, on the other. We emphasise the word 'conscientious', because we have already warned that 'myth' cannot constitute the final endpoint for the present considerations: otherwise, we would be well disposed to recognise that 'myths', whose substance is even more hollow than the abstractions mentioned above, often suffice and have sufficed to move the masses. From the point of view in which we are working, on the other hand, these collectivistic pseudo-justifications seem to us to contain at once an absurd theory and a dangerous practice.

Indeed, it is theoretically absurd to posit as primary reality the collective life and to suppose in it spiritually higher values, when one is incapable of explaining whence this life comes in the first place and what it might mean independent of the individuals that compose it. It is clear that, in this respect, we find here either a mere abstraction, capable of holding at best as a 'myth', or else we wind up in a vicious circle, because this collective, which is supposed to give the individual his sense of higher values, cannot be imagined save as a kind of cumulative sum of individual lives. And it is here that we find the 'dangerous' aspect of all of this. Indeed, on the plane of the real, the psychology of the masses teaches us that, in certain circumstances, *the collective comes to life in terms of an almost autonomous reality: but then it awakens the essentially prepersonal, passional, subconscious, ancestral part in individuals; and in the second place it is such that its spiritual level, far from exceeding that which each individual, or the best of them, as persons, would be capable of attaining, is always inferior to the average itself. In short, it indicates only a dissolution from the higher to the lower.*

Thus it is that in the schools in question, behind their words and their ideologies, there acts a kind of impulse toward spiritual regression and intellectual involution. The 'social', collectivist and 'historical' points of reference would lead the individual who accepts them, in

that appearance of romantic primitiveness and mythological indeter-
minacy which these schools like to take on, only to open himself to
subpersonal and uncontrollable influences, at that very moment when
he believed he was transcending himself, elevating himself and justifying himself with a higher ethical world.

Even the idealistico-immanentistic school presents this virtual and
'vectoral' potential for promiscuity. These ideas of 'society', 'popular
conscience', 'history', etc., which are already rather empty and abstract
in themselves, give way here to other hypostases which are still more
empty and abstract, like the 'transcendental I', the 'Absolute Spirit', the
'Pure Act' and so forth. In general, the so-called principle of immanence or of dialectic identity rules here, which is simply the principle
of confusion. Hence, as is well known, these schools all speak of the
identification of the individual with the universal, of the individual
with the State, of ethics with rights, of 'ideality' with reality and such-
like. In all of this we find either simple word games, or else once again
the clear tendency to dissolve whatever has the value of true personality in the individual, and to undermine the presuppositions of every
true hierarchy. Nor is it without significance that those who years ago
attempted to draw social and legal deductions from premises of this
kind in Italy, in the form of so-called 'pancorporatism', wound up in
a veiled exaltation of collectivism, of the anti-hierarchical, socialised
and technified State.

Anyone who considers the Italian proponents of this school must
recognise that it is Croce who has elaborated the most differentiated
view as compared to any other: he has distinguished between an 'economic' sphere, whose principle would be the pursuit of well-being and
of purely individual utility, more or less regulated by the preponderant
power of the politician and juridical system, and an ethical sphere,
whose principle would be pure reason, the pure universal, and which
would be the sphere of the State, not insofar as it is a simply political and juridical entity, but insofar as it is an ethical State. This would
seem to limit the confusion inherent to the 'philosophy of identity':

in such a philosophy, 'value' and brute fact have the possibility of changing, and the premise to the effect that that alone is real which is rational, and that the fact is only the act of the spirit, is ever ready to furnish excuses for every passive philosophy of the *fait accompli* and to every abdication of the dignity of the person.

But as for that universal of pure reason, which is supposed to be the determinate principle and the supreme point of reference for the entire ethical sphere — and thus for the ethical State and, subordinately, to law itself, given that the ethical level of the spirit absorbs and 'resolves' in itself the pre-moral 'economic one' — as for this pure reason, if one attempts to understand in what it practically consists, one will find nothing but the principles of a kind of liberalism wearing more or less Kantian philosophical garb.

IV. It is in no way uncommon that the universal of Kantian practical reason should make itself the accomplice to such snares as these. The entire so-called 'critico-formal' school begins with an ethical imperative that claims to hold good in and of itself, 'a priori', while it is incapable of defining itself without the surreptitious introduction of absurd egalitarian and levelling premises. Is not this what happens already with Kant himself, when the categorical imperative ends up mandating that one considers any given human creature as an end and not as a means, thus gifting to every man the same dignity and presuming that only those norms of action are valid such as are capable of assuming the levelling traits of a universal law? To which is added the rationalistic abstraction of the view according to which man takes on the value of a person only by way of an abstract *ratio*, which one must conceive as having fallen from out of the pure blue sky, but which really reveals itself practically as an ideological construction, obedient to very clear aims and to a special, and altogether questionable, viewpoint.

This critique holds also for so-called 'legal idealism', understood as a kind of spiritual assumption of natural law. In Italy too this path has had its followers: for example, Del Vecchio follows a not dissimilar road. Natural right, as an innate datum present in every human being, takes on almost an ethical character: it is not so much the simple affirmation of the rights of the individual on the material plane which is innate, but rather the need to respect man as such: hence an ideal and universal right, just as one supposes the rational nature of man to be universal. This right ought to serve as a perennial critique and impetus toward positive right, which presupposes it. In this, the egalitarian and liberalistic premise is once again visible. Although it is claimed that positive right has its original source in the ethicality of this natural right, nonetheless one can always recognise a dualism, or at least an inequality and a certain divergence between on the one hand various positivistic orders, which are necessarily particular and conditioned by history, and on the other the criterion of the immanent *ratio* which tends only toward universality and, at bottom, takes as an ideal limit a unified universal right which embraces the whole of humanity.

Beautiful and 'noble' views, to be sure: if only the purely subversive use to which this *ratio* can be put were not perfectly clear, the way in which this self-styled 'ethics' is invoked in every critique against every positive authority and against every order differentiated by any idea of race or tradition. It seems to us well to insist on this abstractistic-rationalist or collectivistic common denominator, present in all the currents we have indicated here. We must thus be wary of making common cause with those who, while they pretend toward an affinity with our positions, and while they, not possessing any properly creative capacity and wishing nonetheless to treat of the philosophy of right and the science of the State, are constrained to use the material at hand, and so perpetuate in our milieu a climate which has altogether nothing in common with our political conscience and with the problems of an anti-bourgeois and anti-proletarian revolution. We must rather insist on this, that the Kantian, formulistic and neo-natural-law concept of 'rationality' is by its very nature uniformistic and also depersonalising in the worse sense of the word. It was well to speak of a 'standardisation of pure reason', the speculative canonisation proper to an ideal of the liberal-democratic type, in the name of which one demands in good egalitarian fashion the respect and recognition proper to the 'person', even with respect to those who, being 'persons' in name only, have, so far as justice is concerned — *aequitas* and not *aequalitas*[2] — no right whatsoever to this.

But still more evident is it that here we are moving in a world of philosophical abstractions and that, at root, it is precisely for this reason that such theories have managed to do much less ill than they might have done. It is far from clear that one or the other of these schemes — positivism or historicism, sociologism or legal formalism, ethical idealism or absolute idealism or what have you — would suffice to oppose those human forces that possess an anti-bourgeois and anti-proletarian political conscience, or that they would be able to tether these forces any more than can the irrational and hypnotic force of some 'myth' or other.

V. In our considerations here we have ever insisted on the concept of the *person*, because leading man — or at least, a sufficiently large group of men — back to this value of the personality, which a thousand cultural, social and political processes have gravely injured, with an action spanning by now hundreds of years — this constitutes the primary and fundamental task today. The principle of the new ethics, of the new hierarchy, of the new right, of the new State is precisely: *be a person*. Could it be then that we ourselves wind up in a simple word which, though it be promising, is at bottom devoid of any definite and positive content? It does not seem so…

According to the traditional conception, to be a 'person' means to possess an effective superiority in the face of natural being, before everything which is simple instinct, simple life, and, moreover, before

---

2   Latin: 'equity' and 'equality', respectively. The distinction is between giving to every man what is rightly his on the one hand, and giving to everyone precisely the same things on the other. — Trans.

everything which is abstract, in the Aristotelian sense of general, common, undifferentiated, promiscuous. *Now, above all in an epoch and in a humanity like our own, it can be said that to be a person is not a 'fact': it is not the case that the individual, every individual, simply for having been born a man, is* eo ipso, de jure,[3] *a person.* This to provide some understanding of the polemical spirit we have already advanced with respect to a certain more or less Christianistic and rationalistic ethical universalism, which takes as its tacit presupposition precisely the superstition of the 'sacred' and of the 'inviolable' aspect which every single human presents, being as he is already a person, simply because he is a man.

Certainly, nothing comes of nothing, and in every human being one must recognise the *potentiality* of actuating oneself as person. But we must not take this abstract potentiality into consideration when we are dealing with right, with a positive norm for life, with the science of the State, but rather only the levels and conditions of its real development. To be a person implies an internal duality: it implies an 'I' which can command and an 'I' that must obey. The relation between these two 'I's' admits an almost undefined multiplicity of levels: from the coalescence of a higher *I* which entirely adheres to the instinctive and passional part, all the way to an *I* that so to speak holds the entirety of its life in its hand and gives its life the precise form of its own law.

Here we must however prevent every negative 'overman' interpretation, recognising that the solid and true dominion of one *I* over the other is possible only to the extent that the first, in its turn, is referred to a higher order, participates in that order and into that order gradually places the true centre of its whole life. When such a reconnection is not made or is interrupted, there is no way of truly guaranteeing the value and the hegemony of the 'person' before lower forces and elements.

But this participation cannot always have a direct and complete form. And this is the point that leads us to the individual ethical plane — that sphere, in which holds the principle, or rather (since we

---

3   Latin, 'by that fact, by law'. — Trans.

are not speaking of a Puritan and fanatical imperative, but rather of a *vocation* which defines a *dignity*), the invitation: *be a person* — on the level of social organisation, of hierarchy and of the State. That internal differentiation and that internal dominion which we have mentioned are rudimentary at best in the many in their normal state. Thus the necessity becomes clear, for every political order of a higher type, to mobilise with every means at its disposal the 'heroic force' of the individual, his irrationality, so far as to agitate it, to carry it, in one way or another, actively outside of the individual, beyond the individual. This is the task proper to 'myths' and the the action aimed at the leaders of crowds and revolutions and counter-revolutions. To awaken these forces means to awaken something which is on the one hand dangerous, and on the other can lead, under certain conditions, to the actualisation of that 'personality' which is to a great majority of men only potentially 'personality'.

And that this might come to pass, it is necessary that real points of reference exist: otherwise one might bring about a kind of rico-chet. The force which is awakened might propitiate, for its inevitable relations with the collective, that spiritual regression which we have already mentioned.

The function of these points of reference can only be explicated by a group of men in whom appears actualised at a high level, that which in others lives only as an unconscious 'ideal', a 'task' or a potentiality. *The hierarchical reconnection thus assumes the value of a 'participa-tion' and constitutes the very condition for an indirect development of the personality,* and vice versa: the development of the personality creates the interior conditions for a hierarchical reconnection. It is a question of projecting an internal duality externally, if one can put it this way — transferring that higher I, which one does not know how to complete and directly realise, into the person of the leaders or the higher casts, so that obedience to them, sacrificing oneself and super-individualistically fighting for them, no longer takes on the character of servilism, of fanaticism or of mere necessity, but rather expresses a technique and a discipline, and acquires the meaning of an indirect obedience to a higher form of oneself, and a battle and a sacrifice for the realisation of the personality itself.

The ethos proper to every great hierarchical civilisation confirms these meanings, since these civilisations show us that the joy and the pride which the internal takes in serving the higher is inseparably joined, even in the very lowest of the social classes, to a firm sentiment of one's own personality, of one's own dignity and of one's own honour. Thus the value of the personality, from the highest spheres, in which it has its proper place and its direct realisation, is reflected on all levels and even in those ways of being and those forms of life and of work that, without it, seem to have remained in the order of the most formless and opaque materiality — as is seen to happen in the type and the 'ideals' of the modern 'proletarised' worker.

VI. From this fundamental view it is easy to draw an orderly series of deductions, which can furnish the central points of reference to the various branches of a new conception of social order and of the science of the State. Such deductions constitute the object of our next writing, with which we will, therefore proceed so far as various 'specialised' spheres, once we have fully clarified the principles. Here, we yet have space for a few more general considerations.

So as to avoid that the entire system floats suspended in the void, we must always insist on this: that the task of the personality, which is proper to the higher community, to the elites and to the leaders and lords, must lead much less to the dominating Nietzschean type or to the pattern of humanistic principles, than to an effective, transcendent spirituality. 'By divine right' is only a formula, and perhaps also a symbol: however, in its essence it means nothing other than this. For the moment, we do not intend to confront the spiny problem of the relations between State and religion. This problem, however, will be imposed sooner or later on the new science of the State and will require a radical solution. Wherever power is not justified from on high, *there Bolshevism looms on the horizon*, and the metaphysical tension necessary for hierarchical participation is rendered impossible. We will not touch here on the constitutional side of the question, but only the subjective side; it is a question of enclosing within a form and a lifestyle something that, effectively, betrays contact with and even the living presence of a superior order, an idea and a will which is stronger than everything which is merely life, not to speak of that which draws its meaning only from the particular interests of a brief human cycle. An ancient Nordic saying has it that 'Let whomever is lord, be a bridge'. According to an ancient etymology which is perhaps imprecise, but not for that less significant, the *pontifex* was the 'builder of bridges',[4] that is, the man who established the connection between shorelines, between two worlds.

In our previous writing we noted that to speak of an organic order *sic et simpliciter* is not enough, since there are many different kinds of organisms, beginning from those which can barely be differentiated from the stage of an acephalous living mass. The organism of the true State must be well differentiated, even as the human organism is. This means identifying and then hierarchising distinct levels, in correspondence both with various modes of realisation, and with various degrees of perfection, of the personality principle. In this regard, we believe that the traditional conception of a quadripartite order, in respective correspondence with the principle of simple work, the economico-social principle and politico-social principle in the strict sense (administration, organisation), the warrior principle and finally the spiritual principle, most certainly might have some role to play. These principles correspond to very specific ways of being, very distinct vocations; in relation to each of them there is a special way of being a 'person' and also a given quantum of being a person, since, as is natural, not all vocations present equal possibilities with respect to the supreme end. But with the subordination of one plane to another, all the way up to that centre constituted by the lords 'who are bridges',

---

4   The major alternative etymology would draw this word from the Oscan-Umbrian *puntis*, meaning 'propitiatory offering'. — Trans.

the integration and the justification of every partial degree of the whole is established.

The premises of this hierarchical vision of the true state lead to the elimination of ethico-rationalistic universalism and its substitution with a differentiated and functional conception of ethics, of right, of solidarity and of obligation. Indeed, recognising that *equality of rights is an absurdity, and that there do not exist — as if they were mass-produced — mere persons, but rather a variety of differing degrees of realisation, in various men, of the ideal of the person:* from this follows the restriction of equality of rights to those communities or social and political strata which are defined by an equal way of being and an equal function. *In other words, we believe that the traditional conception of the* ius singulare,[5] *if understood in its true essence, still has something to teach us.* It is a matter of putting *aequitas* and the true *suum cuique*[6] in the place of *aequalitas*: solidarity and reciprocity among equals alone is not absurd; among non-equals, the true ethics is not that of the abused 'justice' *à la* humanitarian, but rather that of subordination and of the functionality between higher and lower, between one law and another. To this there naturally corresponds an analogous differentiation and hierarchical implication both of right and of everything which, in the public and private sphere, depend on it.

---

5   Latin: 'singular law', understood in contrast to the *ius commune* or 'common law' which has ruled supreme in modern times. The *ius singulare* suggests different (singular) rights and duties for different (singular) groups of persons. — Trans.

6   Latin: 'to each his own,' meaning classically that each member of the commonweal should receive that which is fit to him by his nature and his quality. As a philosophical precept it traces its origins to Plato and in particular to the *Republic* (Cf. Book 4, 443a). The Latin phrase comes from Cicero (see *De Rerum Natura*, Book III, 38). It is strictly related to the idea of 'distributive justice' which Evola here references, and which was one of Aristotle's political themes (see *Nichomachean Ethics*, Book III, 9.1280a7–22). Aristotle understood by distributive justice 'giving the equal to equals, and the unequal to unequals,' concept connected strictly with the idea of merit, and tied to the aristocratic regime which Aristotle often calls the best regime. — Trans.

7. ON THE SPIRITUAL FOUNDATION OF THE NEW SCIENCE OF THE STATE

PRELIMINARIES

I. IN OUR WRITING on 'The New Science of the State', an order of problems was indicated which are certainly of extreme importance for whomever feels the need to define in a doctrinal system the fundamental tendencies of our vision of the world.

Since the general premises of a 'new Science of the State' were explicated in that writing, we will seek here to draw from this a point of departure to develop a number of considerations concerning the domain which is properly our own competence, and which regards the ethical and spiritual side of the doctrine.

We begin by concurring wholly with Carlo Costamagna,[1] when he denounces the very formula of the '*modern State*'. We must insist that we have and we ought to have nothing to do with the 'modern State'. The 'modern State' stands decidedly behind us. The formula of

---

1 Evola refers here to an article by Carlo Costamagna from *Lo Stato*, VIII, March 1937. Curiously, Evola never once refers to him by name in the present article, but rather calls him merely 'the author'. Note is made of this fact here for what might be inferred from it about Evola's regard for the author in question; but the translator has substituted Costamagna's name for the original circumlocution, in order to avoid confusions. — Trans.

the 'modern State' attempts to pass off the contraband of a mere appendix of that evolutionistico-progressive superstition which brings one to believe that with rationalism, scientism and democracy the history of the world has truly and finally come into its adulthood, leaving behind it a world of barbarisms. We must not delude ourselves: this mentality, which we feel to be so anachronistic, persists to this day in many circles. Not only, but it hides even and especially at the bottom of certain views which we have indicated, which pass for 'technical' and 'scientific', and which in their final sense are not altogether understood by those who use them and consider them as 'acquisitions'. To the extent to which the forces of an anti-bourgeois and anti-proletarian revolution stands at the avant-garde of contemporary history, the 'modern State', along with whatever this term is meant to indicate, is to be considered as something past and residual, which obstructs every reconstructive effort.

Closely considered, the idea of the 'modern State' is moreover connected to that doctrinal dissociation, frequently masked by 'specialisation', which is precisely 'a modern characteristic'. Costamagna has rightly observed that 'so-called modern thought has lost that sense of *unity*, which once constituted, in the previous phases of history, the constant preoccupation of the spirit'. So far as we are concerned, we will observe that this is not simply a question of the social plane, wherein the decomposition is manifested as individualism and liberalism, but that these social effects are only the counterpart of a much more general and essential decomposition, that which, for example, brought to life an abstract right counterposed to form, a faith as a 'private affair' detached from politics, an economy which is superstitiously substantialised as an autonomous reality with its inflexible and indifferent determinisms acting over human forces, a political reasoning that has no truck with ethics, and so forth. It is in this way that from an *organic* world, from a world in which each being and each activity had its rightful place, and maintained thus his proper specific quality and his proper relatively independent function in the order of the whole, we passed over to a world constituted by incoherent atoms. And individualism, rather than a doctrine which is to be studied in and of itself, should rather be conceived of as the *symptom of a state*, which is to say of the very levelling condition which emerged from decomposition and through which the legal fiction and the utilitarian myth seek in vain to gain once more, in some semblance of order, the forms of a world which has passed from the organic plane of quality to the mechanical plane of quantity. Individualism and abstract legalism are therefore two kindred realities, and the same can be said once again for every variant, be it 'sociological' or 'utilitarian' or 'positive', of this famous idea of the 'modern State'.

In connection with this, and repeating what we have already said on other occasions, everything which liberalism proposes should be rejected whenever it feigns to protect and defend the human personality. Liberalism knows nothing of the *personality*, it knows only of the *individual*, which represents the degradation and almost the caricature of the personality; and with its egalitarian and levelling ideology it destroys the very possibility for the person, the very possibility that the individual might have value. Neither liberalism nor legalism nor any other ideology that has sought to furnish a foundation to the type of the 'modern State' is capable of presenting any principle at all such as might resist a deep and unprejudiced critique, in favour of the defence of dignity, of the sense and of the true value of the personality.

II. But this will be the result of a disquisition that we do not wish yet to anticipate, since, for now, we must rest for a moment on the idea that only an organic conception can be considered as the principle of the new science of the State. 'That is a commonplace,' it will be said. 'Not at all,' we will reply, 'if one bears in mind that which we have said regarding a *decomposition*, of which the politico-social chaos is only one of the most external and consequential aspects' — and if one realises, moreover, the abuse that has been made and that is still too often made today of the word 'organic', given that in a great many cases this term is used to express something which should rather and only be called 'collective', 'general', 'organisational' or 'rationalised'.

This is very important: while today we can observe — despite everything — the subsistence of revolutionary anti-bourgeois and anti-liberal positions, we must at the same time recognise that these positions contain, in their turn, various tendencies and possibilities, which are even in some case contrary to one another: and to identify these tendencies and possibilities is a fundamental task for the new science of the State. Let us consider also this: that the positions of which we now are speaking have a predominately activistic and ir- rationalistic tenor. They want nothing to do with previous political, legal and juridical systems, because these latter nourish a strong dif- fidence toward everything which is, in general, the product of abstract reason, this Goddess of the last century. For this reason, these forces are in a certain measure prejudiced by a dialectic: their movement is that of reaction and intolerance, it is a being *against* something before being *for* something. So much for their originary character. According to this character of theirs, such currents are to be conceived of as a *dynamis* or *hylé*[2] in the Aristotelian sense; whatever in them stands against everything today which oppresses or does not know certain fundamental vital values is to be considered, in its turn, only as 'materia prima' compared to the task of a new formation. We must neither forget that the irrational, as a vital emergence, always has fa- tal connections with the pre-personal and the collective. This truth of individual psychology is reflected in the world of contemporary activistic currents: we must indeed recognise that, in one form or an- other, an epoch of collectivism is opposed to the epoch of liberalism. *Now, the collective has little enough in common with the organic; and so long as we oscillate between the two poles of this individuo-collectivist antithesis — poles which, as happens in every contraposition, condition one another and take on each the sense of the other — we will resemble*

---

2   From the Ancient Greek δύναμις (potency, potentiality, power, capability) and ὕλη (matter), respectively. — Trans.

a sick man rolling from one side of the bed to the other, sleepless and hysterical, rather than standing up and leaving.

This, it will be said, is but another platitude, since we well know that these forces oppose liberal individualism as much as they do Marxist collectivism. Well enough: but let us get to the bottom of this platitude, let us seek to clarify its implications, if it is to be something more than a mere stereotypical formula for journalistic proclamations, but rather a true principle of doctrine.

As a consequence of the considerations we have just submitted, let us fix an idea in our minds: the destruction of those schemas which are either positivistic, or rationalistic, or mechanico-sociological or utilitarian, through movements whose watchwords are strength, action and that authority which imposes itself directly by chaining and transporting the irrational, instinctive and sentimental substrate of individuals — this destruction must be considered proper to a state of transition and, in the etymological sense of the word, of crisis. And this state of transition is not to be confused with a solid and positive point. We must on the other hand consider the same phenomenon as negative wherever it leaves open the possibility of a totalitarianism or an integralism based on the overthrowing of those true hierarchical relations which stand between various levels and degrees. This is the tendency of an irrationalist pragmatism which in our opinion constitutes one of the greatest dangers of the world revolution, given that it would lead us, in one way or another, to a materialism not dissimilar to the Marxist vision of history itself. Indeed, when one proclaims the primacy of strength and action, and when one affirms that every idea and every principle has worth insofar as it aids one in reaching predefined ends, it is clear that it will no longer be possible to justify those ends themselves, save in the terms of materialistic realism.

So as to prevent facile objections at this point, we must denounce the sophism which consists in conferring the charisma of a spirituality

and an 'aseity'[3] to certain material ends, the moment that these cease
to regard the individual and make themselves collective. That this
collectivity subsequently assumes various signs, either classist, or nationalist, or internationalist, does not constitute a true divide; the true
divide is determined by *quality*, and quality certainly does not enter
into the question when the individual is overcome in the interest of
projecting the same attributes that constitute the natural, materialistic,
utilitarian or irrational aspects of the individual onto the presumed
super-individual entities.

If the science of the State is, as the author of the above-mentioned
book understands it, 'the science of the common good of a specific
political society', the unique definition of the essence of this good constitutes therefore the very foundation of such a science. But it is precisely here that many 'technicians' get away with saying that this is no
longer 'their business', that this is already 'philosophy' or 'faith', which
for them naturally is equivalent to something vain and arbitrary.
For which reason, the construction rests, so to say, suspended on a
pledge; a whole legion of persons step forth to claim it, and one lets
them say whatever they wish, certain as one is that 'politics' will not be
disturbed by it.

But this is not a little dangerous. *We must persuade ourselves* that,
however large the force of certain forms of collective inebriation is,
however real, on their plane, their practical value might be, still man
will never cease to ask, at a given moment, about the supreme values
of life and, in short, about the justification of practice. We persuade
ourselves again and again of the character of transition proper to the
purely rationalistic, activistic and militant aspect of the global revolution; for we perceive its 'telluric' side (we borrow this expression,
somewhat against our will, from Keyserling), and we consequently

---

3   The term derives from the Latin *aseitas*, which in turn is taken from *a se*, that
     is, 'by itself', and hence comes to indicate that which is in and of itself, that
     which subsists absolutely, that which is uncontingent. It was generally used to
     speak of divinity. — Trans.

feel its purely 'formal' character, in the techico-philosophical sense of the word—which is to say, in the sense of something that holds independently of any precise content or principle, such as might have the qualities of acting disindividually, of a readiness to subordinate oneself, to fight, to sacrifice oneself in the name of something higher than the individual, something which no longer considers either the animal instinct to survive, nor utility. These qualities are characteristic of the new currents of the anti-bourgeois revolution.

III. A contemporary sociologist, Heinz Marr, has come up with the two terms *Bund* and *budisch* to designate the structure of such currents. The *Bund*, in the acceptation of Marr, is the unity proper to the 'heroic minorities'; it is an affective unity and, at the same time, an elective unity, created by individuals who have lost the precedent forms, whether natural or traditional, of social organisation, but who are nonetheless able to transcend the individualistic closure and their own instinct of conservation, rendering themselves capable of a leap, of blind courage, of unconditional devotion to a Leader. This new type of unity has various degrees: it can proceed from a given group up to an entire party, and, from a party, through aggregation ('integral party'), it can work to give form to an entire nation's *modus essendi*.[4] And thus arises a new type of State — precisely that which corresponds with our political vocation.

Now, Marr touches a fundamental point when he says, 'While every *Bund* is a revolt of the *irratio* against the *ratio*, not every *irratio* is also a *religio*'. Which is as much as to say: even having arrived at this point the problem of legitimation in the higher sense poses itself, in the sense, almost, of a *charisma*. And this is the fundamental problem for whomever affronts the problem of the spiritual presuppositions of the new science of the State.

We must not delude ourselves: the affairs of an especially tragic and tempestuous epoch have mobilised a force, in individuals, which

---

4   Latin: 'way of being'. — Trans.

is no longer the force of the simple *Homo politicus* of the previous epoch, and still less of *Homo oeconomicus* or *Homo iuridicus*.[5] This force — the force which is as cement to the *Bund* — has rather much more the character of a *faith*. It therefore has a metapolitical, 'religious' character. As difficult as it is to contest that in many aspects of activistic revolutionary movements, we find, transposed into secular key, facsimiles of those rights of collective participation that were proper to the religions, it is equally easy to see that *there are few political ideas asserted by the advance of the shattered front of Enlightenment democracy, which are not surrounded by a kind of mystical aura, through which they predominately exercise their action.* A grave responsibility therefore falls upon those who must guide these forces, if we are to avoid, at a certain moment subsequent to the high tension, the rise of a crisis, in the form of a collapse, or else a species of short-circuit. For one cannot proceed indefinitely on the basis of 'myths' and of 'idea-forces', that is, ideas which hold only insofar as they 'act', while the very nature of those forces that have been put into motion excludes the possibility of proposing a 'legitimation' for them in the terms of materialism, even should this materialism be collectivist and nationalist rather than individual.

The moment has come for us to return to a point from which it might seem we have distanced ourselves: the point, that is to say, of the determination of the true content of the notion of 'organism'. Some of the most banal analogic considerations can furnish us the surest guiding principle here. To speak generically of 'organisation' does not suffice, if we are to speak clearly: to speak clearly, we must say also *to what kind* of organisation we are referring. The ladder of the organic world goes from the forms of the invertebrates up to those of the human species, and, in it, up to man as 'person', as personality. All of these forms have in common a kind of vital cohesion between

---

5   Latin: 'Political man', 'economic man' and 'legal (or juridical) man' respectively. — Trans.

one part and another, opposed to a simple 'composition' determined, in the inorganic world, by physical and chemical laws.

The inorganic world can indeed be called the ideal model for the various positivistic, economistic and rationalistic conceptions of society, and the author of the aforementioned work is entirely correct in establishing a relationship between these conceptions and the mechanistic views in vogue in the scientism of the last century. Once the generic antithesis has been posited against the mechanical and inorganic, it is a question of defining what, among the various forms of organism, must serve as the analogical model for the new doctrine of the State. It seems to us rather obvious, in this respect, that this type of organisation, if it is to aim at a unity which must have men as its elements, must more or less reproduce the same hierarchical relations which define the human entity itself, which are not indeterminate and generic, but very precise, manifesting in the distinction between and simultaneous coordination of four powers: the power of pure vitality, the power of the general organic economy (vegetative life, sympathetic nervous system), the power of will, and power of the spirit. *No one will seriously contest the fact that, for any man worthy of the name, the normal condition is that of a life demonstrating the hierarchical subordination of these four powers in the very order in which we have nominated them. And neither should it be difficult to observe that the correspondence of these principles of the human entity in a social organism are:* the world of the masses, the world of the economy, the world of the warriors, the spiritual world.

IV. The consequences of these simple considerations are decisive, even as regards the problems that interest us here. The first of these consequences is that every social organisation that 'legitimates' itself with the principles proper to any of the inferior hierarchical planes, though it might have a generically 'organic' character (thus: anti-individualism, anti-mechanicalism, and so on), nonetheless exercises a 'debasing'[6] influence, and it will finally favour, in one way or another, the impairment of the personality (or, let us rather say, of the effort of a man to realise his personality and to have the worth of a personality). This, for the simple reason that if the economy, for example, becomes the principle-basis of this organism, it naturally follows that there will be subordination to it, not only of what is inferior to it (the pure materialised collective), but also of what is superior: and for the individual, to live in an organic state in this sense means to find oneself in an environment in which everything will tend to make of will and spirit mere instruments for those forces in man which correspond to the economy, thus degrading both into an inferior use.

Nor is the danger over when the system rests on a higher principle, such as that of the *will* — which is to say when the organic need brings to the fore, in its social and political correspondences, the warrior principle: which is equivalent, more or less, to the activistic conception of the *Bund*, which we have already mentioned.

Indeed, it should be noted that interferences between will and instinct are almost fatal whenever the will constitutes an end in and of itself, excluding the possibility that something higher might illuminate it and justify it, might confer upon it an unshakable character of continuity and absoluteness. The same thing is observed, likewise, as regards the collective: in the most recent world, which is of an activistic political will, uprooting the *ratio* and professing a gospel of a more or less Nietzschean type (that is, of the worst Nietzsche), here and there we see forms emerging which we would willingly call the forms of a *new totemism*; these signify precisely a paradoxical interference between the 'heroic' plane of will and that of a naturalistic and instinctive primordiality. What indeed is one to think when, in certain contemporary tendencies, such as the 'charisma' of the new heroic irrationalism, things like 'race' or 'people' are proposed, conceived almost as mystical entities, jealous and exclusivist more than the Jewish

---

6   Italian: *inferiorizzante*, lit. 'inferiorising'. — Trans.

god himself—entities which claim an absolute right on the plane of the spirit, elevating blood and the instinct of the blood to the level of a new sacrament and opposing the idea of any kind of transcendence whatsoever?

This is one of the cases in which we can clearly see those dangerous turns to which the religious forces of the masses can be brought for the lack of higher principles, when these forces are awakened beneath a political insignia — a case from which it is evident that a new 'organic', even 'mystical' social type can be conceived, which, however, *mutatis mutandis*, would not elevate itself much beyond the level proper to the collectivistic *pathos* of the clans and of the hordes. And there would be much to say — if the economy of the present essay permitted it — regarding what Leopold Ziegler has called the *mythos atheos*[7] and which truly plays a large role in the contemporary world, as a confused religious surrogate offered to an irrepressible need of the new political world wrought of will, of action and of authority: a surrogate that, with respect to the true spirituality, constitutes an even greater danger than does cold, hard materialism. Taking up once more the organic analogy, the world supported by will alone is undermined by a fundamental contingency: when will is abandoned to itself, when it has lost the capacity to recognise any higher principle, it rests fatally open to every influence from below; and it is to influences of this kind that every variety of *mythos atheos*, every political surrogate for true spirituality, are to be traced back.

Once this has been recognised, the tasks that, on this plane, are posed to the new doctrine of the State appear well enough delineated. It is a question of defining the bases of an integrally hierarchical organic order, bringing the activistic world of anti-bourgeois revolution to truly transcendent points of reference. 'Transcend', according to the Latin etymology, means precisely *going beyond by going over*. It is a Traditional teaching that man as man can be a 'person', and as such

---

7   Transcription of Ancient Greek: 'atheistic myth'. — Trans.

can claim for himself the value of being an end, and not a means, as compared to everything which is, insofar as he participates in a supernatural order: in every other case, he is destined to be acted upon[8] by forces that always have a 'natural', sub-personal and collective character.

These fundamental ideas give the necessary points of reference in order to pass beyond the irrationalistic and 'mythological' phase of the anti-bourgeois forces, to surpass both individualism and collectivism, to be able to adopt the concept of the personality as the basis of an integrally hierarchical and organic order.

---

8   Italian: *egli è destinato ad essere agito da forze.* Lit., 'he is destined to be acted (or moved) by forces', in a sense which is not even passive so much as annihilating of any individual will. — Trans.

EDUCATION AND THE FAMILY

1. FEMINISM AND THE TWILIGHT OF CIVILISATION

THE LEVELLING and depersonalising plague which has brought low our modern civilisation has aspects which are so complex and tentacular that not everyone is able to recognise it behind its various masks, so as to oppose each of its forms with a decisive revolt and a conscious reaction.

And thus it is a fact that the by now almost irreparable compromise of those differences in caste, in nature and in internal dignity which formed the principle of every healthy traditional organisation leads to no good end. In aiming to bring every value under the law of quantity and of the anonymity of the mere social collective, this contaminating ideology now desires that, after the levelling wrought between man and man, we proceed now to that between gender and gender; it sees in this a 'conquest', a sign of 'progress'. From the very same anti-hierarchical and anti-qualitative origin of many forms of modern degenerescence, we now see feminism emerging as if in a retching action; it is taking shape in two countries which have become almost like the two jaws of a single pair of closing vicegrips, from the East and from the West, around ancient Europe: Soviet Russia and America. For the Bolshevik equality of woman and man in all aspects of social life finds its perfect reflection in the emancipation which has already been carried out for some time now on the other side of the ocean.

Here we are not speaking from a spirit of personal aversion, nor of the prejudices of an epoch or of a people. In the feminist phenomenon we find a symptom which can be connected through careful logic to many others, and which indicates the advent of a conception through which the very ideal of 'culture', of civilisation, above all in the classical traditional sense, is dealt a mortal blow.

The fundamental meaning of every civilisation was that of a victory of form over the formless, of the 'cosmos' over the 'chaos'. Thus, at the centre of the classical vision of life and of the State we characteristically find precisely the cult and the valorisation of the limit, of the form, of difference, of the clear personality. The world is 'cosmos' and not 'chaos' to the extent that it, like a harmonious living organism, is constituted by a whole of finite parts, each of which has a precise function, proper to it and unmistakable in the whole; its good, its 'truth' therefore does not consist in the cessation of its individuality and in its receding toward the non-qualified, the identical, the indefinite — toward that in which all things mystically and atomistically become a single thing — but rather in being ever more itself, in expressing ever better its proper nature, in carrying its individuation ever deeper, thus rendering the great body of the whole richer, more various and determinate.

Our best traditions always set this valorisation of difference, of the limit, of individuation against all evasionistic and pantheistic visions, which posit the good to lie in the impersonal, in the undifferentiated, so that they almost understand being an individual as a fault or a punishment. Thus they established the principle through which a hierarchical order could arise, on the basis of the natural differences between the beings, and constitute itself in the *gens*, in the city, in the State and, at the extreme, in the Empire.

At present, nothing is 'itself', no natural being is 'itself'. But this condition of 'intermixing', which was traditionally recognised to 'the things below', was always considered to be a condition of imperfection, and the task was given to institutional norms, to morality, and finally to ascesis, to overcome it and to clarify distinct types, genres, classes and individuals — precisely as the artist draws his figures from formless material. Such was the traditional concept of culture or civilisation: form — let us say it again — victorious over 'chaos'.

* * *

It is altogether evident what a contradiction of this point of view is constituted by the principles of egalitarianism, mindless fraternalism, pallid humanitarianism and impersonal universalism which, in various forms, wind through the modern world, undermining not only the concepts of society, of the state, of right, but even the ideals of knowing and acting. Returning to our point of departure, the spirit and the face of *modern feminism* is equally clear on this basis, so far as its particular applications are concerned.

So far as the genders go, feminism, in its demand for equality, subscribes to the view according to which every difference and every distance is to be held an evil. It would abolish the specificity of functions and types, it would tend to something uniform, which however we will not say lies (as is believed) 'beyond', but rather 'within', individuation and the differentiation of the sexes. The result is precisely either the altogether new neutral and Amazonic type of American women and of the sportive European *'garçonnes'*[1] — or else the presexual, camaraderie-communist promiscuity which is so characteristic of the Slavic race, established today by the Bolshevik 'Zag': that promiscuity which almost tempts us to say that the Slavic sexual relationship is only rarely detached from a certain incestuous tinge. These are the two possible conclusions — either uniformistic (standardised) or 'mystical' (promiscuous-communist) — of anti-difference.

Precisely where our morality would command to man and to woman to be ever more themselves, to express ever more decisively and daringly that which makes the one man and the other woman — precisely here, these retch-like movements press backwards. They adulate

---

1   French: 'tomboys'. — Trans.

the developmental stage in which difference no longer exists — and in this they even make the claim of envisioning an 'evolution' of which our 'antiquated' minds would not be capable of following.

The truth is rather that at the bottom of feminism there hides a 'radical pessimism': that is, the tacit premise that woman 'as woman' cannot find value in herself, for which she must, insofar as she can, make herself into a man, claim the same social and intellectual prerogatives of man. In this sense, we call it pessimism: the presumed feminist 'vindication' of woman conceals an abdication of modern woman, her impotence, or her mistrust, at being and at having value as that which she is: as woman, and not as man. It conceals in short a degeneration, in the most rigorous sense of the term. To which, moreover, modern man analogously brutalises himself into a purely physical and animal ideal — at most, a pallidly intellectual one — which represents his own decline from the zenith forms of life, which consecrated his effective 'virility', to which corresponded in our greatest traditions the two highest castes of the social hierarchy: that of the 'Ascetics' and that of the 'Warriors'.

It is as woman — and not as man — that woman realises herself, elevates herself to the same level as man as Ascetic and as Warrior insofar as she is 'Lover' or 'Mother'. To us, the lineage of every value is one and the same: heroism, the overcoming of oneself. But there is an active heroism and a negative heroism: there is the heroism of absolute affirmation and there is the heroism of absolute obedience — there is the heroism of absolute affirmation and there is the heroism of absolute dedication, which each stand in an identical light and at an identical level of greatness.

Thus, this differentiation decrees the natural difference of ways toward interior consummation for man and for woman. To the gesture of the Warrior and of the Ascetic who pass from life to a 'more than life', the one by means of pure action and the other by means of a clear and virile renunciation, ideally corresponds in woman the heroism of the leap to be wholly *for* another being — to give herself wholly to another being, be he the man whom she loves and who is her Lord (the type of the 'Lover'), or be it her child (the type of the 'Mother') — finding in this the sense of her life, her own joy, her own justification and liberation. And in realising oneself ever more intensely and luminously according to these two distinct and unmistakable directions of heroism, attenuating everything in man that is woman and everything in woman that is man — in this stands the internal rule which can give form and order according to nature and spirit.

The modern world, on the other hand, with its '*boxeurs*', with its fanatics of passion and of the most wretched ambitions, with its gold-mongers and car salesmen and 'chauffeurs' in the place of the Ascetics and the Warriors — or, on the other side, with its '*garçonnes*', with its working girls and its 'intellectuals', its 'girls'[2] and all the other forms of naturalised women forced pathetically into the crossroads of public life and of modern corruption — this modern world proceeds at a running pace in precisely the opposite direction of the above ideal. But this cannot help but be accompanied by the twilight of love itself in the deepest, 'organic' sense, a phenomenon connected in turn to the biological destiny of the races itself: for love, like electricity and magnetism, is based on polarity. It is all the stronger and more creative the more decisive is the polarity, the differentiation of the types and of the sexes: absolute woman and absolute man, without intermediary forms.

In the world of the 'evolved', 'emancipated' and conscious woman one might find the promiscuity of an equivocal camaraderie or of pallid intellectual sympathies; there might be encounters of pleasure, just as one might accord to a game of 'bridge' — but there cannot be love in its true and elementary sense, in which the ancients saw the manifestation of an originating and awesome force and a cosmic significance. Just as social egalitarianism has killed the ancient, living, virile relations between man and man, between warrior and warrior,

---

2   This was given in English in the original. — Trans.

between Lord and subject — so pure feminist egalitarianism will lead us ever more toward an insipid and perverted world in which, perhaps — as can already be seen in the banal exhibitionism of American women — women can 'even' seem chaste, so as not to so much as brush the complications of sinfulness.

2. THE SPIRITUAL PROBLEM
OF THE FAMILY

I N THE OCTOBER ISSUE of *Gerarchia*, Arturo Assante expounds
on several considerations on the family as a cell of the organism
of the 'State'; his thoughts merit particular notice and comment.
Assante maintains the following fundamental thesis: there exist two
fundamental conceptions which, in their opposition, seem to constitute an insurmountable dilemma. According to the first, the primary
element of society is the single individual, 'and there is a natural, incoercible discord which is eternally immanent between the individual
and the State, a limit put on his proper activity, a pressure deriving
from preponderant power'. The second conception, 'on the other
hand, negates in a simplistic way the discord and antagonism between
the individual and the State, maintaining that every individual should
be negated, destroyed and resolved into the statal organisation or the
State ethics, which supposedly represents the unique reality'.

Modern political currents seem to be locked into this limiting
antithesis, and they oscillate between the one and the other error,
often enough failing to oppose anything to the individualistic and liberalistic deviation other than a mortifying statolatric and totalitarian
levelling. Yet there exists a synthetic middle term, and only with reference to it can one arrive at a healthy and normal vision: this term is
the family. To conceive of the individual, not in himself, atomistically,
but in terms of the unit and lineage to which he naturally belongs,

his family; to integrate and strengthen the ethical significance of this last and to recognise in it therefore the true cell of the national political organisation — this is the presupposition for the construction of a solidly articulated State, such as overcomes both of the dominant conceptions indicated above. Assante takes his cue for such considerations from the recent norms regarding Fascist family law, which seem to proceed from a persuasion of the kind.

The theoretic and traditional value of this point of view is, for us, not a matter of discussion. The problem rather consists in seeing to what extent it is possible to think such ideas through to the very end, and to what extent we are constrained by the conditions of today's society and civilisation to stop up half way.

It should be observed that the reform and the new political meaning of the family already constitute the subject of a recent book by G. A. Fanelli, entitled *Preliminari per un codice domestico*.[1] The thesis is developed here courageously in all of its principal consequences, and at the same time Fanelli seeks every possible path toward making felt an almost integral revival of the ancient family and the ancient Roman *gens*, not as a utopia and a nostalgia, but rather as something susceptible to harmonisation with the reality of the Fascist State. Fanelli touches on a delicate, but fundamental point, when he observes that 'the omnipotence which has been reached in the modernised States of the most recent national revolutions, the historical grouping of the nation itself, threatens, to be sure, a weakening of the domestic grouping'. This consideration could easily be extended: it is a fact that in the modern contemporary world in general the centre tends ever to shift from private life to public, political or at least associated life. Bolshevism seeks with every means at its disposal to accelerate this process, pushing so far as a kind of *reductio ad absurdum*. But the same process is equally at work in America, in Germany: there is the tendency to withdraw the individual from the familial unit as soon

---

1   'Preliminaries for a Domestic Code'. This book does not appear to have been translated into English. — Trans.

as possible, by causing the life that he lives in collective organisations seem to him ever more important and ever richer. This collective life comes in various kinds, but they are always by their nature super- and extra-familial, if not even statal.

It is undeniable that we are proceeding toward standardised forms, forms of qualitative construction, against which reactions — like that of Fanelli and various Catholics of the Right — are fully justified. But we must not forget this fact: the *collectivist attack on the family arose only after the individualistic dismantling of the same.* The new forms of centralisation seek to recover and to organise individuals, in one manner or another, for the greater part of whom neither family nor tradition nor blood nor class any longer exist, save as mere words, surviving remnants and conventions. These are individuals devastated by the laical and rationalistic modern culture; they have been carried by this culture to no longer consider as a principle anything beyond individual material well-being, careerism and the search for pleasure.

Is it possible to lead individuals once more back to organic and living forms of unity without having to recur to general principles of totalitarian, collectivist or national unification, education and discipline? This is the problem which both Fanelli and Assante should consider in its innermost psychological and spiritual aspect; for with institutional provisions, legal paragraphs, sanctions and external incentives, never, never we will succeed in establishing a living reality.

Fanelli delineates all the presuppositions for the hierarchical-qualitative articulation of the State with respect to the family: a return to the *patria potestas*; the absolute economic and moral cohesion of the family; the overcoming of its materialistic and conventional aspect; the affirmation of its concrete political significance; the primacy of family education, understood as character formation and the awakening of a clear sense of honour; the corporative familial economy with an inalienable domestic axis; the direct responsibility before the State of the father, as head of the family, for all the members of the same; the progressive organisation of the various familial groups of one and the same bloodline into greater units, which Fanelli calls 'foci' and which would be more or less equivalent to the ancient *gentes* — juridical and political units which articulate and decentralise the State, included as they are in a final unity of supreme directive power, which Fanelli identifies with the Party in the Fascist sense of the word, but which at bottom corresponds to the Senate of Priscan Rome.

This is a coherent and complete scheme. But precisely because it is a scheme, it is fatally prejudiced. Indeed, either it is a reality which we find before ourselves, arising organically from the deepest spiritual forces of a tradition, or else it is nothing: 'to build' this reality is an absurdity. Fanelli writes: 'The family, as a natural association, is a materialistic and utilitarian deformation of a *super-rational reality*, whose causes and effects are confounded' — which is to say that the family is a *heroic and sacred fact*. Precisely this is the decisive point. The entire ancient organic-hierarchical order and the Roman familial right itself proceeded from essentially spiritual premises — premises present only wherever the *pater familias* appeared also as the priest and the leader of his own; when the cult of the ancestors and of the heroes gave to every injury of his absolute authority the character of a sacrilege; when the corporations and the *gentes*, rather than units of common interests and production, were rather units determined by a common mode of being and by a common, differentiated sense of honour; when *fides*, conceived as an immaterial and almost transcendent bond of fidelity, made a man capable of connecting the various partial unities with higher unities, all the way up to the universal unity of the Empire, without in any way impairing his own life thereby.

To detach institutions, juridical schemes, and political structures from this living reality, and to presume to be able to establish their meaning without these things and without any possibility of their existing, is a grave error, a rationalistic confusion. But to recognise this fact means to recognise also that whoever today wishes to fight for a truly normal order, detached from every modern and contingent creature of necessity, must not delude himself regarding the true path that he will have to follow, supposing only it is still possible for him to do so. Interior forces and sensibilities which are almost extinct must be reawakened, a new man must be called into life. With every means at our disposal we must impede the varieties of a profane, laical, rationalistic and anti-aristocratic culture from leading us to the end of a work of destruction which truly began centuries ago. This is a difficult task, a task which goes far beyond the reach of every direct political and social action; but it is a task whose fruits will be therefore all the more fecund and precious. The condition holds as regards the problem of the family, of its dignification, of the overcoming that might be attained through it of individualism and of collectivism in a truly articulated and 'Roman' State; and only if this condition is met will all of this not be reduced to a sterile utopia, or to forms wholly void of substance.

3. CONSIDERATIONS ON DIVORCE

ON OCCASION of the discussions surrounding the introduction of divorce in Italy, which have given place to the referendum now underway, some have posed the question of what a man should think so far as the Traditional point of view is concerned. In point of fact, we have spoken more than a single time on this subject, and most especially in the chapter of a recently republished book, *Ride the Tiger*. Nonetheless, for the sake of convenience we can summarise the essential ideas here.

In the first place, the question would expand considerably if we were obliged to refer to 'traditionality' in the general sense, which is to say, with reference to the various societies and civilisations which have or have had a 'traditional' imprint, and therefore a spiritual and sacred basis. But it is clearly advisable here to examine the problem only so far as Italy is concerned, considering both 'traditionality' in its predominate form in this country, which is above all Catholic, as well as that which might concern values not tied to the limitations of this same 'traditionality'.

To deal with the problem at hand requires prior clarification of two others: firstly, that of the family as an idea or an ideal; and secondly, that of the family in its factuality, in one or another historical situation. So far as the second point is concerned, it is useless to hide the fact that today we find ourselves in a period of more or less pronounced dissolution of social structures — structures which, moreover, have already for some time presented a less 'traditional' character, in the rigorous sense, than a predominately bourgeois one. As for the processes which have brought about or are bringing about this dissolution, some must be considered irreversible.

Catholicism confers on marriage (and with it the family) the character of a sacrament, and therefore divorce is excluded (apart from in the exceptional case of the annulment of matrimony). This character is actually not original. In the early days of Christianity marriage was reduced to little more than a 'benediction', and its repudiation was not excluded. With the definition of the Catholic doctrine of sacraments, marriage came to be considered one of these. Note that in designating it, the term 'mystery' was sometimes used — *mysterium*, not without relation to the term *teleion* already used in Greece in relation to the initiatic conception of man with woman as the image of the *hieros gamos* (holy marriage).

However, the situation ended up in the following state of affairs: the Catholic attempt to sacralise the profane (in the present case, marriage, understood as a naturalistic fact) had as its consequence a profanation of the sacred. This is not the only case in which Catholicism has brought about a similar overturning, by way of a kind of democratisation. In fact, matrimony rendered sacred by a rite such as would, in principle, deeply bind two beings so far as to make of them an indissoluble union, ought to have been conceived only on a higher plane — not for any given little couple, unfit, in general, for dedication and an almost heroic and superindividual tension. This stood naturally in relation to the traditional idea of the family. But this matrimony-rite was admitted for, nay it was finally imposed upon, any given union, with an evident and inevitable fall in level. Sacrament ceased to be such in the deepest sense (of the sacred mystery), and assumed rather a mere social functionality *terre-à-terre*: the function of reinforcing and defending a temporal reality, of protecting the unity of a family, whatever it might be, regardless of its particular situations, and thus protecting it as well from the possibility that religious matrimony was used solely for the benefit of social conformism. But this is precisely profanation of the sacred.

On the basis of these considerations, the problem of divorce, too, can be adequately framed, in the context of our times. It is useless to underline that in these times the family of the traditional type has almost disappeared, and that some of the spiritual presuppositions for which divorce might have appeared inconceivable, if not even blasphemous, have similarly vanished. Those who stand against divorce to the bitter end wish to rigidly maintain the indissolubility of the family even when the family is already *de facto* dissolved — when it is shaken by quarrels, when it is conquered by nothing more than apathy, bare tolerance, indifference, if not even worse, given the centrifugal forces prevailing here. Such persons can justify their views only by empirical considerations, not by a realistic, existential and, overall, spiritual point of view. Everything is reduced to an artificial constraint.

By instituting divorce, a *possibility* is offered. It would obviously not be the traditionalist and observant Catholics who will make use of it, and so they should have no interest whatsoever in the corresponding polemical. There remains only the difficulty relative to the clauses of the Concordato (which, however, seems to be in want of downsizing or updating). In view of these, great care should be taken here.

We hold that in this regard the best solution is offered by the duality of religious marriage (marriage-sacrament) and civil marriage. By overcoming the aforementioned profanation of the sacred, marriage-sacrament should be chosen by couples who still feel the disposition for a deep, almost super-individual union, correlated to a higher type of family, as has been said; this religious marriage should remain indissoluble, and those who wish to enter into it should have this well in mind, so as to regulate themselves in full responsibility. No divorce should be conceivable for this kind of marriage, and it should be the State itself to adjudicate its indissolubility.

Otherwise, a couple should choose civil matrimony, such as is sufficient to regulate the practical and legal problems connected to family.

For this kind of matrimony, we see no reason why the institution of divorce should not be admitted, in carefully considered forms. And this would be also a reason to invite thought on the future, whenever a couple is brought to marry before its members have expressed mental, erotic or sentimental reservations, or if they marry on account of the prevalence of contingent factors.

That those who marry civilly can, *after a certain time has passed*, also marry through marriage-sacrament, would represent an altogether positive addition, because in this way a preliminary verification could be carried out to see if there exists the proper premises for taking a further step, from which it would no longer be possible to return. In this manner provision would be made for that which some have called a 'trial marriage', which however might seem somewhat redundant, given the great diffusion of preconjugal relationships.

The law on divorce which has been approved in Italy, save as it is eventually reformulated through the results of a referendum, does not appear to be particularly clear in its aims. The obvious limit-cases (the imprisonment or the permanent mental damage of one of the members of couple, etc.) are naturally to be set aside here. Only that divorce which is so to speak in current usage enters into question here. The legal details fall beyond the theme of the present writing. We observe only that the legal framework here is rather bulky and not particularly functional. Originally, a period of seven years of separation between the members of the couple was decreed before divorce could be obtained, more or less along the lines of the pre-existing annulment of marriage. It appears that this period is to be reduced to five years. But even so it is unclear what end this period could possibly serve. It might well serve as a time to further reflect and ponder. But in truth this period might encourage, in many cases, libertinage. Those who remain 'wed' in that long period can do as they please, especially now that adultery has ceased to be criminally indictable. One of the two members of the couple might have a sincere interest in divorce so as to make a new matrimony. But the fact that divorce cannot be obtained before the end of that period could also serve that same individual as a pretext to untie himself, to indulge in a lifestyle of free love, taking refuge in this legalisation of new relations.

We do not believe that sufficient emphasis has been placed on the existence, or the lack thereof, of children — a factor which ought to have negative effect in the first case, and positive in the second, leading to a less mechanical conception of divorce. If a great deal of weight is given to this as to an *interlocutory* factor, a couple would be constrained to bear it in mind from the very start.

Some have advanced the wholly sensible idea that divorce should be permitted only a single time, and not in a chain, as often happens in the United States, and to a lesser degree also in England. One can comprehend that a person might commit an error a single time or that a person might be unfortunate once; but this error or misfortune should serve as a lesson to not find oneself sooner or later in the same situation, save as truly unforeseeable circumstances intervene. In America, on the other hand, especially in the highest social strata, many marriages followed by as many divorces is possible, and manifests a typical hypocrisy, because in reality the situation is more or less one of free love and promiscuity, to which one insists on applying the conformistic and 'respectable' label of marriage.

But all of this at bottom exceeds the boundaries of the argument in the present article, which concerns above all the existential presuppositions of indissoluble marriage and of divorce.

4. THE FAMILY AS HEROIC UNITY

ONE OF THE PERILS which menace all reaction against the forces of disorder and of corruption that are devastating our civilisation and our social life, is the tendency to wind up embracing forms which are little more significant than those of mere bourgeois domesticity. More than once have we heard denunciations of the decadent character of moralism as compared to every superior form of law and of life. In truth, if an 'order' is to have value, it must not signify routine nor depersonalised mechanisation. There must exist forces which are originally untamed, and which conserve in some way and to some extent their nature even in the most rigid adherence to a discipline. Only then does order become fecund. We could express this in an image: an explosive and expansive mixture, when constrained to a limited space, develops its efficacy to the extreme, while if it is placed in boundless space it almost dissipates. In this sense, Goethe could speak of a 'limit which creates', and could say that in the limit the Master is shown. It is also necessary to recall that in the classical vision of life the idea of the limit — πέρας[1] — was taken as perfection itself, and was posited as the highest ideal, not only in ethical terms, but even in metaphysical terms. These considerations could be applied to a variety of domains. In the present essay we consider a particular case: that of the family.

---

1   Ancient Greek for 'limit', 'boundaries', 'extremities'; hence the perfection of a thing, its end or its object. Hence also a final decision. — Trans.

The family is an institution which, eroded by the latest cosmopolitan civilisation, undermined at its foundations by the very premises of feminism, of Americanism and of Sovietism, is in want of rebuilding. But even here the alternative indicated above arises. Institutions are like rigid forms in which an originally fluid substance has crystallised: this is the original state that one must reawaken, whenever the inherent vital possibilities of a specific civilisational cycle appear to be exhausted. Only a force which acts within, as a meaning, can be creative. Now, to what meaning must one refer the family? In the name of what must one desire it and preserve it? The usual, bourgeois and 'respectable' meaning of this institution is known to everyone, and it is less worthwhile to point it out, than to observe the wholly insufficient support it might furnish to a new civilisation. It might be well to safeguard the existing vestiges, but it is useless to hide the fact that this is not the real pith of the matter, that this by itself is 'too little'. If one wishes to find one of the earlier causes of the corruption and the dissolution of the family which have arisen in the most recent times, it can be indicated precisely in the state of a society wherein the family is reduced to signifying nothing more than convention, bourgeois respectability, sentimentalism, hypocrisy and opportunism.

Here as elsewhere, simply by carrying ourselves directly and resolutely, not to yesterday, but to the origins, we can find that which is truly required. And these origins should be accessible to us, particularly if our Roman tradition of the family stands among those that have brought the highest and most original expression of the concept.

According to the original conception, the family is neither a naturalistic nor a sentimental unity, but an essentially heroic unity. It is known that the ancient denomination of *pater* derives from a term which designated the leader,[2] the king. The unity of the family already

---

2   The word here translated 'leader' is *duce* in the Italian, from the Latin *dux*. It means he who guides, he who leads, he who commands; it is obviously etymologically connected to our English 'duke', and in modern times has most

for this reason appeared therefore as that of a group of beings joined in virile manner around a lord, who to their eyes appeared invested with a brute power, but also with a majestic dignity, such as to arouse veneration and fidelity. This character is moreover confirmed if one recalls that in the Indo-European civilisations the *pater* — as well as the leader — is the man who exercised an absolute rulership over his kith and kin, insofar as he was at one and the same time absolutely responsible for his kith and kin before every superior hierarchical order; he was also the priest of his *gens*,[3] for he more than any other represented his people before the divine; he was the custodian of the sacred flame, which in the patrician families was the symbol of a supernatural influence invisibly joined to the blood and transmitted with the same. No soft social sentiments nor conventionalism, but something between the heroic and the mystical therefore founded the solidarity of the familiar or popular group,[4] transforming it into a single unified thing through relations of participation of virile dedication, such that it was ready to rise up united against whomever might injure it or offend its dignity. With good reason did de Coulanges, in his studies on this matter, conclude that the ancient family was a religious unity, before it was a unity of nature and of blood.

---

famously been associated with Mussolini, known universally as *il Duce* during the *Ventennio*, the twenty years of Fascist rule. — Trans.

3   Latin for 'people, populace, folk, race', originally 'generative power or origin'. The centrality and extent of this term can be indicated by noting several of the English terms which derive from it: geniality, genius, ingenuity. Evola makes some brief observations on the Roman concept of the *gens* in *The Bow and the Club* (Arktos, 2018), pp. 41–42. The Italian *gente*, 'people', is obviously directly derived from it, and wherever this word appears in the present essay I have translated it with 'people'. The temptation to use our word 'folk' has been resisted on account of the radically different etymological weight of this last word, which originally was connected to the concept of the warrior. (It might originally have meant a 'host of warriors'. — Trans.

4   Italian: *gruppo familiare o gentilizio*; that is the group based on family ties or ties of *gens* (see footnote 2 above). — Trans.

That marriage was a sacrament much earlier than Christianity (as for example in the Roman ritual of *confarreatio*)[5] is perhaps already known to the reader. Less known, however, is the idea that this sacrament did not hold as a conventional ceremony or as a juridico-social formula, but rather as a kind of baptism which transfigured and dignified the woman, bringing her to participate in the same 'mystical spirit' of the people of her spouse. According to one Indo-European rite, itself very expressive as a symbol, before marrying, the woman was Agni, the mystical fire of the house. But this is no different from the original presupposition, by which the husband was identified with the Lord of the woman, establishing a special relationship, of which bourgeois fidelity is naught but the decadent and debilitated shadow. The ancient dedication of the woman, who gives everything and asks nothing, is the expression of an essential heroism — much more mystical or 'ascetic', we are tempted to say, than passionate or sentimental — and, in any case, transfiguring. According to an ancient saying, 'There is no special rite or teaching for the woman. Let her venerate her husband as her god, and she will obtain her own celestial place.'

The conception of another tradition has a near parallel here. According to that conception, the Solar House of immortality was reserved, not only for the warriors fallen on the field of battle and for the lords of divine lineage, but also for the women who died bringing a son into the light of day: in this was seen a sacrificial offering as transmutational as that of the heroes themselves.

---

5 The *confarreatio* was a patrician form of marriage, notable in the present context for its religious and spiritual overtones. For instance, a woman could only become a Vestal Virgin if she were born of parents wed through the *confarreatio*, thus indicating that it was connected with a certain view of spiritual purity. It is also noteworthy (given the prequel here) that it was at least originally considered indissoluble — something of a rarity in marriage rites, which, until what can rightly be regarded as the Christian revolution in marriage, tended (to greater or lesser degrees) to permit divorce under well-defined conditions. — Trans.

This might bring us to consider the very meaning of generation itself, save that that topic would lead us too far. Let us recall only the ancient formula according to which the first-born son was considered to be the son, not of love, but of duty. And this duty was, once again, of character both mystical and heroic. It was not a matter only of creating a new *rex* for the good and the strength of the family,[6] but also of giving life to him who could absolve his people of that mysterious obligation to the ancestors and to all those who produced large families (in the Roman rite, these were often recalled in the form of innumerable held aloft carried during solemn occasions), symbolised by the perennial familial flame. Therefore, in not a few traditions we find formulae and rites which bring to mind the idea of authentic conscious generation, of generation, not out of a dark and semiconscious act of the flesh, but through the body and at the same time through the spirit, literally giving life to a new being; with regard to his invisible function, it was even said of this being that by virtue of his existence the ancestors would be confirmed in immortality and glory.

From these testaments, which are but a few from among the great many that could easily be gathered, issues a conception of familial unity which, as it stands beyond every conformist and moralist bourgeois mediocrity, and every abusive individualistic presumption, stands equally far removed from sentimentalism, passion and everything relating to brute social or naturalistic facts. The family receives its highest justification when set upon a heroic foundation. To comprehend that individualism is not a strength, but a renunciation; to recognise in the blood a steadfast basis; to articulate and to personalise this basis through the force of obedience and of command, of dedication and affirmation, of tradition and of a solidarity which

---

6   Italian: *ceppo*. This word has a much wider acceptation than mere family, meaning as it also does 'lineage', 'stock' and 'family' in the more scientific sense of a group of genetic relations. — Trans.

we will go so far as to call warlike, and, finally, through a force of intimate transfiguration — only by all of these means will the family come once more to be a living and powerful thing, the first and essential cell for that highest organism, which is the State itself.

5. THE CASE OF MONTESSORI

ONE OF THE TRAITS of tolerance and of internal security of Ancient Imperial Rome was constituted by its acquiescence to accommodate, in the Pantheon of the city, every sort of cult and of creed, even those that had little enough in common with the true and original tradition of Rome, with its innate *mos et fas*.[1] This was the sign of a calm surety and superiority — even if in a later period it can be observed how the foreign guest not rarely ended up transforming himself into a real Trojan horse.

Something similar comes to mind with respect to the hospitality which Fascist Rome has conceded to a whole variety of 'conferences', often of international character. These are almost always launched in the middle of the Campidoglio, presided over — albeit only in 'honorary' or 'nominal' fashion — by the higher personalities in the Regime.

In this we see come alive once again the ancient hospitality of the Imperial Pantheon, but, at the same time, perhaps also something of the old danger. One can understand that today the most varied currents might aspire to gain a kind of chrism from this Roman hospitality; and, on the other hand, what best befits the new Italian tradition is not an attitude of narrow-minded exclusivism, jealous of its turf, but rather of open breath, of conscious universality and of supernational mediation. However, once these two points have been stated and lain aside from the discussion, it is still legitimate to ask oneself if in this

---

1   Latin: 'Mores and divine law'. — Trans.

casc it would not be opportune to cultivate a bit more of an attitude
of prudence, or, at least, of distance — not, let us say, out of any love of
clarity, but simply to avoid the possibility that, under our very noses,
someone might come round to thinking his all-too-liberal host a little ingenuous, and supposing Rome apt to let itself play the *marché
de dupes*[2] before the forfeiture of the honorific presidencies and the
'Roman' celebrations.

We pass on from these generalities to a concrete example.

By pure accident we came to learn that Rome was very recently
to host an international 'Montessori' congress, which was to be held,
as usual, 'officially', in the Campidoglio. And equally by pure accident
we ourselves came to attend a conference held, for this Congress, by
Ms. Maria Montessori herself. We were struck by the curious atmosphere of this event. The audience, composed primarily of that usual
out-of-commission feminine public which gathers ecstatically around
the theosophists, the feminists, the vegetarians, the proclaimers of
universal brotherhood and the protection of animals, appeared visibly
restless. At a certain moment someone (we later learned that it was
several of the fascists of the GUF)[3] cried out: 'Enough!' Montessori
soon after hastily concluded what she had to say, and her son, announcing the next conference of the Congress (first in English, then in
French, then in German, and finally had the good grace to announce
it also in Italian), added these strange words: 'If it will not be a bother.'

In truth, in patiently following the slow exposition of Ms.
Montessori, and of her 'doctrine', about which we had only the vagu-
est notion, we ourselves felt a certain surprise, not disconnected — let
us admit it — to a rather decisive instinctive aversion. That rather
nervous atmosphere was therefore altogether comprehensible to us,
and we do not doubt an instant that if analogous expositions were

2   French: 'parade of dupes'. — Trans.
3   The 'Gruppi universitari fascisti', or 'University Fascist Clubs'. These were young
     men of university age who allied themselves with the Fascist Party and engaged
     in many Fascist-related activities. — Trans.

made, not before that public of curious attendees and of international 'scholars' and of women adoringly gathered before the 'doctor', but of pure and aware fascists, things would have proceeded in an altogether different fashion.

But why? Here we do not wish to bring the antecedents and the political vicissitudes of the 'Montessori Method' into particular, and unfriendly, relief. Let us just barely mention how this 'method' has passed from one to another of the most suspect exponents: from those militant socialists like Labriola and Nathan, to Don Sturzo; or how, standing at the very threshold of certain Catholic organisations, this method all at once leapt over onto Protestant ground, where, under the auspices of the famous Wilson and through the 'animal ideal' of 'civilisation' held across the ocean, it found its fortune, its own rich gold mine, and at the same time a way to ricochet back to the old continent and to take hold here in Italy. Before these pacific observations, or various others of a more delicate nature, which we will not discuss, we well know what response is certain to be made. 'We do science, the "Montessori method" is a scientific method, indeed an experimental one, and so has no truck either with political parties or with religious confessions.' We might then add that it has no truck either with nationalities or regimes, and, in short, we might garner a declared agnosticism as the conclusion to these remarks. Now, what man does not know that every agnosticism is only the instrument for affirming, whether consciously or unconsciously, a certain content, which is itself in no way 'agnostic', and which, even *à rebours*,[4] ends up assuming an ethical or political meaning? We well know what it meant, just yesterday, to be agnostic. It meant to be militants — and how! — in the framework of the liberalistic and Masonic-Enlightenment ideology. Matters are even clearer in the case of Montessori, since her 'method' does not refer to the culture of flowers or the production of chemical fertilisers, but rather to human education. Now, how is it possible, in

---

4   French: 'backward' or 'against the grain'. — Trans.

something as delicate as the education of a child, to prescind from a position which is at once ethical, and *also* political?

Here we certainly encounter the decisive point. The Montessori Method could effectively be an agnostic method and, if it wishes, even a 'scientific' one — in the negative sense of the term — since its its premises and its criteria find their beginning and their end in a purely naturalistic plane; in a plane, that is, to which all higher elements, by which alone man is an 'ethical', 'political' and finally 'spiritual' being belonging to a hierarchical order different from that of the animal or of the plant, are foreign.

Montessorianism forms a part of that new superstition of 'nature' and that optimistic primitivistic ingenuity, which already made its appearance — in the meaning wed to natural right — in Jean-Jacques Rousseau, but which also has various and very precise modern branches: on the social plane, liberalism and anarchic optimism; on the intellectual plane, the Bergsonian revolt against reason; the attack of psychoanalysis against the defences and the censorship of the conscious personality; the irrationalistic psychology of a Klages; finally, the idea of a 'liberated life' of Krishnamurti.

Anarchism says: man by his nature is good, social, capable of order. Every evil comes from the State and from authority. Let's obliterate both the one and the other, and everything will spontaneously improve. Liberalism repeats: *laissez faire, laissez aller,* do not disturb the spontaneous rhythm of the economy and everything else with your own unsought interventions. According to the Jew Freud, barriers, moral prejudices and the controls of the ego are nothing but the founts of illness and neuroses; true life is to be found in the unconscious and in the irrational, presupposed and accepted — just as for the Jew Bergson reason has only an altering, limiting and falsifying function as compared to the spontaneity of the *élan vital.* According to the new psychological typology of Klages, every life has its biologically conditioned type, and our 'style' does not come to us from a reality superior to reality, but from nature itself — hence the connection with the whole paraphernalia of racism. Finally, according to Krishnamurti, the path toward total happiness and 'fulfilment' is found in liquidating every principle of authority, every tradition, every particularism, to liberate the life from the ego and to render it 'unconquerable'.

The 'Montessori Method' enters with mathematical exactitude into this decadent ideal world — this world in which the apparent and naturist optimism of 'well-being' is nothing, at bottom, but a mask for a profound pessimism, for a (not always confessed) profound mistrust in the possibilities and in the higher values of the personality in the face of mere nature: a mistrust which then finds its compensation in the gratuitous supposition that nature is in itself capable of form, of education, of liberation.

The 'Montessori Method' indeed leaves the child to himself; it declares every direct intervention on the part of the educator to be deforming and destructive; it gives to the child alone every opportunity to instinctively choose and to materially execute an action or a work which is supposed to reveal him to himself, and to form him; it maintains the uncoercability of the infantile nature, and, departing from this erroneous premise, adulates that nature and reinforces it. For this method, the adult is never capable of true comprehension of child, is full of limitations and prejudices which he imposes on the child. The affection of the educator supposedly influences the child as little as his authority and his punishments. The child is almost conceived in the image of a 'windowless' Leibnizian monad. Nothing enters it that it does not draw from itself. The pedagogical model therefore passes over to a type which is not precisely naturalistico-animal — since the animal develops itself in the state of nature, yet is full of irrationality, of improvised and dangerous elements, of the fears and instincts of prey, which open it dramatically to its fellows — but which rather could even be called naturalistico-vegetal. Nor yet is the child an amorphous mass, a raw material to mould according to a form and a style that this substance does not already have in itself — and therefore according to a determining action for education and culture — but rather he is like a plant, which has already in its pith the foreordained development; whence it is a matter only of leaving it to its soil, of making it leaf out, of not obstructing its growth through any external actions.

This image summarises the final meaning of the Montessori Method and permits one to measure precisely what horizons are reached by Ms. Montessori's sense of the dignity of the human personality.

Moreover, in Montessorian circles this optimistic type of the child-plant takes at times the significance of a glorious universal ideal. We have heard certain good young women — and it would be much better for them if they gave their raptures more normal feminine paths of expression — speak to us enthusiastically of the Gospel of the Child, and of the child even as a kind of Messiah. That is to say: it is no longer the adult who must serve as model for the child, but the child, developed along Montessorian lines, which must serve as the model for the adult. The man-plant becomes therefore the eschatological ideal of a higher humanity which is no longer 'compressed', disturbed, deformed, put into conflict with itself: thus, an ideal which has been restored.

It might be that Ms. Montessori will not recognise herself in these observations: but they would not for this reason be less legitimate or less illuminating so far as the final sense of her method and her pedagogical views go. Carry these views over into the social and political field, and then tell us how much space and how much justification there remains for the whole of authority, hierarchy, action from on high, domination, State as a supernaturalistic reality and the centre of reference for a transfiguring commitment. Montessorian education is nothing but liberalism and anarchical optimism applied to the pedagogical field. There remains only to ask ourselves if, in the framework of a State like the Fascist State, pedagogy can possibly constitute an agnostic zone, in which every method, so long as it leads to certain material results, is to be considered equal to every other, and can be applied undisturbed; or put otherwise, we must ask ourselves if a

certain consistency might be desirable between the principles of pedagogy and those that, in general, form the basis of a specific conception
of political life and of human personality in general.

We have heard Ms. Montessori state the image of the parallelogram of forces as an argument. The child, with those very clear inclinations one supposes in it, consititutes a force in a certain direction.
The non-Montessorian educator is a force in a different direction. If he
intervenes, the result is neither the one thing nor the other, but a 'resulting' force that follows the diagonal direction of the parallelogram
of forces, differing from both. This image lends itself equally well to
its own confutation. Before anything, why believe that the resulting
direction is a deviation, while it might, even if it does not coincide
in every case with the direction of the educator, be a rectified direction? We return ever to the usual hypothesis of the initial goodness of
infantile direction and of the superstitious decree of its intangibility:
as if even among plants one did not see that grafts sometimes lead to
better fruits than those single species which nature produces. Beyond
this, if we are to keep to the mathematical comparison, the result of
the interaction of these two forces, apart from its direction, in many
cases represents a force greater in its intensity than that of its lesser
component.

This is true — one might however counter — just as true as the fact
that in other cases the divergence of the components dissipates and
even neutralises the intensity of the two forces. But here, for our part,
we find the limits of this disanimated and abstract image in the face of
living reality. In truth, not only in the case of the child, but also in that
of an adult and even a race of people, it is altogether yet to be demonstrated that all contrast, dissension, and antagonism resolves ever in
dissipation, and might not rather be an occasion for the unleashing
of something higher, of a force yet more alive and more irresistible.
Let us lay aside consideration of lesser natures, the domesticatable beings: these bear witness neither *against* us, nor *for* Ms. Montessori. We
rather consider the case in which there is present in a child the germ

of a true temperament, a true innate will. This germ has two possibilities in the face of the will of the educator: either a toughening of that germ, its being rendered little by little still stronger and more decisive, up to the point of revolt, or else — when it finds itself before a true educator, such as one might truly call a Maestro[5] — there will be a true recognition, a fortifying adhesion, something like the current which flows into another and greater current, in which it does not lose itself, but finds rather a vaster homogeneous element, and so strengthens itself, carrying itself beyond that point it might have reached alone, or from which it might have been deviated by every kind of contingency.

Now, the 'Montessori Method' has no regard for this creative alternative. It therefore has no regard either for that faculty which is truly the central point upon which every true education should leverage: the faculty of veneration. There is a vision in which the master or the father, rather than standing behind the curtains like a shadow watching over the development of the child's spontaneity in whatever regards it materially, should rather be a model silently imposing respect, veneration, desire for emulation and spontaneous obedience; this vision, which transports us to a higher plane, is the very basis for every true authority and every virile hierarchy, falls altogether and wholly beyond the horizons of the Montessorian method. And the latter thus neglects, and in neglecting atrophies, the infantile faculty of veneration, that most precious latent germ of all; it closes the road to every classical and Roman conception of culture (culture for us having ever the meaning of style and form imposed on a given material, as *cosmos* upon *chaos*); prepares for adults who are perhaps 'pacified', without 'defences' or 'deformations', but, in the best of cases, who are in this way just vegetables, and in the worst of cases individualists incapable of inwardly feeling the ethical meaning of discipline, absolute dominion of the spirit over the body and over sensibility, and thus also liberation and virilism.

---

5   It bears recalling here that the Italian 'maestro' literally means 'master'. — Trans.

Some have told us that, if we would lay our hands upon the effects of this method, it suffices to witness the results which it has brought in certain cases which are particularly near to Montessori herself, and to her application. We leave aside these contingent references and thus we stave off every argument of a crudely experimental type. It suffices for us to observe an incompatibility of doctrinal positions, a fundamental error of premises, a complete incomprehension of the meaning which the ideal of the personality and of culture, and thus of the pedagogical action itself, has traditionally always had for us. It is for all these reasons that the 'star-struck' atmosphere of that Montessorian conference, which was itself held, albeit in international guise, in Mussolini's Rome, did not surprise us, and that indeed, recalling the Capitoline inauguration of this Congress, what we have indicated at the beginning came to mind: the magnanimous hospitality of Ancient Rome, even with regard to those things which had nothing in common with Romanness.

LIBERTY AND DUTY

1. 'SERVICE TO THE STATE' AND BUREAUCRACY

A CHARACTERISTIC SIGN of the decadence of the idea of the State in the modern world is the loss of the higher significance of service to the State.

Wherever the State presents itself as the incarnation of an idea and a power, an essential role in it is played by political classes defined by an ideal of loyalty — classes that feel a high honour in serving the State, and that on this basis participate in the authority, in the dignity and in the prestige inherent in the central idea, thereby differentiating themselves from the mass of simple, 'private' citizens. In traditional States, these classes were above all the nobility, the military, the diplomatic corps and, finally, that which is today called the bureaucracy. We would like to offer some brief considerations on this last.

As has been defined in the modern democratic world of the latest century, bureaucracy is naught but a caricature, a materialised image, faded and displaced, of what ought to correspond to its idea. Even leaving aside the immediate present, in which the figure of the 'state worker' has transformed into that squalid figure in perennial struggle with the economic problem, to such a degree that he has become the favourite object of a kind of mockery and bitter irony — even leaving this aside, the system itself shows deplorable qualities.

In today's democratic States, we are confronted with bureaucracies deprived of authority and prestige, deprived of a tradition in the best

sense of the term, with bloated, grey, underpaid personnel, specialised
in sluggish, listless, pedantic and cumbersome routines. A horror for
direct responsibility and slavishness before one's 'superior' are other
characteristic traits here; and higher up, we find another trait still,
namely empty officialism.

In general, the average state functionary today is almost undistin-
guishable from the general type of the modern 'wage earner'; and in
fact in recent times 'state workers' have assumed precisely the role of
a 'category of workers', which follows the other categories in making
social and salary demands through protests and even strikes — things
that are inconceivable in a true and traditional State, as inconceivable
as an army that one day up and goes on strike in order to impose
its demands on the State, understood as an 'employer' *sui generis*.
Practically speaking, one becomes an employee of the State when
one has no initiative and when one has no better prospect, in order
to achieve an income which is, to be sure, modest, but also 'sure' and
constant: that is to say, one becomes an employee of the State in a
spirit which is petty bourgeois and utilitarian in the extreme.

And if in depraved democracy the distinction between he who
serves the State and any given worker or private employee is therefore
almost inexistent, in the upper spheres the bureaucrat is confounded
with the type of the insignificant politician or 'underling'. We have
'honourable' and 'influential persons' invested with governmental
power, but for the most part without the counterpart of a true and
specific competence — men who, in the ministerial reshuffle, grasp at
and exchange the portfolios of some ministry or other, hastening to
summon friends or fellow party members to similar posts, keeping in
their sights less service to the State or to the Head of the State, than
the question of how to profit from their situation.

This is the sad picture which the entirety of the bureaucracy today
presents. Part of this might be due to technical reasons, the dispropor-
tionate growth of administrative structures and superstructures and
of the 'public powers': but the fundamental point is a fall in level, the

loss of a tradition, the extinguishing of a sensibility — all phenomena which run parallel to the twilight of the principle of a true authority and sovereignty.

We are reminded of the case of a functionary who belonged to a noble family, and who resigned his post when the monarchy of his country collapsed. He was asked in bewilderment: 'How is it possible that you could be a functionary — you who, being a millionaire, had no need of an income?' The bewilderment of one who felt the need to ask such a question was certainly not inferior to that of the man who responded to it by saying that he could not conceive of a greater honour than that of serving the State and the sovereign. And, from the practical point of view, there was nothing of 'humility' in this, but of the acquisition of prestige, of 'rank', of an honour. But today who more than the bureaucrat himself would be amazed and would laugh if, for instance, the son of some fat capitalist had ambitions in this spirit to become... a 'state worker'?

In Traditional States the military, anti-bureaucratic spirit of serving the State had almost its symbol in the uniform that its functionaries soldier-like donned (we notice the desire to take up this idea once more in Fascism). And contrary to the style of the high functionary who makes his post serve his various practical ends, there was, in these former, the disinterest of an active impersonality. In the French tongue the expression *On ne fait pas pour le Roi de Prussie*[1] means more or less this: one does nothing save in return for coin in one's purse. It is a contrasting reference to the style of pure, disinterested loyalty that constituted the climate in the Prussia of Frederick II. But also in the early English *self-government*,[2] the highest posts were honorary and were entrusted to whomever enjoyed economic independence, precisely so as to guarantee the purity and the impersonality of the post, and, to no lesser degree, its corresponding prestige.

---

1 French: 'One does nothing for the King of Prussia' (lit. 'One does not do for the King of Prussia'). — Trans.

2 Evola gives this term in English. — Trans.

As has been indicated, bureaucracy in the lower sense is formed parallel with democracy, while the States of Central Europe, being the last to conserve traditional traits, conserve also much of the style of the pure, anti-bureaucratic 'service to the State'.

To change this state of affairs, especially in Italy, makes for a desperate venture. There are exceedingly grave technical difficulties, also financial ones. But the greatest difficulty is that which derives from the general fall in level, from the bourgeois spirit, from the materialistic and profiteering spirit, from the absence of a true authority and sovereignty.

2. SOME THOUGHTS ON
ELECTORAL POLITICS

NOW THAT THIS whole 'electoral' business has come to an end for better or worse,[1] we would like to express the discomfort that this spectacle has aroused in us, for reasons which it will perhaps not be useless to offer up for brief consideration.

Before anything, it has been demoralising to see all these men — all of them without exception totally lacking in any sense of restraint or examination of conscience — hurling themselves into the fray so as to win some parliamentary seat. As regard those parties which are democratic by their own declarations, there is of course no reason to expect anything else. But so far as a position of national opposition is concerned, which is permitted to be democratic, not in its spirit or ideals, but only in the form imposed on it by this period of interregnum (for there is no other way of characterising the present Italian regime), the situation has been depressing. Paraphrasing an evangelical saying, we can summarise our idea as follows: '*It is necessary that the MSI*[2] (or any other party, be it present or future, that is inspired by

---

1   That is to say, the election of June 7, 1953. — Trans.

2   The Movimento Sociale Italiano was a party of the Right in Italy which was formed after the War primarily by the remnant figures of the fallen Fascist regime, including Giorgio Almirante, who was for many years its secretary, and who can likely be taken as a representative of the kind of dutiful individual that Evola mentions favourably toward the end of this article. — Trans.

the same ideas) *should have its deputies in Parliament, but woe to those who feel the ambition to become deputies.*

What sense is there in disdaining democracy, even while gambling everything in order to win an office that can have significance, and can be desired, only in democratic terms? And what matters the diversity of ideas — these patriotic ideas on the right instead of the left — when the *style* is identical, which is as much as to say, when it is quite clear that, in the case of not a few of these candidates, the person is not in the service of ideas, but the ideas in service of the person, as a mere aid in the achievement of his aims? Or when these candidates, lacking in any scruples, should feel it necessary to throw sucker punches, using sabotage against inconvenient and dangerous 'representatives', as contestants in the electoralistic arena? And for how many of these candidates is it wrong to suspect that they profess to despise the democratic system, even while striving to attain those advantages that can be procured by anyone knowledgable in the generic arts of the politicaster?

More: to what extent do they maintain a line of true dignity and severity in that contest? We have had the chance to leaf through more than one of these propagandic pamphlet-autobiographies, written by one or other candidate of the opposition parties. 'Prostitution', in the rigorously etymological sense of the word, means *exhibition* — setting something on display toward the end of offering it up or selling it, as when one puts an object in a shop's showcase. Well, we would not know where to find a meeter expression for the style that we have witnessed, and more than a single time, in these aforementioned instruments of personalistic propaganda. To be sure, in all of this we might be utopists: but in our opinion it is not by this path that true selections can be made, or that recognition of a man can have serious and solid foundations, rather than frivolous ones such as are fit for 'the proud politics of the vanities'.

Some will ask what, then, ought to be done. The entire system must be changed by banning the wrong kind of ambitions. A party which corresponds to our ideal would be organised according to a true hierarchical structure, and should acquire ever greater prestige and strength as a *movement* awaiting its decisive hour, ever aware that, given the present situation, both domestic and international, it is certainly not at Montecitorio[3] that resolution will be achieved, in the sense that we desire.

This ideal party must be quite clear regarding the *radical opposition existing between the type of the leader and that of the 'honourable gentleman'*;[4] it should aim to have and to form leaders, not to produce these 'honourable gentlemen', and a clause of its statue should decree *the incompatibility of simultaneously belonging to the supreme hierarchy of the party and of being an 'honourable gentleman'*. The 'honourable gentlemen' should simply be detached persons, designated by the leaders of the party as 'observers' and curators of the petty business connected to parliament in the period of the interregnum. This is our point of view. Nor can anyone who truly says 'No' to the present system affirm any other.

Returning to what we mentioned at the beginning, it would be unjust not to recognise the exception constituted by those who have accepted the electoral battle, not so much out of personal interest,

---

3   The Palazzo Montecitorio is the seat of the Chamber of Deputies, one of the branches of the Italian Parliament, together with the Italian Senate. Montecitorio is also where joint sessions of the Chamber and the Senate take place, so in that sense can be taken as representative of the Parliament as a whole. — Trans.

4   'Leader' here is the translation of the Italian *capo*, which comes from the Latin word for 'head', and can also be rendered 'lord' or, more colloquially, as 'boss', both in the sense of employer and in the sense of the head of an organisation like the Mafia. (It is used in current Italian primarily in these latter two senses.) 'Honourable gentleman' translates the Italian *onorevole*, which is used to this day in address of Parliamentarians in formal settings. Though the use of the title 'honourable' for parliamentarians is fairly vestigial in the United States, for instance, *onorevole* in Italian is used with similar frequency to the epithet '(right) honourable gentleman' in the British House of Commons, and is used here in the translation in that sense. — Trans.

but because they, after having stood aside in expectation that truly meaningful figures would set the party on the right track, and finding themselves deluded in these hopes, felt it was their duty to intervene.

We should also bear in mind what certain friends of ours have said so as to justify their candidacy: for them, it was not a question of aspiring for a parliamentary seat in and of itself, but of using this position as a means to an end with regard to the internal affairs of the party: for letting others be elected would mean letting others use the prestige they have thereby obtained to make their group or their ideological tendency prevail within the party. Perhaps this is really how matters stand. But is the necessity of recurring to this 'indirect action', which is itself favoured by the democratic system, not perhaps a sign that things within the party 'are not in order'?

Now that the hubbub has died out, and the disappointment of the one side and the euphoria of the other have passed, the time has come to see to what extent the premises are in place for a new phase — one which is truly, and silently, constructive.

3. THE TWO FACES OF LIBERALISM

A COALITION OF Right-wing forces has already been desirable in Italy now for some time; today, it has become a crucial need for whomever has any sense of political and moral responsibility, given the growing deterioration of the internal situation. Unity in terms of an entire national movement, which attempts to gradually win over ever greater strata of the population, would be the best-case scenario. But we must also consider the consensus of those parties which are today generically considered to be of the Right, for the weight that such a well-organised coalition would have, even in a simply tactical way, in the political battle that ought to be waged in the democratic parliamentary framework.

However, the obstacles that even this very simply tactical and pragmatic unity encounter cannot help but indicate the prevalence of particular interests, often enough belonging to individual persons or very restricted points of view, as compared to a higher, impersonal and common interest. Here we will not consider this strictly political aspect of the problem. Instead, we would rather venture a brief analysis of a doctrinal point of view. Though it might, in the present state of affairs, appear unreal and solely academic, nonetheless it will perhaps not be without a certain interest so far as a discussion of ideas and a certain orientation are concerned.

We propose, that is, to look at what valid elements might be gathered from each of the parties that today are indicated as belonging to the Right. In other words, we will consider what might be the contribution that these could give ideologically and by way of principles to the definition and the construction of a true State, a State of the Right.

The relevant parties are the Italian Liberal Party, the Italian Democratic Party of Monarchist Unity, and the Italian Social Movement.[1] There does not exist in Italy a conservative party (such a character can certainly not be ascribed to the DC,[2] whose lacklustre clericalising bourgeois traditionalism is presently giving way to a decided opening to the forces of the left). In any case, there would be rather little to 'conserve' in Italy. Laying aside the Fascist period, there would remain that post-Unification period in which the so-called historical Right was very far from representing anything comparable, in terms of its meaning, to the conservative parties above all in central Europe and in part also in England.

Let us begin with the examination of liberalism. There is something symptomatic and almost amusing in the fact that the Liberal Party today presents itself as a party of the Right, while in the previous period the men of the Right saw in it the black beast, a subversive and corrosive force precisely in the way that nowadays Marxism and Communism are thought to be (even by the liberals themselves). In truth, since '48, liberalism, revolutionary nationalism and the anti-traditional Masonic ideology have appeared strictly connected in Europe, and it is always interesting to page the old annals of *Civiltà Cattolica* to see how its writers used to express themselves with regard to the liberalism of their time.

---

1   Evola obviously uses the condensed and common names for these parties in the original text (for example, he refers to Italian Liberal Party as the 'Liberale'); I here furnish their complete names in English in the interest of those who might wish to research these matters further. In Italian, their names are Partito Liberale Italiano, Partito Democratico Italiano di Unità Monarchica, and the Movimento Sociale Italiano (later Movimento Sociale Italiano — Destra Nazionale). None of these parties exists today. — Trans.

2   'Democrazia Cristiania', the Christian Democrats. — Trans.

But we will leave aside these circumstances. Let us indicate, as briefly as is necessary to our ends, the origins of liberalism. It is known that these origins are to be sought in England, and it could be said that the antecedents of liberalism were feudal and aristocratic: we refer to a local nobility which was jealous of its privileges and of its liberties and which, establishing itself as a body in the Parliament, determined to defend itself against any abuse of the Crown. Following this, and parallel to the advance of the bourgeoisie, liberalism was reflected in the Whig wing of the Parliament, which stood in opposition to the conservatives, the Tories. But it should be observed that up to yesterday the party had the role of an 'organic opposition'; its loyalty to the State remained firm, to such an extent that one could speak of 'His Majesty's most loyal opposition'. Its opposition exercised the simple function of a brake and a control in the two-party system.

The leftist ideological factor did not penetrate into liberalism save in a relatively recent period, and this event was not disconnected to the first Spanish revolution; hence the original designation of the liberals was Spanish, *liberales* (and not the English 'liberals'). And it is here that the decline commenced. It is to be taken for granted that early English liberalism had an aristocratic character: it was a liberalism of gentlemen,[3] the liberalism of class. Such liberty as any man might claim for himself was not so much as dreamed here. To this day, there subsists this healthy and, at bottom, a-political aspect of liberalism: liberalism not as a politico-social ideology but as the requirement that, irrespective of the particular form of the political regime, the individual should enjoy a maximum of liberty, that the sphere of his privacy,[4] of his personal private life, should be respected, that the interference of any extraneous and collective power therein should be avoided. In principle, this is an acceptable and positive aspect of liberalism, which ought to serve to distinguish it from democracy, since

---

3   Evola uses the English word here. — Trans.

4   Here again Evola uses the English word, since Italian is curiously (and most suggestively) lacking in the noun form of the adjective *privato*. — Trans.

in democracy the social and collectivising impetus predominates over that of individual liberty.

But here we find another turning point, because a generalised and indiscriminate liberalism, in the guise of an ideology, fused on the European continent with the Enlightenment and rationalistic movement. Here comes to the foreground the myth of the man who, to be free and to truly be himself, must disown and reject every form of authority, must follow his reason alone, never admitting any other bonds than that bare minimum of external ones without which no social life would be possible. In these terms, liberalism became synonymous with revolution and individualism (just one step beyond this, and it arrived at the anarchical idea). The primary element is seen in the single individual. And here two heavy mortgages are introduced under the sign of what Croce had denominated the 'religion of liberty', but which we would rather call the fetishism of liberty.

The first was that the individual has now become 'evolved and conscious', thus capable of recognising or creating every value by himself. The second is that a sound and stable order can miraculously arise from the mass of single individuals left to their freedom (*laissez faire, laissez aller*):[5] for the which, however, it would be necessary to recur to Leibniz's theological conception of the so-called 'pre-established harmony' (of Providence), such that, to use a comparison, even though each of the cogwheels of the watch moves in its own way, still the watch works and always gives the correct time. In the economic sphere, neo-liberalism[6] derives from liberalism; one can call the former the application of individualism in the economico-productive field, affected by an optimistic egalitarian utopia concerning the order that will spontaneously emerge therefrom and that will truly protect

---

5   French: 'to let alone' and 'to let be', respectively. — Trans.

6   The term here is obviously somewhat anachronistic, as it really came into its present use in the 1970s and especially the 1980s, some years after the writing of this article. But Evola is clearly critiquing the notion which would later come to be expressed by this term, and given the word he uses here (*liberismo*) which has no cognate in English, the translator has thought it best to use the clearer term, rather than opting for an awkward neologism (liberism). — Trans.

this celebrated freedom. (However, the fate of the freedom of the weakest in a regime of untrammelled and pirate-like competition is well known.) But the spectacle offered by the modern world demonstrates just how arbitrary both these assumptions really are.

At this point we can arrive at certain conclusions. Ideological liberalism, in the terms just indicated, is evidently incompatible with the ideal of a true State of the Right. Neither its premise nor its fundamental intolerance of any higher principle of authority can be accepted. The individualistic conception has an inorganic character; its presumed vindication of individual dignity at bottom leads to a maiming of the same, on account of its egalitarian and levelling premise. Thus in the most recent times liberalism has made no protest against the regime of universal suffrage of absolute democracy, where the parity of any given vote, by which the person is reduced to a simple number, is a grave offence against the individual in his personal and differentiated aspect. So far as liberty is concerned, the essential distinction between liberty *from* something and liberty *for* something (that is, to do something) is neglected. It is senseless to so jealously guard the first kind of liberty, external liberty, when one is not even capable of indicating ideals and higher political ends by virtue of which the use of this liberty might acquire true meaning. The conception underlying the true state, the State of the Right, is 'organic', not individualistic.

But if liberalism, taking inspiration from its pre-ideological and pre-Enlightenment tradition, were to limit itself to promulgating the greatest possible liberty in the private individual sphere, to combating every abusive and unnecessary interference in this sphere by public and social powers; if it served to distance 'totalitarian' tendencies in the negative and oppressive sense of the term; if it defended the principle of partial liberties (thus defending at the same time the idea of intermediate corps, gifted with partial autonomies, between the zenith and the bottom of the State, which would lead it toward corporatism), if it were disposed to recognise a State *omnia potens* but not *omnia facens* (W. Heinrich),[7]

---

7   Latin: 'capable of everything' and 'doing everything' respectively. The distinction is between a state which has the power to intervene in any given situation

which is to say a state exercising a higher authority without interfering in everything — if it were to do all of this, the 'liberal' contribution would be indubitably positive.

Especially given the present Italian situation, the separation between the political sphere and the ecclesiastical sphere proposed by ideological liberalism might even be positive, so long as this does not implicate the materialistic laicisation of the first. Here we encounter however, in all likelihood, an obstacle difficult of the overcoming, because liberalism has a phobia for anything which might ensure to the state authority a higher and spiritual foundation, and professes a fetishism for the so-called 'rule of law' and a State built on abstract legalism; almost as if legalism existed outside of history, and law and constitution alike fell ripe and ready from the sky, with the character of irrevocability.

The spectacle of the situation to which the party-ocracy has led us in this demogogic mass regime should lead us to reflect on the ancient liberal (and democratic) thesis that the disorderly pluralism of parties guarantees liberty. And so far as that freedom goes which is demanded at all costs on every plane, for example that of culture, a number of clarifications would today be necessary, if we do not want everything to go definitively and swiftly to the dogs. We can clearly see what modern man, who has finally become 'adult and conscious' (according to liberalism and progressivist democracy) has become capable of in recent times with his 'freedom', which has often enough proved to be a freedom such as systematically produces the ideological and cultural bacilli that are bringing ruin to an entire civilisation.

But this would make for a long discourse, and it would lead us beyond the purview of our present examination. Let us suppose that with these notes that which liberalism might present of the positive and that which it might present of the negative from the point of view of the Right is brought to light, if only in an extremely summary way.

---

on the one hand (i.e. a 'strong' state), and a state which actually does intervene wherever it can on the other (i.e. a 'totalitarian' state). — Trans.

4. IDEAS ON A STATE AS POWER

FOR US, the concept of hierarchy and of State as power[1] is founded on the idea of an absolute liberty. To be *absolute*, it is necessary for this liberty to be *unconditioned*.

---

1   Italian: *Stato secondo potenza*, which could also be translated as 'the State according to power'. The word *potenza* is one Italian word for 'power'; more common is *potere*, which Evola also uses here, though, as is not unusual for him, he prefers the less common *potenza*. It is difficult to say whether there is any difference intended between these two very similar words, or whether they are used synonymously. I offer a supposition regarding a potential distinction that Evola might be encouraging us to draw. The two terms derive from two different Latin roots, *potere* coming from the identical antique Latin verb, meaning 'to be able' or 'to have the power to' or even 'to be powerful', and thus is connected to the Latin *potestas*, the Roman juridical concept of 'that power which can effect its will through coercion', and which culminated in the highest form of *potestas*, the *imperium*. *Potestas* is thus necessarily linked to the political, and more than anything to the structural or official power of the state. *Potenza* comes rather from the Latin *potentia*, a kind of immanent power or might, which suggests the real presence of power, quite separate from the question of its formal presence or proper institutional framework. *Potenza* by this understanding would thus bring one back most emphatically to the powerful individual, his inherent, his immanent power, his might, not primarily of body, but primarily of soul. Unfortunately, it is difficult to render this word in English, because 'might' has implications of physicality, and 'potency', our nearest derivative, while it sometimes can suggest 'the state of being potent', on the other hand suggests a mere *potentiality*, an inherent capacity which may or may not be realised in full. It is moreover somewhat awkward to use in many contexts; the 'State as potency' is not quite so clear as one would like, and confuses rather than clarifying. I have therefore translated both of these words as 'power'. For the benefit of the reader, however, I have noted the two instances in this essay in which Evola recurs to

But there can evidently be only one unconditionally free individual. Several free beings cannot help but limit one another and negate one another — save as there is in the depths of each one a *law*, by which individual freedoms are regulated and harmonised. But since a law does not cease to be a law for being internal, and given that this law is moreover, by definition, something that transcends every single individual, in this case the result is still not an *unconditional* liberty.

Therefore: it is either impossible to conceive of such a liberty, so that one arrives at compromises which, as such, contradict it (liberalism: *the* liberty is negated in order to permit life to *the* many, single, atomistic liberties); or else one must conceive of a being which, for its interior superiority, ceases to be *one* force *among* many others within a dynamic system — namely the society of men[2] — and actuates itself in that which, as *determiner* of the law of the aforementioned unity, is itself free from the law which others hold in authority. And so in the free legislator, in the dominator, the idea of State as power is formed.

And indeed: that hierarchy which is able to culminate and burn in a single being reflects the value mentioned above, but only when it is comparable to a unified organism synthesised in a soul, a *spirit*.

Such an organism converges in the unity of a higher life which is an end-in-and-of-itself, which does not live for the needs of the body, but takes the body rather as its instrument; it is not the product of the body, but vice versa, in the sense that the soul is the end, the deep organising principle of the body itself (Aristotle). This means: the Lord[3] will not be a mere *representative* of his inferiors (the democratic

---

potere. It is interesting to note both the context of these appearances, and the fact that Evola chooses to emphasise them; facts both of which, in my opinion, suggest some validity to these considerations. — Trans.

2   Italian: *umanità sociale*, literally 'social humanity'. — Trans.

3   Italian: *capo*. As iterated earlier, this word can mean 'lord', 'head', 'leader', and is most commonly used today in the sense of 'boss'. Evola obviously intends it in one of the prior senses, and it is probable that 'Leader' would be the most fluid; nonetheless, the sense of both the Italian term itself and Evola's use of it in particular is considerably stronger than this. — Trans.

thesis), the impersonal symbol of a self-organisation of which these inferiors are already capable, but vice versa: the mass, the people are not organised; they receive form and order only by virtue of the superior man, who is qualitatively distinct from all others, whom he strenuously tends to express; and he, far from living for that people, would subordinate the interest of the masses to his own interest — to those vaster horizons that he alone can determine — and would recognise no man's right to limit his law (in neat opposition to the democratic principles of popular limitations on power,[4] and of the dedication of the government to the general interest). Otherwise at the apex there would not stand a free being, but rather the first among servants — not a spirit, but the voice of the body.

But to posit that means also to posit that *power is the least of the freedoms*. As the soul — in which the various parts have their end, while it itself is its own end — will consider the conditions and the limitations that come to it from the body as imperfections and will not tolerate them but will tend to overcome them in a perfect dominion and in an organism which is entirely malleable to the spirit, so the dominator will comport himself with regard to the various conditions (political, social, economic, etc.) that are proper to the masses.

His freedom, his right, his being a value — as an end in and of himself — will therefore extend precisely so far as he has the *power*[5] to do as he is fain; for 'responsibility', in any sense of the word one pleases, has meaning only when one finds oneself before a *stronger* power. Losing such a *power*,[6] he will lose to the same extent the right to command, and will have to give way to that man who, being stronger, will know how to impose his own law. Thus, without *power*,[7] the legislator, the zenith of free being, has no foundation and, however he might succeed in subsisting, he will subsist in a contingent

4   Italian: *sanzione popolare*, lit. 'popular sanction' or 'popular penalty'. — Trans.

5   Italian: *potere*. — Trans.

6   Italian: *potere*. — Trans.

7   Italian: *potenza*. — Trans.

and precarious way, basing himself not on himself, but on the other, not on his own strength but on the other's weakness (readiness to compromise[8]).

Violence, however, is the lower form of such power. Violence expresses, indeed, a 'standing against' (and thus, a state on the same level) and never a 'standing over'; it presupposes that other wills might resist, and thus bears witness, in the last analysis, to an impotence, an extrinsic, polemical, dependent relation, which is not truly hierarchical and dominating. Whoever truly *can*, has no need of violence: he has no antithesis — he imposes himself, by virtue of his interior, individual superiority, directly on that which he commands — and so has it been with all true dominators revealed to us by history, all the more at the limits of this road, where it skirts upon the Master or the Creator of religions.

Whence violence (and, with it, everything which is material force) will appear as naught but a rudimentary and provisional phase. Beyond it lies *dominion through ideas*, which are considered not as pallid abstractions, but rather as forces, as principles susceptible of unleashing energies and social currents through a variety of factors which are moral, suggestive, emotional, faith-based, etc. It remains the case, therefore, that the legislator will not assume the various ideas or *myths* (right, justice, etc.) insofar as he *believes* in them, insofar as he recognises in them a superior validity to which he himself submits, but rather as pure *means*, as simple aspects of that power which must be dominated (anti-devotionalism,[9] anti-idealism).

But even this step implies compromise and must be transcended. The various force-ideas or myths should not serve the dominator as

---

8   Italian: *compromessismo*, or 'compromisism'. This neologism does not sound so well in English as it does in the Italian, and has been avoided. — Trans.

9   Italian: *antirettorismo*, a curious neologism evidently indicating opposition to *rettori*, which might mean the rector of an institution or university, a ruler, or an officiating priest. This last alone would make sense in the present context; the meaning appears to be that the single ruler will not subject himself to the peculiar and peculiarising tendencies of any specific faith or church. — Trans.

a prop and a condition; rather, *he alone must be the condition.* Thus, such ideas — whose maximum culmination is in the idea of 'fatherland' — perforce imply something transcendent and impersonal, so that when others reveal social situations which correspond to these ideas more wholly than does the situation of the ruling group, he can turn the forces upon which he bases his dominion against this group.

Whence the dominator, in the end, will abolish the very idea of 'fatherland'; that is, *he will make it immanent,* and will spare nothing but his self, his naked being, the sufficient centre of every responsibility and of every value. '*I am* the State, the Fatherland'.[10]

And here commences the point of true power: *not to draw superiority from power, but power from superiority* — this is the principle.

The dominator is he who has at his disposal a greater quantity of *being,* by which others are fatally — almost without his, in a certain sense, even *desiring* it — kindled, attracted, impelled; he is the one who imposes himself, so to speak, with his mere *presence,* like that deeper and more fearful gaze which others do not know how to resist, like that calm greatness which magically paralyzes even armed, proud men[11] and directly arouses respect, the need to obey, to sacrifice oneself, to place one's truer life within this vaster life. In him an entire line, an entire tradition, and an entire history burn, as if in their *act*: they cease to be abstractions, they cease to be transcendent, generalities; they become individual reality, concreteness, *life* — an absolute life, because it is a life which is an end in and of itself, because it is pure liberty — spirit, light.

---

10 This last sentence clearly echoes the (possibly apocryphal but certainly spiritually true) statement of Louis XIV: '*L'état, c'est moi.*' — Trans.

11 When Napoleon broke his exile on Elba and landed on the shores of France, to all appearances a wretched and desperate adventurer invading a massive sovereign state with a rag-tag contingent of men, he was immediately confronted by the French military. He approached the entire French army alone and entered into its gunfire range, inviting them to shoot their Emperor if they would. The army submitted to him with cries of '*Vive L'Empereur!*' and side by side with him marched on Paris. — Trans.

And thus, at the summit, it is this man who can say: '*I* am the way, the truth, the life',[12] and who gives to all the multitude of beings, to the entire system of lesser determinisms in practical life, his unity, his *sense*, his *justification*. For the higher never lives its own life so perfectly as when it has its end in the higher: the part, when it knows itself to be member of a body that exists not in itself, but in a soul — in a soul which is a reality, an *I* and not a pallid ideal or abstract law — has its own *raison d'être*.

The generic possibility for the achievement of all this, as for any other organisation and hierarchy, lies in the so-called 'principle of the indiscernibles' (Leibniz),[13] which is to say: Any being which was *absolutely* identical to another, would be one and the same thing with it. In the concept of *multitude* there is thus implicit the idea of a *fundamental inequality* of single individuals — and if of inequality, then also a possible hierarchy among them. The Christian principle of equality naturally leads to the opposite — to anti-authoritarianism, to democratism, to socialism, to anarchy — to disorganisation (and this is precisely the way in which it operated on the Roman Empire).

Insofar as Christianity builds a *hierarchy* instead (such as that of the Church, and, specifically, the Catholic Church), *it must* betray the principle of equality — but then it becomes an enemy of that State whose concept has been delineated, albeit in the roughest way, above. For it would constitute one authority against another, one empire against another — while the principle must be *one*. An empire whose dominion is purely material can coexist with a Church which gives it the soul which it lacks; but an empire which is what it is insofar as it is permeated with an immanent spirituality — a spirituality which however is not the object of dreamy faith but of effective immanent value in an individual — must supplant, absorb, subordinate

---

12   This is an evident reference to the Gospels: John 14:6; the musical key in which Evola sings this tune, however, is decidedly another. — Trans.

13   This is also known as Leibniz' Law. See Leibniz' *Discourse on Metaphysics*, § 9. — Trans.

to itself every Church (anti-Guelphism).[14] Such is the Roman concept of empire — the *Caesar Augustus*, the royal and priestly Dominator; a concept which is every bit as much Pythagorian, Mithraic, Dantesque.

We have delineated the present concept of the State in a rather *a priori* manner, independently of any historical reality. But 'apriorism' does not signify abstractionism. The idea must judge reality, not vice versa. The task of speculation is not to observe that which is, but to determine, in the uncertain world of men, that which, as value, must be. And if that which must be does not correspond with reality, one must not for this reason call it abstract; we must rather call abstract and indolent that will and power of men, which are insufficient to their own realisation.

Whence it would not be devoid of interest to examine to what point the concept of the State which today has been reaffirmed in Italy might be reflected in the views which we have so summarily presented here, or might consider these same views in its possible attempt at further fulfilment.

---

14 Reference to the long contest between the Guelphs and the Ghibellines which framed so much of the last period of the High Middle Ages, particularly in Italy. The struggle was between the Pope, to whose favour fell the Guelphs, and the Holy Roman Emperor, supported by the Ghibellines. Evola often references this question. Dante was a staunch Ghibelline — fact which caused him no end of mischief. — Trans.

MONARCHY

1. NECESSARY MONARCHY

I N OUR INTENT to identify the contributions which, from a doctrinal point of view, those principle Italian political parties today thought to be part of the Right might eventually give to the definition and the construction of a true State of the Right, we will now follow our analysis of liberalism with analysis of the monarchical party. In the third and last we will concern ourselves with the MSI.[15]

Regarding the monarchical party, we must observe an incongruity between its numerical weight — compared to the other parties we are considering here, it today has the least number of members — and the weight which its corresponding idea might possess. The decline in number of supporters of the monarchy in Italy is rather enigmatic. Indeed, it is known that in the institutional referendum the republic won the day quite narrowly — even through manipulation of the results, it would seem, and a failure to await, albeit for good reasons, the return of any great number of prisoners of war who would have almost all voted for the monarchy. Where then did that considerable minority go — a minority of many millions, who even in a republican regime would have been able to furnish a very strong basis for a unified monarchical party?

Some would like to maintain that the dispersion is owing to an abject inurement to the general shattered and materialistic climate

---

15 This third article has yet to be republished in an accessible form, even in Italian. — Trans.

which immediately came to prevail in the new 'free' Italy. Others see the cause in the incapacity and division of the monarchical parties themselves; this, however, would put a great deal of responsibility on the shoulders of the exiled sovereign, who would thus have the duty of resolutely putting things back to their rightful place and of entrusting his cause to qualified and courageous men. Apropos of a lack of courage, it is characteristic that the denomination 'monarchical' was even diminished in the party name, while, in a servile homage to the new idol, the word 'democratic' was highlighted.[16]

But what is perhaps worse, there was no one in Italy who took upon himself the duty of formulating a clear doctrine of monarchy and of the monarchical State. In exception to our general rule, we listened in the last political elections to certain propagandic discourses on the part of certain monarchist leaders. While they levelled critiques against the centre-left government (critiques analogous more or less to those levelled by the liberals and the MSI), monarchy was not so much as mentioned; it was not stated in what terms the existence of a monarchical regime would bring about an essential modification of the present state, in what way monarchy should be conceived, what its form and its function ought to be. But everything apart from this is at bottom secondary, consequential and contingent.

There can be no doubt that a nation which has passed over from a monarchical regime to a republican regime is a 'demoted' nation, and no one who has any sensibility for values which, while they are subtle and immaterial, are not for this any less real, can possibly have failed to sense this 'downgrade.' The ideological contribution of a true monarchical party would be of essential importance because, in our view, the true State of the Right cannot be aught else than monarchical, as has predominately been the case in the past. Only that, in accord with

---

16   On 7 March, 1961, the original Partito Nazionale Monarchico, or National Monarchist Party, changed its name to the unwieldy Partito Democratico Italiano di Unità Monarchica, or Democratic Italian Party of Monarchical Unity. — Trans.

what we have said, the form and the functions of the monarchy must be well defined.

In a well-known study on monarchy in the modern State, Karl Loewenstein came to the conclusion that, if monarchy were even still possible today, it might be 'democratic' and of the kind presented by the smaller states of Western Europe such as Belgium and Holland. If this is truly how things stand, one might as well close the party, and the monarchy with it. In times like the present, monarchy as a kind of ornamental and inoperative mantelpiece placed on the top of the 'system' would be something frivolous and devoid of any true *raison d'être*. We rather needs must defend a courageous and revolutionary conception of monarchy.

With the advent of the Third Estate the monarchical idea was completely depotentialised and hollowed out. The well-known formula that the king 'rules but does not govern' expresses this impairment in a characteristic way. The meaning and the fundamental function of traditional monarchy is to assure 'transcendence', the stability and the continuity of the political authority, so as to create an immutable and supreme point of reference and of gravitation for the entire political organism, quite beyond any particular interest. In normal times, the purely symbolic aspect of monarchy could suffice for this task; there once existed an atmosphere of loyalty for which the function itself in a certain sense dominated the person who incarnated it, such that it could not be compromised by the possible insufficient human qualification of that person.

One must be wary however of confounding this detached, and we would almost say 'Olympian', character of true monarchy with the limitation imposed on the institution according to the aforementioned formula of ruling without governing, which was introduced precisely during a period in which the opposite would have been required — that is, an activity on the part of the Crown that might order diverging forces and rectify the deficiencies of the standing institutions. Moreover, Benjamin Constant was quite right in wanting

to attribute to the Monarchy a fourth power, subordinate to the three
known to constitutional doctrine (the legislative, judicial and execu-
tive powers): the power of an arbitrative and moderating character. In
any defence of the monarchical idea, this point ought to stand in the
forefront.

Next, we must consider the limits of constitutionalism. We should
certainly not backtrack so far as to wish to defend the type of absolute
monarchy (which is, however, usually presented one-sidedly, emphasising only its negative sides). But there is constitutionalism and
then there is constitutionalism. Above all, one must not make of the
constitution a fetish and a taboo, as we have noted in our examination of liberalism. Constitutionalism maintains its value only so long
as the waters of the political world are not agitated. As the supreme
power, the Crown ought to have the right and the duty to intervene, in
the case of emergencies, and it is precisely by these means that every
upheaval, be it dictatorial or revolutionary, can be prevented. In the
second place, we must distinguish between constitutionalism such as
subsisted up to the First World War in Central Europe, and that which
has prevailed in those Western states which have been democratised
to the bitter end and placed beneath the sign of the so-called 'popular will' and parliamentary sovereignty. In the first case, the political
representations of the nation might well have been elected with a
democratic system, but in their functions they were responsible to
the sovereign above all, and not to the parliament. Thus the sovereign
enjoyed the right to uphold and confirm a certain political line, even
when it did not receive the approval and the so-called 'faith' of the
parliamentary majority. To cite a well-known example, this is what
occurred in the case of Bismarck. He had the support of the sovereign,
and for years he carried out a programme of appropriations despite
the adverse parliamentary majority. After his victorious wars and the
creation of the second Reich, Bismarck was hailed as a national symbol, and a new constitution, which bore well in mind recent experience, substituted the prior one.

If the monarchical principle is to make any sense, it would be necessary therefore to restore an analogous situation. The king ought to have an active part of the government and, through those powers proper to him, ought to act as check to the system of parliamentary absolute democracy, to its deviations and its excesses. Beyond his significance as a symbol and as the custodian of the abstract idea of a supreme authority, he ought, in the modern epoch, to be sufficiently qualified that he can control the system of the political forces of his nation and contribute to the determination of the political line. And in this function of his, which is to be exercised to varying degrees depending on the circumstances, he must never forget the ancient maxim: *Rex est qui nihil metuit* ('He is king who fears nothing'). That even blood might flow in extreme cases (which in all likelihood cannot be avoided in the case of the resurrection of any nation in which the Marxist and communist gangrene has had a strong presence) — this should not anguish him, in his consciousness of his own forever representing and defending a superior and impersonal idea.

After this, we should highlight that which is referred to the intrinsic dignity of the monarchy and to the general spiritual climate that must be its necessary counterpart. When there exists a true monarchy, those values are brought out that in any other regime can only be parodied. 'To serve one's sovereign', to fight for him, to be the representative or the minister of a king, etc. — all of this becomes but grey and impoverished when one refers it rather to the president of a republic. A president of a republic is, as the tribune of a people, 'one of us'; there exists no 'distance', and therefore neither that majesty which is conditioned precisely by such distance, rather than by democratic popularity. The oath of a sovereign is totally different than swearing on some abstraction, like the constitution. The ethics of 'service' assume, in the monarchical regime, a particular dignity: to see in service to the state and to the sovereign an honour and a privilege, not paid employment. There is no need to mention that special prominence that all of this has in the official corps. The sense of responsibility, free dedication, active impersonality, fidelity and honour find in the monarchical climate the natural soil for their development.

Indeed, the decline of monarchy proceeded essentially in parallel with the materialism and the apathy of modern mass society, and with the decline and disappearance, in the many, of superior forms of recognition and of sensibility. A true monarchy could have, therefore, a rectifying influence on the national political climate. However, on the other hand we find here something of a vicious cycle, because every return to such a situation must have as its existential condition a change in climate, and this can perhaps only arise if the present disorder grows still more acute, and the disanimate and absurd character of everything which today is called the 'system' is finally perceived, up to the point of producing a rupture and crisis, and thus leading to the positive overcoming of that 'system'. Then perhaps a higher idea might be able to attract, might be able to take hold. A positively revolutionary restoration (revolutionary with respect to the present condition of subversion) can be realised on this presupposition alone, never by abstract juridico-procedural paths.

If the ideas that we have here briefly indicated are essential for the monarchical cause, who can we find, among the Italian monarchists, who really cares for them and makes them the declared counterpart of the current of oppositional political action? Unfortunately, even in the case of the monarchists, it is possible to speak of 'nostalgics'; they maintain a respectable generic loyalism, often founded on sentiment, characteristic of the older generation, but without employing any impactive force, nor any animating myths. On the other hand, bearing in mind the alternative to which we have previously alluded — namely, that we must either definitively put the monarchical cause on the shelves, or else restore to the monarchy a goodly portion of its meaning, of its dignity and of its original function, even when the times, thanks to a conjunction of circumstances such as that we have indicated, offer a favourable situation — where are we to find the hands truly capable of holding the sceptre? Someone has written that 'it takes a great deal of faith to believe in monarchy despite the kings of our days'.

But this is another question, which exceeds the boundaries of the present considerations, in which we wished only to consider the doctrinal aspect of the problem.

2. ON MONARCHY

I N A P E R I O D of doctrinal uncertainty, of confused aspirations, now innovative, now reactionary, now revolutionary — in a period, that is to say, like that in which the better part of Europe presently finds itself — every profession of healthy and enlightened traditionalism constitutes a contribution of indubitable value and of salutary efficacy, once the expression 'traditionalism' has been withdrawn from the abusive assumptions resulting from a certain demagogic polemic. By 'tradition' is meant, to be sure, conservatism, but conservatism which would conserve the living and not the dead; affirmation of the principles which, on account of their superior dignity and nature, can be said to stand beyond time, and which are therefore not of yesterday but of perennial currency; in short, to state the matter with De Reynold and Maritain, it is a vision of the future subordinated in an orderly way to a conception of being.

On this basis, a recent work dedicated to the monarchical problem in relation to the international situation merits recommendation.[1] This book is by a personality of today's England, one Sir Charles Petrie — a name already known to the Italian public both for his having been among the first to recognise the European significance of fascism, and for the interesting presentation he made two years ago or so at the

---

1   C. Petrie, *Monarchy*. A controversial and outspoken book on the future of Monarchy in Europe, London, Eyre and Spottiswoode, 1933.

Volta Conference.[2] With his work, which makes for clear and interesting reading, Sir Petrie places himself decisively on the antidemocratic and traditionalist avant-garde of those who today fight in Europe, with consciousness of views, for a better future, declaring their fidelity to those principles to which we once owed the greatness of our prior civilisation. Petrie observes that a defence of the monarchical principle is all the more necessary and timely than many believe. Indeed, there are not a few circles in which it is believed that monarchy is nothing more than a 'vestige of the past', an anachronism 'of which every truly civilised and evolved society of the twentieth century must necessarily be ashamed'; or that, after the war, hereditary monarchy is a 'lost cause', and that, for right-thinking folk, 'to declare oneself a royalist is equivalent to inviting that condescending commiseration which men would concede to anyone who had called for the abolition of mechanical transport or asserted that the earth is flat'.

Petrie justly indicts, as the premise of this ideology, the progressivist superstition. It is seriously believed that every change which has occurred over the course of the centuries signifies progress and that the modern world therefore represents the final word on civilisation. If our predecessors in the 'nightmare of the dark ages' lived beneath a hereditary monarchy, this was only because in those times they were not capable of perceiving any better possibilities, 'even as they admired van Dyck and Velázquez only because these knew nothing of the superior art of the futurists'. Beginning from 1918, Petrie continues, contempt for the past became ever more pronounced, and the obsession with 'new times', 'new eras', 'new pages' to turn in the book of history came ever more to the surface. Hence, to return to normality, what is required in the first place is a radical renewal of mentality, a renewal which takes as its first condition the liquidation of such attitudes. The illusion of 'progress' is in reality based on the limited vision

---

2   The Convegno Volta was an international conference held three times in the interwar period by the Royal Academy of Science in Rome to discuss topics and science and the humanities. — Trans.

of those who assume as their supreme criterion what can be referred to the purely material — and thus inferior — aspects of civilisation. In short, it is the technical and scientific spectres, with their relative and more or less Enlightenment appendices, that have given birth to this myth. 'After all, while we travel in automobiles, our ancestors travelled in stagecoaches, and knew neither the wireless telegraph nor aeroplanes. Thus it is entirely natural to suppose ourselves superior to them from every point of view'. But the times of 'progress' were also times of crisis, of decadence or even of the fall of the European monarchies. In this fact, it is thought, one finds an irresistible argument against the monarchical principle as such. Progressivism, here, makes alliance with 'historicism', in its aspect as an impotent, passive, anti-revolutionary apologia for a *fait accompli*. Save that even when one wishes to arrest oneself at so low a level, one can still perceive elements which are apt to provide foundation, at least to the same extent, for quite different deductions. This is what Petrie does in a certain sense, when he observes that historically speaking 'the eclipse of hereditary monarchy coincides ever with an era of regression and chaos'. Even restricting himself to the most recent times, he says:

> [W]hat has France in particular gained in its adopting, for the third time, the republican regime? Does it counts for more, perchance, in the European assemblies? Is its public life clearer and its citizens happier, than when the most Christian King ruled over Paris? The tempestuous and oscillating course of the German Republic does not do much to convince one that the *Reich* finds itself in better case in the absence of an Emperor or his constitutive members in this or that particular dynasty. The collapse of the monarchy of the Habsburgs was hailed as the harbinger of the dawn of a new era for what would become the Austrio-Hungarian empire, and now the statesmen of all the world are seeking in vain any kind of solution to the problem of its successor states. What boons has democratic government brought to Spain, to Portugal, to Brazil or to Greece? Is it not possible that the existence of a monarchy in Washington would have contributed to arresting the social and moral disintegration of the United States? The democrats must respond to these questions before they can repulse the

accusation that the advent of the republican principle itself is nothing other
than a backwards step in the history of humanity.

These considerations of Petrie seem to us eminently just. Only that, in
our view, one must recognise that there exists a variety of criteria of
measurement for judging better and worse. To hold firm at the politico-social criterion alone can be dangerous. As we will shortly see, the
principal foundation of the monarchical principle and of its superior
right is to be found in its possibility of spiritualising and dignifying
political life and of granting a higher justification to the principle of
authority. On the other hand, in the terms of mere economico-animal
well-being, which is to say, on the basis of the trivial equation well-
being = happiness, the utopian prospects proper to the technological
Marxist or Soviet messianism could well be called a political regime
or ideal in which, through the rational destruction of every higher
human interest, even the premises for the right of a monarchy would
not be posed in the least, nor could they hold good. If he does not
stand upon a purely spiritual plane, Petrie surely stands upon an ethical one when he observes that to liken the monarchs to something like
hereditary presidents, is to demonstrate a fundamental ignorance of
the highest attributes of regality. A President assumes his office more
or less as a high-ranking functionary fills his post. Altogether different
is the attitude of a monarch who fully assumes his responsibility and
his dignity. 'A President who swears obedience to the principles of a
constitution created by men and a king crowned by the Church of his
country as God's representative on earth are things as different from
one another as a diamond and an artificial stone'. And 'the fact that
monarchy is something that money cannot ever purchase exercises a
beneficent effect on the overall level of the public life, which is invari-
ably lower in a republic'. For Sir Petrie, monarchy draws its original
significance from a 'corporative' type of state, in which the individual
has no value save in function of his group, with each group finding its
progressive place in a hierarchical series.

At the zenith of this pyramid stood the monarch as the symbol of the nation as a whole, and, after the incoronation, as the anointed of the Lord, as the Lord's representative. He was not a despot, subject to no other law beyond those that he himself had made, but was rather an integral part of the system which he headed. His crown was an emblem of fidelity to his people and his rights and duties were defined in this way precisely, as much as those of his subjects. This was truly the distinctive character of the feudal regime: everyone had his defined place in the social whole, a place which corresponded to him and for which he was responsible.

With this, Petrie approaches certain essential points, and one can only wish that he had integrated them and specified them through a wider development, and that he did not subsequently fall into concessions which are dangerous and even contradictory, such as the following: 'today, in the twentieth century, *it is not necessary* that the monarchs raise the question of divine right' (p. 263). So far as we are concerned, precisely the opposite is true, and, if anything, it should be said that the theory of 'divine right' is still too little.

Indeed, if we seek the highest traditional justification of regality, we find it in a conception according to which the State (and still more the Empire) has a meaning of its own, its own transcendent purpose, and appears as a triumph of *cosmos* over *chaos*, as an efficacious formation operated by a force from on high — as the ancients said, by a force of the 'overworld' — within the naturalistic element of the *demos* and, in general, of everything which is merely ethic, biological, and, in a restricted sense, 'human'. Some will discover in this also a relation with what we have recently written in these very pages[3] regarding the relation between *race* and *culture*, between the naturalistic conception and the aristocratico-spiritual conception of race and of the nation. Now, precisely the King, the Monarch, is the point in which this force from on high eminently manifests itself, gathers itself, renders itself

3   'Razza e Cultura', in *Rassegna Italiana*, n. 1 of 1934. Not yet translated into English. — Trans.

efficacious, conferring on the State the aforementioned transcendent significance. Moreover, there is a profound meaning hidden in that reminder by Servius: '*Majorem haec consuetudo ut Rex esset etiam sacerdos et pontifex*,'[4] testimony of the primordial unity of the regal function with the 'pontifical' function (which is far from corresponding to the forbidden little formula of the scholastic manual: 'theocracy'). Indeed, according to the ancient etymology of, for instance, Festus, taken up in turn by St. Bernard, *pontifex* means 'maker of bridges' and was almost a bridge between the natural and the supernatural — *lex animata in terris,* according to the Ghibelline expression — and thus the supreme point of reference for every action of transfiguring devotion on the part of the various elements of the social whole which he headed — and the supreme basis as well for a true hierarchy.

Through the widest possible documentation, we have elsewhere[5] demonstrated the *universality* of this primordial conception of regality and we have equally demonstrated that in the highest form in which the two powers are united, that is the temporal and the spiritual, the virile and the sacred, the doctrine of divine right, as in nearer times it has been professed in Europe, refers already to a period in which the original teaching to a certain degree had already undergone a darkening, and, in the place of a regality spiritual or 'divine' in and of itself, and having directly in itself the principle of its transcendent 'legitimacy', there had come about a regality which was spiritual and legitimate only through the mediation of a priestly caste or Church, which were in turn distinct from it. The task of this distinct, priestly institution was therefore to transmit to the monarchs a specific group of 'spiritual influences', which are to be understood not as vain abstractions, but as effective supersensible powers, through which the regal function is confirmed, for all the elements that it governs, in its office of an ordering force from on high, of the centre of stability and

---

4   Latin: 'Greater is this custom, were the King both priest and pontifex'. — Trans.

5   See *Revolt Against the Modern World*, Part One, §§ 2, 3 et seq.

of 'tradition' in the higher sense — as well as 'health' and 'victory'. It is therefore natural that the continuity of a select blood should constitute the best condition for the regular and uninterrupted transmission of these spiritual influences from generation to generation, even if, for each single representative, the rite of investiture must be called upon to reconfirm these influences and to bring them, so to speak, from the virtual to the actual. Thus it is also natural that the hereditary dynastic concept should have often been the counterpart of the highest and most regular forms of monarchy.

From such considerations it therefore appears that one cannot separate the doctrine of 'divine right' (supposing of course that this is not reduced to a political instrument *ad usum delphini*,[6] but is understood on the plane of that *spiritual positivity* which we have just indicated) from the monarchy, without destroying the higher, more traditional justification. Here we might take up the observation already alluded to at the beginning. The superiority of the hereditary monarchical system over democratic systems or any other type of systems, neither *can* be nor should be defended in simply secular, political or practical terms. Wherever one ceases to demand that the intimate cement of the statal unity be something spiritual and transfiguring, rather than an opaque discipline, a statolatrous mechanism, an anodyne obedience or a vulgar unilateralism — wherever one ceases to demand that this cement of state be *fides*, the living and virile rapport between inferior and superior, which is to be gradually increased to such a point of attaining the sense that with this *fides*, this dedication, one has come to participate in something superindividual and superworldly, which in its turn is not the mere 'soul' of the nation as a naturalistic entity, but rather the point at which the nation

---

6   The Latin name of the *Delphin Classics*, a series of annotated Latin classics reproduced — and duly censored for the benefit of Louis the French Dauphin, for whose education they were intended — in the 1670s. Given this censorship, the expression passed into the popular lexicon to mean expurgated. In the present context, it of course means that the doctrine might be commandeered for political purposes. — Trans.

becomes the body in which a force from on high victoriously manifests itself—wherever, I say, this ideal loses its force, monarchy can be nothing more than a mere surviving remnant, a voided symbol, and the monarchical system descends, in its dignity, to the same plane as any other political regime, against which it no longer possesses and higher right. *A secularised monarchy is a monarchy which has dug its own grave.*

Nonetheless, it is necessary to add something at this point: the principle alone is not sufficient, but an *environment* is also necessary, every bit as much as the seed requires for its development a suitable soil. Petrie notes that the present is the era of a materialistic *forma mentis*[7] which is prevailing in every way. Now, modern man, if he is not able to rid himself of that *forma mentis*, if he is not able to revolutionise in a 'traditional' sense, which is to say in a spiritual sense, by reawakening forms of sensibility and types of interest that have fallen into atrophy, then this secularised, bureaucratised modern man, reduced to nothing more than a 'political animal' in the lowest sense of the term, will lack the suitable soil for the monarchical principle to bear fruit, or to seriously—and irresistibly—reaffirm itself in the face of inferior and fatal ideologies, rendering itself truly effective and healing.

These are the very premises which permit us to approach the *problem of the relationship between monarchy and dictatorship*: a problem to which Petrie provides the correct solution more by instinct than by direct knowledge of the doctrinal premises we have indicated above. For his part, Petrie observes however that today there exists a current which, while it affirms that the era of democracy is by now coming to a close, 'believes that monarchy, in the etymological sense of the word, is, more than hereditary regality, a form of government responding to the needs of the twentieth century'. That a dictatorship is probably the only effective way of repairing the evil brought by democratic

---

7   Latin: 'mental form', in the sense of mentality, or way of thinking. — Trans.

administration is true, responds Petrie, but 'the whole of human history demonstrates that dictatorship is generally a temporary expedient. There were very few tyrannies in Ancient Greece that lasted more than a single generation, and none survived the second: while in medieval Italy only those dictators who were able to found a hereditary monarchy were able to conserve the power they had in their hands.' The fact is — continues Petrie — that in the vulgar dictator we find a creature 'not of a stabilised law, but of an immature *demos*.' Dictatorship is positive when it does not have the sense about it of a risky experiment, but of a counterpart and complement to hereditary monarchy: and this, for its very nature and function, represents traditional continuity through the generations and through their various historic contingencies.

Very much apropos of this, our author recalls the ancient Roman constitution which reconciled the two institutions and limited dictatorship to a determinate period, to be used in exceptional political situations. Moreover, we might adduce examples proper to entire kindred cycles of civilisation. There is, for example, the constitution proper to the ancient Nordic races, in which there was originally a fundamental and significant distinction between the king and the *dux* or *heretigo*: the first was such on account of his 'divine blood', symbol which indicated his incarnating a spiritual and a properly traditional superbiological influence with respect to his race; the *dux* on the other hand — who corresponds more or less to the dictator — was the person chosen and acclaimed as a temporary head by the warriors for a specific enterprise of defence or of conquest, and not on the basis of 'divine right', but rather on the basis of his human capacities and qualities in the temporal realm. In the traditional concept there is therefore no antithesis, but rather a complementarity between the two functions: the king represents the 'divine' element — we are tempted to say, the *Olympian* element — which assures the stability of the centre and the influence of a higher nature in dynastic continuity. The dictator is a fateful apparition, in whom the force of the *demos* is gathered for decisive action during points of crisis or danger in the laical history of a nation. Thus Petrie can rightly say that dictatorship is regularly 'a complement, not a surrogate, to hereditary monarchy: at the closing of the dictatorship, the king remains in place to ensure that no violent break in continuity might arise'.

And it is natural that Petrie should indicate, in the constitution of Fascist Italy, a living and salutary example of the application of these ideas. The fact that Mussolini did not hesitate to recognise in monarchy 'the sacred, glorious, traditional, millennial symbol of the Fatherland'; that for him 'the Nation is summed up in the august name of the King' whose majesty 'represents the continuity, the vitality and the health of our race'[8] — this in truth demonstrates how much Fascism is interpenetrated with a healthy traditionalism and how much it presents to the world the example of a dictatorship purified of this demagogic, contingent, irrational element, which in other cases ever accompany it. In point of fact, another fact mentioned by Petrie is also not without relation to the regular relationship standing between monarchy and dictatorship; Petrie says that monarchy is the safeguard against every extravagant nationalism and even against the disintegrating particularism inherent to such nationalism. Indeed, we must have the courage to recognise that there exists a nationalism, direct creature of Jacobism and of the revolt of the masses against every higher principle of authority; and this nationalism, even when it takes on authoritarian, pseudo-hierarchical or dictatorial garb, is nothing other than a deviation and a kind of 'collective pandemonium' breaking out of the ruins of the traditional world; it finds in Soviet ideals its logical conclusion and, at the same time, its *reductio ad absurdum*.

Since we cannot linger too long on this point, we will only note that what we have already mentioned regarding the spiritual foundation of regality directly leads to this conclusion: while Jacobin nationalism

---

8   Quoted from the *Discorso di Forlì* (31 October 1932), the *Discorso di Milano* (on the first anniversay of the March on Rome) and the *Discorso ai Fanti* (12 August 1925).

expresses the limit of something simply natural, something enslaved to the blood, to space, time and history in the confined and plebeian sense, monarchy expresses a force of a different quality, which arrives to give to the 'nation' a spiritual, and no longer collectivist and materialist, meaning. In this way one might say that monarchy represents *the supernatural and immanent element of a nation*. For which reason it is quite natural that, in any group of monarchically constituted nations, the path remains virtually open to their higher spiritual unity, to an understanding attained between their national summits, which is precisely contrary to every democratic-internationalistic promiscuity. It is effectively this which we find in the Medieval Period, symbolised by the Holy Empire: here, there no longer existed nationalisms, but *nationalities*; not formulae of abstract submission, but rather living loyalties to Principle. For this reason, Petrie is right to say that 'before the French Revolution there did not exist among the nations that harshness of relations that we see today. Democracy is the negation of true internationalism, and there was much more cosmopolitanism in the eighteenth century, and before in the Medieval Period, than in the twentieth — despite all the international conferences that are continuously being held'.

We must effectively recognise that the greatest difficulty standing between us and a new European unity of civilisations is to be found precisely in this degenerative transition of peoples of *nationalities* into *nationalisms*; these nationalisms, constituting the various races in so many secularised entities and moreover making of them divinised and antagonistic concepts, thus create an embattled and unbridgeable schism in the unity of European culture. This experience reminds us that it is precisely beneath the insignia of nationalism that the world has known those wars which have assumed, more than any others, the low aspect of hatred, of violence, of embitterment, of denigration of the adversary by every means, in the place of the higher aspect of chivalry, of loyalty, of recognition of one's adversary, such as one finds in the better epoch of monarchical Europe.

These brief considerations regarding the relationship between monarchy and nationalism, at bottom, permit us to define principles for consideration of the nature of the processes which have led to the collapse and to the decadence of the monarchical regime in Europe, as well as those which might let us approach that regime's healthy restoration once again. Indeed, it is this which Sir Petrie treats of in the better part of his book, speaking to us of the past and of the future of the monarchical idea in the principle European and also extra-European nations. However, it seems to us that this part of Petrie's book is the weakest, since, despite his good intentions, the author seems lacking in those elements of doctrinal order that might furnish him a firm orientation with regard to such ponderous problems as these, on the basis of a general philosophy of history in a traditional key. Rather than this, we find many detailed considerations which are certainly interesting, but not conclusive, nor even of such a kind as might avoid occasional dangerous turns. For example, when Petrie says, 'It is no exaggeration if we state that the enormous progress made by civilisation between the sixteenth century and the Revolution is owed directly to the Kings of France in general and Louis XIV in particular' — when Petrie says this, he confounds the positive with the negative. It is rather the case that the Kings of France, not only in that period, but beginning already with Philip the Fair, unconsciously prepared the collapse of the monarchical principle above all in their country; for this reason France was the first to have a revolution, which then proceeded to the other peoples in a kind of backlash. Here we find the point of reconnection with the considerations already made on secularised nationalism, since the sense of that process which Petrie believes led to an 'enormous progress of civilisation', was nothing other than 'nationalisation' and 'laical centralisation'.

In the first place, the Kings of France lapsed from that purely symbolic and spiritual function they once had possessed; they passed over to absolutism, destroying, bit by bit, the articulation proper to the feudal regime, laicising their right and patronising the vanity of

'humanistic' culture, and aligning themselves against the aristocracy without disdaining the support of lower social strata, by coming, through a progressive centralisation, to the constitution of those
'public powers', formed of the mere *demos*, the mere national decon-
secrated collective. Along this path, the decadence of the monarchical
principle, its collapse and its mortifying reduction to a state of mere
survival (*le roi règne mais il ne gouverne pas*) was an inevitable consequence of logic and historical necessity. — We cannot dwell on this
order of questions here — which, moreover, the interested reader will
find expounded elsewhere at due length:[9] but what we have already
mentioned will suffice to give a glimpse of the true fracture point
which overcame the ancient European aristocracy, as well as the sense
of that path which might lead us back to a new traditional Europe.

Regarding this second point, it would have been desirable if Petrie
had courageously confronted the constitutional problem by study-
ing the relation between the true monarchical ideal and the various
modern forms of national unity at greater length, so as to demonstrate
which of these last, in their reduction to mere centralisation and mechanicalisation on the basis of simply ethno-national values — if not
even economico-administrative ones — remain, despite all appearances to the contrary, altogether opaque, and irreconcilable with the
traditional ideal of living relations based on ethics, personality, spirituality and loyalty. In any case — passing over into another level — Sir
Petrie arrives at a *punctum pruriens*[10] when he observes that 'it is not
true that the problems of the world are greater now than yesterday, but
it is rather true that men today are smaller', and when he indicts a real
'inferiority complex' in certain monarchies with respect to the altered
political conditions of recent times. This is a decisive point, albeit one
which concerns more a foreign people, if the traditional saying is true,
according to which it is more the king who gives force to regality than

9   In *Revolt* (Part Two, § 12 et seq.,); cf also 'The Fall of the Idea of the State' (in
    Recognitions).

10 Latin: a burning issue, lit. 'an itching spot'. — Trans.

it is regality — in the abstract — which gives force to the king. Petrie is convinced that the 'salvation of the world is connected to the triumph of the monarchical principle'.

The twilight of the parliamentaristic regime, the growing force which the idea of the corporate State is gaining — and which, in the opinion of our author, in his integrity, cannot help but take a monarchy as its zenith — are for him the harbingers of a new ascending arc. That that man who represents 'the most decided contrast with the mediocrities who presently head the affairs of many States, which is to say, Mussolini, the greatest figure of the twentieth century, is a convinced monarchist' is, for Petrie, another symptom of that higher meaning, which leads him to confidently declare, 'The political insight of the present generation will be judged by its attitude with respect to the monarchical principle within the next decade'.

This is a noble and courageous profession of faith, that we cannot help but share. Even if we are not as optimistic as Petrie regarding the internal and external possibilities remaining to Western man, nonetheless we recall that *quod bonum faustumque sit*[11] is part and parcel of our Roman tradition, and we ourselves subscribe to the hope that the worthiest royal figures of our time will be joined by others, in Europe and in the world, others whose hands are truly capable of holding once again, in all their power, sword and sceptre, that the living reality of the ancient myth of the Monarchs might be restored — Monarchs as the manifestation of a force from on high of glory, of 'health' and of victory.

---

11   Latin, usually *quod bonum faustum felix fortunatumque sit* and often abbreviated *Q.B.F.F.F.S.* Meaning is 'May it be successful, favourable, happy and fortunate', this phrase was often invoked by the magistrates before undertaking an action of public scope. — Trans.

3. THE MEANING AND FUNCTION OF MONARCHY

THE BOOK OF K. LOEWENSTEIN offers to its reader a vision of the whole of the various forms of monarchy and of the possibilities which, according to this author, remain to a monarchical regime in the current epoch. Monarchy, as has been seen, is here not taken in the literal sense of the term (the governance of one alone, power concentrated in a single man), but rather is understood rightly in its traditional and most current sense, which is to say with reference to a King.

Loewenstein's conclusions are rather pessimistic. If it is to exist in our days, monarchy must resign itself to being a shadow of what it once was. It could be conceived only in a democratic framework and, more precisely, in the form of a constitutional parliamentary monarchy. Apart from England, which constitutes a case all its own, the model offered by the monarchs of the smaller States of northern and western Europe — Sweden, Norway, Denmark, Belgium, Holland, Luxembourg — is that which one must keep before one's eyes.

In the analysis of the scope of the various arguments adopted in favour of the monarchical regime, Loewenstein has sought to be objective, though he does not always succeed in this. A clear aversion to every principle of true authority is visible in his work, while an insufficient emphasis is placed on factors of an ethical or immaterial character. Now, we believe that if we are constrained to conceive of monarchy only in the aforementioned empty and democratic forms — which is moreover possible only because we are dealing here with small and marginal States, such as have not yet been sucked into the dynamism of the great forces of the epoch — we may as well give up the game as lost.

It must be recognised, on the other hand, that pessimistic conclusions regarding monarchy appear in large part justified, if one hypothesises the situation of the present world and holds that it is irreversible and destined to carry on indefinitely. This situation is defined by a general materialism, by the prevalence of base interests, by the egalitarian error, by the regime of the masses, by technocracy and by the so-called 'consumer civilisation'. And the signs of a profound crisis in this world of well-being with its fictitious order begin even now to multiply. Various forms of revolt are already perceptible, for which reason the possibility cannot be excluded that we will arrive at a state of tension or a breaking point, and that, especially when faced with certain possible limit situations, tomorrow might come to reawaken various forms of sensibility, and reactions might emerge which are similar to those which might arise in an organism when it is mortally menaced in its deepest being.

The appearance of this new climate would be the decisive element, also as regards the problem of monarchy. In our opinion, this problem should be posited in the following terms: What meaning could monarchy have, if such a change in climate arises, and in what form could it constitute a centre for the reconstitution of a 'normal' order — normal in the higher sense? Certainly, the presence of a true monarchy in a nation would have a rectifying power; but we find ourselves in the grips here of a vicious circle. Without the premise which we have indicated, every restoration would have a contingent character; it would be non-organic and, in a certain sense, unnatural.

The present disorder in the political field, all the ways in which it is unstable and dangerously open to subversion — to Marxism and communism — derives substantially from the lack of a superior principle

of authority and from an almost hysterical intolerance for such a principle; and it is sure that certain political experiences of recent times
afford the many convenient pretexts for such intolerance. When we
speak of a higher principle of authority, we refer to an authority which
has an effective legitimation and a somehow 'transcendent' character;
for without this, its authority would be deprived of all basis, it would
be contingent and revocable. It would be lacking in a truly stable
centre.

It is important to clearly establish this essential point, so as to
differentiate between that monarchy which we here mean to discuss
on the one hand, and monarchy in the broad sense of power in or
governance by one man alone on the other. Indeed, spurious, counterfeit forms of authority are conceivable, and have also been realised.
Even the communist regimes stand *de facto* on an authoritarianism
which can assume the crudest and most tyrannical forms, whatever
justifications one might mendaciously give to them. One can put the
dictatorial phenomenon in the same terms, if one conceives of it in
any way other than the consequence of emergency cases — a conception of dictatorship that can originally be found, moreover, even in
Ancient Rome.

On the other hand, the antithesis, so often advanced, between
dictatorship and democracy is relative, supposing only that one ex-
amines the existential foundation of these two political phenomena.
That foundation is a 'mass state'. If a dictatorship does not have purely
functional and technical characteristics (the regime of Salazar in
Portugal offers one current example), if it stands on *pathos*, as in certain of its recent plebiscite and populist forms, it is galvanised by the
same element which is activated by every democratic demagogy. The
dictator becomes a bad surrogate for the monarch, appealing to forces
that confusedly seek a point of support, a centre (whatever it might
be) in order to gain the upper hand over chaos, disorder, situations
which have become intolerable. This also explains the phenomenon
of possible swift changes of polarity following some trauma which

has suspended the cohesive and animating force of the system, just as when in a magnetic field the current suddenly ceases. The most evident case for this is perhaps offered by the amazing change in the political climate which can be observed in present-day Germany, after the almost frenetic mass enthusiasm which characterised the previous dictatorial period. It is significant on the other hand that no analogous phenomenon of inversion arose in Germany after the First World War, because what had preceded it was not a dictatorship, but rather a monarchical tradition.

By the 'transcendence' of the principle of authority proper to regality, the monarchical regime constitutes the single true antithesis both to dictatorship and to absolute democracy. We must indicate in this the foundation of its higher right. The various forms which this transcendence might adopt according to the times, and the ideas or symbols by which it might legitimate itself, do not touch the essential: the essential is the principle. Loewenstein is right to say that in a world desacralised by the natural sciences, in which religion itself has been undermined, there can no longer be any question of that mysticism of monarchy which in other times rested upon certain theological conceptions and on a certain liturgy. But if we turn our gaze to the bearers of the crown in all times and in all places, we observe as a common and constant motif the recognition of the necessity of a stable centre, of a pole, of something that to be truly stable must have, in a certain way, its own principle in itself or from on high, and that must not have a derivative character. In this context one might peruse, for example, the excellent work of F. Wolff-Windegg, *Die Gekrönten*. Someone has rightly written that '*A purely political regality has never existed*'. We can affirm this without any doubt. In times not distant to our own, the 'for the grace of God', the sovereignty of divine right, did not imply, in its subjects, any specific theological considerations; it held, so to speak, in existential terms, and corresponded precisely to the need of a higher point of reference — a point that failed utterly when the king was king solely by the 'will of the nation' or 'of the people'. On the other hand, only by that presupposition could those dispositions develop in the subjects, in the form of loyalty, of which we will soon speak: dispositions and forms of comportment and of custom of a higher ethical value.

Thus we cannot help but share Loewenstein's opinion that the 'ideal' argument in favour of monarchy has by now been invalidated. To be sure, what he says is true, that the decline of the monarchy is owed not so much to democracy as to the advent of machines and aeroplanes, the automobile and television — in general, we can say, the technological industrial civilisation. But here it must be asked if this civilisation must simply be presupposed; it must be asked to what extent man wishes to accord to all of this a value higher than that of a mere complex of simple, banal means, which leave an absolute interior emptiness in this 'consumer civilisation'. Let us say it again: we are speaking above all of the 'dignity' of monarchy, of a prestige and of a right which ever and everywhere were drawn from a superindividual and spiritual sphere. Sacred investitures, divine right, mystical and legendary filiations and genealogies and so forth, were naught other than forms used to express a substantial and always-recognised fact, namely, that a political order, a truly organic and living collective, is possible only where there exist a stable centre and a superelevated principle, higher than any particular interest, higher than the purely 'physical' dimension of society — a principle which has in itself a corresponding intangible and legitimate authority.

Therefore, in principle, that which Hans Blüher wrote is absolutely right: 'A king who lets his sovereign function be confirmed by the people, and admits, in this, that he is responsible to the people — rather than being responsible *for* the people and *to* God — such a king has renounced his regality. No infamy which a king might commit — and God knows that they have committed such — destroys the objective mystical sanction of the sovereign. But a democratic election destroys it immediately'.

While in other times the bond of fidelity which united the subject and the devotee to the sovereign could be likened to a sacrament — *sacramentum fidelitatis*[1] — something of this was preserved even later as the rather perceptible foundation for a special ethics: the ethics, that is to say, precisely of loyalty and of honour, which could acquire a particular strength in the presupposition, just now indicated, of the presence of a personalised symbol.

In normal times, the fact that a sovereign as individual was not always capable of living up to the principle[2] was little important; his function remained unalienable and intangible because obedience was owed not to the man but to the king, and his person held essentially as a support toward the awakening or the propitiation of that capacity for superindividual dedication, that pride in free service and possibly even that readiness to sacrifice (as when in dramatic moments an entire people gathered around its sovereign) which constituted at one and the same time a path to elevation and to the dignifying of the individual, and the most powerful force to hold together the compages of a political order and to reduce whatever remained in it of the anodyne and disanimate — precisely that which, in recent times, has taken on a dangerous extension.

It is evident enough that all of this cannot be realised to the same extent under any other form of political regimentation. The president of a republic can be revered, but one can never recognise in him anything other than a 'functionary', a 'bourgeois' like any other, who only extrinsically, and not on the basis of an intrinsic legitimacy, is invested with a temporary and conditioned authority. Whoever conserves a certain subtle sensibility perceives that 'being in the service of one's king', 'fighting for one's king' (even combatting for 'one's fatherland', its Romantic hues notwithstanding, has in comparison something less

---

1   Latin: 'the sacrament of the faithful'. — Trans.

2   The Italian — *all'altezza del principio*, literally 'at the height of the principle — is much more evocative here, but is based on a common Italian expression which has no perfect translation in English. — Trans.

noble, more naturalistic and collectivistic), and 'representing the king' have a specific quality. All of these actions present rather a parody-like, not to say grotesque character when they are referred 'to one's president'. Above all in the case of the army, of the high bureaucracy and of diplomacy (not to speak of the nobility), this fact appears quite evident. The same oath, when it is given not to a sovereign but to a re-public, or to some abstraction or other, has something flat and empty about it. With a democratic republic something immaterial, but even essential and irreplaceable, is fatally lost. The anodyne and the profane prevail. A monarchical nation which becomes a republic is, in a cer-tain way, a 'degraded' nation.

While we have observed that this kind of fluid which forms around the symbol of the Crown is wholly different from what might be referred to excited 'crowd states', which can be aroused or favoured by the demagoguery of a popular leader, the difference exists also with respect to a simple nationalistic mystique. Certainly, the sovereign incarnates the nation as well; he symbolises its unity on a higher plain, almost establishing with this a 'unity of destiny'. But here we find the opposite of every Jacobin patriotism; there are none of those confused collectivising myths which prattle on about the pure *demos*, going so far almost to divinify it. It can be said that modern monarchy limits and purifies simple nationalism; that, as it prevents every dictatorship by advantageously supplanting it, so it also prevents every nationalis-tic excess; that it defends an articulated, hierarchical and equilibrated order. It is known that the most calamitous upheavals of recent times are to be attributed essentially to unleashed nationalism.

After what we have said, it is evident that we do not at all share the idea that monarchy must now be democritised, that monarchy must almost assume bourgeois traits — that it 'must descend from the au-gust heights of former times and present itself and act in democratic mode', as Loewenstein claims. This would mean nothing more than destroying its dignity and its *raison d'être*, which have been indicated in the preceding. That king of the Northern-European countries

who carries his own suitcase, who goes shopping in the shops, who
consents to having his well-behaved familial life, including his babies
and their tantrums, presented to the people on the radio or the television, or else who allows that the Royal House should lend itself to the
curiosity and the gossip of the tabloids, and favours whatever else it
is believed might bring a sovereign nearer to his people, including at
bottom, possessing a certain good-natured paternal aspect (with the
father being conceived in a bland bourgeois form) — all of this cannot
help but injure the very essence of the monarchy. 'Majesty' becomes
then truly an empty and purely ceremonial epithet. With good reason
has it been said that 'the powerful man who, from a poorly understood
sense of popularity, permits himself to approach it will end badly'.

It is clear that to stand firm in all of this means to stand against
the current. But an alternative is once more presented to us: do we accept as irreversible a state of affairs whose continued existence means
that monarchy can only exist in inane vestiges? One of the elements
to consider here is the intolerance of the present world for distance.
The success of the dictatorships and other spurious political forms is
owing, in part, precisely to the fact that the head of state is considered
'one of us', 'Big Brother'; only in these terms will he be accepted as a
guide and obeyed. With things standing like this, the preoccupation
for 'popularity' and for 'democratic' modes is quite comprehensible.
But this, at bottom, is anything but natural; it is hard to see why one
must subordinate oneself when the leader is, at the end of the day,
simply 'one of us' — when no essential distance is felt, as in the case of
a true sovereign. Thus a 'pathos of distance' — to use one of Nietzsche's
formulations — should be substituted for the pathos of nearness, in relations which exclude every haughty arrogance in the one, and every
kind of servilism in the others. This is a basic and essential point for
any monarchical restoration.

While avoiding both exhuming anachronistic forms, and a propaganda which 'humanises' the sovereign so as to endear the masses,
almost along the same lines as the American presidential electoral

propaganda, we should attempt to discover up to what point, given an adequate framework, the traits of a figure characterised by a certain innate superiority and dignity might produce effect. A kind of ascesis and liturgy of power might play a role here. The traits precisely, while they reinforce the prestige of that man who incarnates a symbol, ought also to exercise on any non-vulgar man the force of an attraction, and even pride in the subject. And it should be said that even in fairly recent times we have had the example of the emperor Francesco Giuseppe who, though he interposed between himself and his subjects the ancient strict ceremonial, and though he in no way imitated the 'democratic' kings of the little Nordic States, enjoyed a particular and non-vulgar popularity.

In summary, the main presupposition for a rebirth of monarchy in the dignity and the function that we have discussed, remains, in our opinion, the reawakening of a new sensibility. This sensibility must be of an order that detaches it from the most material and even simply 'social' plane, and tends toward all things connected to honour, fidelity and responsibility, because such values find their natural centre of gravity in monarchy; while the monarchy in its turn would be degraded, reduced to a simple formal and decorative vestige, when such values are no longer living and operating above all in an elite, in a true ruling class. Those chords that the defender of the monarchy must cause to resound in the individual and in the collective are not identical to those which sound in any other system. It is thus absurd to entrust the destiny of the monarchical idea to a propaganda and a system of parties which in turn copy, in the same manner, the very methods of the opposite side in our democratic climate. Even the sense that tendencies are emerging toward an authoritarian centre, toward a 'monarchy' in the literal sense (= monocracy), does not suffice, given what we have noted on the profound differences that might appear in the various externalisations of the principle of unity and authority. The sense of that which cannot be sold nor bought nor usurped is a decisive fact in the dignity of and participation in political life, and runs like water through the hands of whomever thinks in merely material terms, or in the terms of personal advantage, of hedonism, of functionality and of rationality. If we are not supposed to speak of this sense on account of the famous Marxist 'sense of history', which, it is claimed, is irrevocable, then we may as well definitively table the monarchical cause. This would be equivalent, however, to professing the bleakest pessimism with regard to that appeal which can yet be made to something within the man of these last times.

After having considered the spiritual aspect of the problem of monarchy, it is necessary to indicate the aspects which refer to its positive, institutional and constitutional plane. On this plane we must now clarify the specific function to attribute to monarchy and that which differentiates a monarchical system from all others. It is incredible that this problem is not even remotely touched by the propaganda of the monarchists. In the late elections, even in Italy we heard discourses from the monarchists, who indicted, more or less on the same lines as other sectors of the opposition, the dysfunctions of the democratic and party-cratic republican State, as well as the danger of Communism, taking care however not to indicate, fearlessly and without mincing words, in what terms the presence of the monarchy would positively eliminate those dysfunctions and that danger alike — or rather, in virtue of what particular prerogatives monarchy would be capable of as much.

If one is truly monarchist, one cannot admit that the monarchy is reducible to a simple decorative and representational institution, a sort of nice bibelot or, following an image suggested by Loewenstein, something like the gilded figure which was placed on the prow of the galleon; the State would remain concretely a parliamentary republican democracy, and the king would have the single responsibility of countersigning anything that the government and the parliament decide upon, just as the president of the republic would do. The restoration must rather involve a kind of monarchical revolution (or counter-revolution).

To the well-known formula that 'the king rules but does not govern', another should be counterpoised: 'The king both rules *and* governs' — governs, naturally, not in the terms of the absolute monarchies of elder times, but rather, in the normal way, within the framework of an established right and constitution. In this respect the best example is offered us by the previous central-European monarchies, for which Loewenstein does not hide a decided antipathy. To the sovereign should be reserved not only a regulative, moderating and arbitrative power with respect to the various other political forces, but also the power of the last resort.[3] One must not make a fetish of constitutions and rights. Constitutions and rights do not fall ripe and full from the sky; they are historical formations, and their intangibility is conditioned by the normal course of things. When this course fails, when confronting emergency situations, a superior power must make itself positively felt — a superior power, that is, which, though it has remained latent and inactive in normal conditions, has not for this ceased to constitute the centre of the system. The king is the legitimate subject of this power. He can and must exercise it whenever such becomes necessary, saying, 'This far, but no farther', thus preventing both any subversive revolutionary movements (and preventing them in particular through a 'revolution from above'), and any kind of dictatorial upheaval, whose single justification is the lack of a true centre of authority.

It is not necessary that such a power be exercised directly by the sovereign; it could also be exercised through a capable and decisive Chancellor or prime minister who, strong in their support of the Crown and essentially responsible to it alone, are able to confront the situation. The case of Bismarck in the 'institutional conflict' recalled by Loewenstein corresponds to this possibility. Firm in his fidelity to

---

3   Italian: *ultima istanza*. The meaning of this, as Evola subsequently clarifies, is that the king should have the final say, particularly in states of emergency. This can be usefully compared to Carl Schmitt's idea of the 'state of exception'. — Trans.

his sovereign, Bismarck was able to disregard the opposition of the parliament and, in by this route, succeeded in bringing about the greatness of Germany, receiving only subsequently, in a new constitution, the sanction for his work.

We might risk suggesting that an analogous situation was partially at first realised when the king of Italy supported Mussolini, conceding to him powers in order to impose order on an Italy that had been shaken by subversion and the social crisis — powers that he himself, Vittorio Emanuele, would have been able to exercise, had he not felt himself constitutionally limited from doing so. Had he been able, he might have imposed this order through new structures, without having need of Fascism, and thus would have prevented those developments, defined by some in the terms of a 'diarchy', which in the end undermined his position to some extent, by bringing about almost a State within the State.

In the decisive hours a sovereign must never forget the saying of an ancient wisdom: *Rex est qui nihil metuit*, 'He is king who fears nothing.' Against a badly understood humanitarianism, in extreme cases he must not tremble even before the danger of battle in which blood may be shed, because it is not a question of persons, but of bringing authority, order and justice to reign above all things, and against possible partisan agitations. We have already indicated the formula for this: '*This* far, but no farther.' In non-exceptional situations, we can accept the conception of Benjamin Constant of the Crown as a 'fourth power', with an arbitrative and equilibrating function. So too the rights recognised by Bagehot to the Crown — the right to be consulted, the right to encourage, and the right to warn — are irreproachable.

Thus it is that, with a monarchical restoration, a relocation of the centre of gravity should be effected. There can even be a national representative body elected by the 'people', according to one modality or another (we will return to this), but it must be responsible, *in primis et ante omnia*, before the sovereign, according to a personalised responsibility that already in itself would close the way to many forms of democratic corruption. The king must be the supreme point of reference, and the aforementioned values of loyalty and honour must be manifested in the representatives, rather than their being the instruments of parties and of that mysterious, changeable entity known as the 'people' which is exploited by the same, and to which alone is granted the power of confirmation and revocation in the system of absolute democracy, or the system of universal equal suffrage.

On the other hand, for a true monarchical renovation, the ideal of an organic State must be present, for which the problem of the general compatibility of monarchy with the system of absolute parliamentary democracy cannot be avoided. The superimposition of the one on the other can produce only something hybrid. It is to be considered that if the hoped-for change in mentality comes about, we will arrive little by little at recognising also the absurdity of this system of representation, based as it is on indiscriminate universal suffrage, on the law of pure number, which takes as its obvious presupposition, not the conception of the citizen as a 'person' but rather his degrading reduction to the status of an undifferentiated interchangable atom.

In this context we must bear in mind that democracy in its absolute modern form is one thing, while the system of representation is another, the second not necessarily coinciding with the first. It is known that a system of representation existed even in the traditional monarchical States, but in general as an organic representation, which is to say of bodies, of orders, of *Stände*,[4] and not of ideological parties. So far as the party system goes, the two-party system is the best, admitting as it does an opposition which acts constructively and dynamically within the system, not outside of or against it. (It is a true absurdity, for instance, that a communistic or revolutionary party, so long as it observes certain purely formal statute norms, can be considered 'legal' and can be admitted into a national assembly when its

---

4   The word is German, and can be translated, in this context, as 'classes' or 'social bodies'. — Trans.

programme, whether declared or tacit, is the overturning of the existing social order.)

Apart from the two-party system, which was already beneficially
adopted in monarchical England, the organic representative system
which best harmonises with the monarchy would be the corporative,
in the widest, traditional sense, without intending any reference to the
attempt, which was made by Fascism with its creation of a corporative rather than party-cratic House. Perhaps the present Portuguese
system — and to a lesser extent the Spanish — approaches a desirable
order.

Loewenstein has brought to light the alternative that would present itself in the case of a restoration: either the sovereign would seek
support in the upper classes, which are more inclined to maintain the
monarchy, and so play the game of those who are ready to accuse him
of conservative reactionism; or else he would seek the support of the
working classes and, in general, set himself up as 'the king of the people', and thus would dangerously alienate that support which the other
part of the nation might give him.

Now, such a dilemma obviously presupposes the maintenance of
the state of struggle of the classes, in the terms of Marxist ideology.
But we hold that one of the presuppositions for a new, organic and
monarchical order is to be seen precisely in the overcoming of this
antagonistic division of the national forces. The corporative reform
should aim precisely at this, and once it has been actuated the aforementioned alternative standing before the monarchy would largely
disappear. Even if opposite tendencies arose within the corporations
(or however else one wishes to designate the primary representative
organ), one can suppose that the pre-eminence which would be given
to the principle of competencies would largely reduce the ideological
factor in these divergences.

Given the importance which the technological and economical
sector has by now acquired, the system of corporative representation, based on competencies, could appear quite current, given the

almost cancerous development of the technocratic element and, in general, of the economy. There have been well-known critiques advanced against the technological civilisation of consumerism in the most advanced industrial society; the destructive aspects that are proper to this society have been indicated, and the need to put a halt to economic processes which have become almost independent has been expressed, as in the image of the 'unchained giant' which W. Sombart has used. Now, no halt can be conceived for the system, no containment, without the intervention of a higher political power. The task of adequately slowing and ordering the forces moving within this society on the basis of a more complete hierarchy of interests and values, thus also obviating a paradoxical situation which has arisen in recent times — namely, that of a State which is ever stronger, with a head which is ever weaker — this task would evidently find a more favourable environment for its realisation in a true monarchical State.

Institutionally, the organ for this could be furnished either by a single assembly — which, however, side by side with the representation of the economic and productive forces, would include also the representation of the spiritual and cultural life (as was seen, for instance, in the 'General Estates' and in the analogous assemblies or Diets of the ancient monarchical traditional regimes) — or else by the two house system, with its Upper and Lower Houses, the second being the properly corporative body, and the first the bearer of superordinate claims. It is known that the last 'triumph' of absolute democracy was that of having reduced the Upper House, or the Senate, to a useless duplicate of the lower, because the principle of mass election and of term restrictions was brought to hold also in it (at least for most of its components). The definition of the Upper House should rather be, as it was even yesterday in Italy, one of the essential tasks of the monarchy, however it might be most conveniently assisted in this, so that the formal character of the nomination from on high is preserved.

In this way, the Upper House would remain the political body nearest to the Crown, and it would be natural that loyalism, fidelity and impersonality would be active in it in the highest possible degree. It ought to have a power, an authority, a prestige and a meaning different from that proper to the Lower House. As the custodian of higher values and interests, it would constitute the true central and active nucleus for codetermining the political line. That characteristic would differentiate it profoundly from the form taken by the Senate in post-unification monarchical Italy — this Senate being an assembly of worthy persons, of 'high talents', of notables according to the census, which however have an essentially decorative capacity, without any true, vigorous organic function.

Without lingering on the details, it is clear that a system of this kind would overcome the aberrations of absolute democracy and of the republican party-cracy, and would have its natural integration in monarchy. Here monarchy would not be something heterogeneous, almost the vestige of another world, superimposed on the parliamentary system. Therefore, rigorously speaking, the problem of monarchy stands within a vaster problem, that of the 'revolutionary' redimensioning of the entire modern State.

But for the functions of the monarchy that we have sought to outline, and if this monarchy is to have the power not only to 'reign' but also to play an active role — more or less determined according to the circumstances — in 'government', it is clear that there would be required a particular qualification of the sovereign not only on the level of his character, according to his strict traditional education in principles, but also so far as his competencies, knowledge and experience are concerned. This is rendered necessary by the character both of the epoch and the modern State.

The ancient Far Eastern conception of the *wei-wu-wei*, the royal 'acting without acting', is suggestive: it alludes, not to a direct material action, but to an action 'through presence', as the quintessential centre and power. This aspect, though it maintains its intrinsic validity in the terms we have noted above, has need of integration (thus making certain that it not be impaired), when, as is the case both in current times and probably still more in those which are to come, everything is in movement and forces tend to depart from their normal orbit. As we have said, in other times the symbol of the monarch could hold pre-eminence over the person of the monarch himself; given the general climate and the force of a long tradition and a legitimacy, the symbol could not be judged by the merely human aspects of the person that in this or that case happened to incarnate it. If today or tomorrow a monarchical restoration should come, this would no longer be possible: the representative must stand as much as possible at the heights of the principle,[5] and not through any ostentation of his person — indeed, the contrary. He must have the qualities of a true lord, of a man capable of holding the sceptre more than symbolically and ritually. Such a qualification in our times can be that of the warrior dynasties alone. The gifts of character, of courage and of energy, though these remain the essential basis, must unite to those of an enlightened mind and of essential political knowledge, sufficient to the whole structure of a modern state and of the forces which are presently active in contemporary civilisation.

The decline of the traditional regimes has had two causes, which acted together even before the materialistic climate of modern civilisation and of industrial society was added. On the one hand, above, there was the increasing incapacity to completely incarnate the principle, especially when the general structures began to break apart; on the other, below, there came the failure of the peoples, who became more or less mere 'masses', a failure in a specific kind of sensibility, in certain capacities of recognition. Thus the possibility of a monarchical restoration suffers a double setback, and appears to be conditioned upon the removal of both of these negative factors. On the one hand,

---

5   Here again, the Italian is *all'altezza del principio*, which primarily means that he would be up to reflecting the principle. Evola often plays on common expressions, however, and this is a clear case of this tendency. The translation renders the play on words without rendering the commoner translation, as it seems to the translator that the 'play' is the real pith of the meaning here. — Trans.

sovereigns would be required who do not owe their prestige merely to their superelevated position, to the symbol that overshadows them, but who are also capable of confronting each situation as the exponents of an idea and of a higher power. On the other hand, there would be required a change in the general mental and moral level of the masses — a necessity which we will never tire of emphasising.

In the present day and age, both conditions appear hypothetical. But if one is not to reach the essentially negative conclusions drawn from studies on monarchy in the modern State, like that which Loewenstein has carried out — if monarchy is not to be considered exclusively as an institution which, as the pallid shadow of what monarchy once was, is now almost entirely deprived of its meaning and its essential *raison d'être* — then there is no other way of posing the problem. It would therefore be well to repeat that the destiny of the monarchy appears to be, in a certain way, wed to that of the entirety of modern civilisation, and more properly depends on what might be the solution to a crisis which, as is evident from a great deal of evidence, is infiltrating the very foundations of that civilisation.

4. ALTERNATIVES FOR CIVILISATION

THE CLASSICAL and Mediterranean world exalted the sense of individual dignity, of difference, of aristocracy and hierarchy: it set, above every other, the ideal of culture, in the sense of the realisation of the self, of the creation of 'types', of living works of art expressing complete persons. And in the autarchy, blooming out of the superb dominion of those who possess themselves, of the Doric and Homeric type, whose purity is strength and whose strength is purity, it recognised *virtus*, which brings the human to communicate with the non-human.

Our tradition has never known aught of stones enchained in the ever-elusive cement of collective bonds, of mechanical laws, of social despotism: it has rather known vales and peaks, forces alongside forces and forces against forces, organised freely in direct and organic relations — warrior, heroic and sacrificial, in acts of absolute command and absolute devotion; strongly individuated solar centres culminating wherever Imperium was felt as the presence of a force from on high. Thus organisation in the true and living sense — no amalgams, no composites. The individual here is not an impersonal part, but a *member connected directly to the whole* and constituting a function and a modality of distinct and irreducible life, which is not to be erased or levelled out, but is brought to become ever more perfectly and intensely itself, for the greater wealth and determinateness of the great body of the whole.

Our tradition has celebrated the 'heroes', has celebrated the dominators, has celebrated the human-gods. And while, in contrast to certain Semitic and Asiatic conceptions, it has never detached the spiritual from this terrene world, it has nonetheless in an unequivocal way affirmed the *sovereign right of quality, of the idea and of wisdom* over everything practical and conditioned: that these must dominate through the act of complete persons in the same way that meaning dominates the word, and the soul the body. And in the *pax profunda* brought about by Roman power, the luminous civilisation of Hellenism was diffused throughout the entire Mediterranean basin.

In the sensation of immanent unity, it awakens other eyes, other ears, other limbs of our power than those known to the most recent barbarians. Rather than materialising and mechanising even man himself, it felt *living and immortal forces* in act behind that which modern man calls material and mechanical law, and it established real contacts with these through rite and symbol, whence it awoke in him, to whom it gave the name 'god incarnate' (*en sarki peripolón theós*) the sense of being 'all in all, composite of all powers'(*Corpus Hermeticum*), free as 'a world in the world' (Plotinus) in the hierarchy of beings, even while he remained himself. And it is *Empire* — not Bolshevik promiscuity, not the federalism and the democratism of modern societies — which logically crowned this conception; and its harmonious hierarchy acquired the sense of reflection and symbol of the hierarchy of the intellectual and divine world.

It is wholly another conception of the world, of things, of life, not as a philosophical excogitation, but as something living in the very blood, and transposing itself as meaning in the breast of all the activities, variously articulated but organised all around a single axis. The contingency of the times has gradually buried this, and the great shadow of the 'Formless Being' looms at last as its definitive negation.

EMPIRE

1. ON THE PROBLEM OF SPIRITUAL RACE

ON VARIOUS OCCASIONS, and above all in our work *Synthesis of the Doctrine of Race*,[1] we have maintained the idea that a totalitarian racism, one understood to embrace man in his fullness, is bound to consider race, not only as a merely physical reality, but also as an interior one.

More particularly, we have proposed the distinction between the *race of the body* (somatic race), the *race of the soul* and the *race of the spirit*. In the present writing we intend to clarify this distinction and to explain both its doctrinal justification, and its practical and political justification.

With the formulation of a racism understood as being the study of race as an interior as well as exterior reality, we have essentially sought first to prevent every attempt to limit racism itself to a material and scientistic plane, and second to contest its right to enter as well into a spiritual and cultural field. In reality, we know of certain circles which, tendentiously interpreting certain declarations of the racist manifesto from three years ago, rejoice when they hear that the problem of race in Italy ought to be placed on a merely scientific and biological plane. 'Excellent,' they say, 'then let us by all means leave it to the anthropologists and the biologists to measure facial angles and cranial indices, to compile lists of these or that typical characteristics with respect to

---

1   Yet to be translated into English. — Trans.

eyes, hair, noses, etc., to seek even to get to the bottom of the complex ethnic reality contained within the Italian people.' None of this troubles us. Let them by all means face the biological and 'zoological' problem of race. But let them not dream of making pronouncements on the plane of intellectual, cultural and spiritual values. There, they will find our barrier awaiting them.

Now, to affirm that race exists not only as a biological and somatic fact, but rather also as an interior reality, means to thwart any such manoeuvrer on their part and to accommodate oneself to the deep exigency which first led to the incorporation of the racial idea in Fascist doctrine. In Fascism, which intends to form a new man and to be the beginning of a new civilisation, it is absurd to think that race might be conceived only as an affair of the anthropological niche, without having also a living, spiritual meaning, such as to *impinge*[2] decisively on the world of moral and cultural values. The political value of racism would be otherwise gravely injured. It is therefore worth our while to posit the problem of race, beyond the purely biological scope.

Now, the doctrine of interior race holds good also in the prevention of another false turn, one which has aroused many prejudices against racism. We refer to the thesis of a one-way dependence, of man's higher values and higher faculties, on the simple race of the body, a thesis which is on the one hand humiliating and animated by the very spirit of materialist Darwinism and Jewish psychoanalysis, and on the other hand is problematic in itself, because it is not easy, given the present state of ethnic intermixing characteristic of every contemporary people, to precisely identify in each man the various components of the race of the body which actually condition the rest. Such a false turn is avoided so soon as the reality of an interior race is admitted. Higher values and faculties do not depend on biology, but

---

2   The original text as it was printed in *Vita Italiana* had the Italian word *indicare* ('indicate') here, which is most likely a misprinting of *incidere*. The word has been translated in the latter sense. — Trans.

on internal race, to which somatic race normally serves as the instrument for manifestation and action.

What is the relation between internal race and somatic race? It depends. Speaking in normal cases, and indeed in normative cases, they are two manifestations of a single reality, two modes of appearing on two different levels of a single reality. It has been written that race is the exterior aspect of the soul, just as the soul is race seen from within. Leaving aside certain reservations, which are altogether comprehensible given what we will say below, we can subscribe to this point of view. Therefore, we propose neither the one-way dependency of the internal race on that of the body, nor of the dependency of the body on internal race. The true point of reference is a reality which is prior and superior both to somatic race and to interior race, given that both are but the modes in which this reality appears on two different planes.

But this, as we have said, is to be found in a condition of normalcy and of racial purity. Where this condition is not to be found, things naturally go differently. And just as interbreeding leads to a state in which the somatic traits of a given racial type are mixed with those of another, so it can also bring it about that the correspondence between somatic race and interior race is interrupted. In this case the physical figure ceases to be a sure index for the presence of a corresponding interior race. And here we find justification for what we have called racial investigation of the second and third degree, which is to say that which considers, not only the somatic race, but also the race of the soul and the race of the spirit. Such investigation, beyond being scientifically necessary, has clear political importance. Indeed, Fascist racism evidently intends to awaken a sentiment of internal unity; it desires the unity of race just as the unity of will, of feeling, of acting and of way of being, quite different from the hypothetical uniformity of the greatest number of individuals who reproduce a given somatic racial type. Without injuriously neglecting the race of the body, we must therefore consider, with adequate means of investigation, the race of the soul and of the spirit as well.

But here arises another difficulty. It might be asked: What is this distinction between soul and spirit? Is it not an idle, or at least an artificial, distinction? Let us by all means speak, if such seems useful, of an 'internal race': but is it really necessary to distinguish in this between a 'race of the soul' and a 'race of the spirit'?

We say that it is. Such a distinction is possible, is indeed necessary, if we are not to noticeably restrict our horizons, and if we wish to prevent other false turns within the racial doctrine itself. Certainly, it is not easy for contemporary man to distinguish between the 'soul' and the 'spirit'. But the cause of this is only the state of involution in which we find ourselves — which is as much as to say, the fact that contemporary man knows almost nothing any longer of what is truly spirit, and is liable to confound it with certain surrogates and reflections that he might find on the plane of the simple 'soul'. Things stood otherwise in antiquity. The ancient Aryan-Hellenic man clearly felt the difference between the *noûs*, or the spiritual principle corresponding to the 'Olympian' and 'solar' element in us, and the *psyche*; the ancient Aryan-Roman man likewise guarded against confusing the 'sovereign mind', the intellectual power, the *mens*, with the simple *anima*, which for him almost bordered on the sensitive-animal life (*animal*, from *anima*); the ancient Indo-Aryan man, then, went so far as to conceive between the spirit, the *âtmâ*, and the animico-mental life the same difference which exists between this life and the physical body; and so forth and so on. With the distinction in words that we have made here, we have therefore invented nothing, nor are we merely woolgathering; indeed, we take our bearings by a very clear tradition, which is the only one capable of leading us to comprehend the human being in his completeness and his true dignity.

From the most immediate point of view, how do we distinguish then between the race of the soul and that of the spirit? The race of the soul corresponds to the form of character, to the collective and hereditary style of each person's bearing with respect to the external world and to his peers. We remain however in the 'temporal' world: the historical, sensible, social world. There exist two typical ways of conceiving the things that surround us, of exercising a given activity, of comporting oneself with other men. These typical ways are reflected in customs, in literature, in art, in law, and betray precisely the 'race of the soul'. This is also a problem of psychic 'style': there are various ways of being an individual who hates, who loves, who is faithful, who is courageous, even who betrays a not merely biological heredity, and many of these nonetheless never go beyond the human element, or the order that unfolds in time and in history. Wherever one speaks of the 'races of the soul' almost as super-individual collective entities, this order is not surpassed.

The 'race of the spirit' is something else, because it regards the form, no longer of a man's attitude with respect to the sensible, historical and social world, but rather his attitude with respect to the divine and supersensible world: the point of reference is no longer life, but that which stands beyond life.

It regards therefore also the form and the 'style' of spiritual vocations, in the highest and strictest sense of the word. Just as the world of custom, of thought, of art and of individual and collective psychology shows us certain 'invariable' features, which is to say certain common denominators, certain typological uniformities that we can trace back to the 'race of the soul', so the world of cults, of myths, of symbols, of rites, of paths toward ascetic, mystical or initiatic realisation, can be offered up to a discrimination which itself can be traced back to a given number of primordial and original spiritual forms. Even within a given religion there are ways of conceiving the divine and the relations existing between it and man. It is in this diversity that we discern 'spiritual race': it belongs, so to speak, to the vertical direction (toward the heights), just as the 'race of the soul' regards rather the horizontal direction (the world around us, our environment).

We hope that the distinction, when put in these terms, will be clear. And it is evident that with it we prevent a deviation which is analogous to that belonging to the thesis of the one-way dependency of the psyche on biology. As a sign of the intellectual abasement of the modern world, there do indeed exist schools which desire to reduce every view regarding spirituality and the transcendent world to something simply human, something conditioned by 'history' — by the social environment, by temperament, if not even by obscure atavistic instincts and by the subconscious of the psychoanalysts.

This is one of the reasons why the distinction between soul and spirit seems thorny or artificial to many: for in point of fact they put the sacred and the profane into one and the same box, mixing together that which belongs to the temporal world and has a simply 'humanistic' character with that which rather reflects a really transcendent principle and constitutes the true crux of human personality.

And precisely on this basis we find the timeliness of the distinction between the race of the soul and that of the spirit. That is to say, so far as regards this problem, and indeed in our positing it *as* a problem, it must be said that it is not possible, save as one distinguishes between the race of the soul and the race of the spirit, even to understand the exceedingly important distinction between *natural race* and *race in a higher sense*, or what we might even in a certain sense call *super-race*.

Everyone will more or less admit that race does not signify precisely the same thing when we are dealing with cats or horses on the one hand, and when we speak of men on the other. And, reflecting on this, everyone might also be convinced that the difference here leads us back to the first two degrees of the idea of race, which is to say: in a cat or in a horse everything is exhausted in somatic and biological race, while in man one must consider beyond this the race of the soul as well. Now, an analogous distinction can be made within the human race. There are races which can be called 'natural', because their very interior and cultural life is exhausted in the human element; it has a simply historical and social reality, against a collectivistic background.

Biological heredity is here complicated by a second heredity, historical heredity, in which, beyond external factors, the 'race of the soul' plays a large role: however one cannot speak in this case of truly spiritual influences, not even where one finds oneself standing before a *sui generis* mysticism. As we have often had occasion to state, the savage communities of the 'totemic' type represent the limit-form of the 'natural races': in them lives the sense of the caducity of the individual before the collective type of the stock, which is put into relation with the forces that also manifest in given species of the natural world. We are thus on the plane of an immanentism devoid of all light. Other races might, *mutatis mutandis*, recede to this same level — races which are believed to be altogether other than savage, on account of their having created every form of exterior civilisation, of science and of art. But wherever man has lost the capacity to sense that which stands beyond man, both as individual and as collective, his civilisation effectively falls on this level.

In contrast to this, the superior race, or super-race, is characterised by the presence and by the power of a spiritual race, which goes, at bottom, to constitute its centre. Whatever ancient Aryan tradition we consider, we always find this idea. Race is taken here from a 'supernatural' plane: it is not exhausted in the zoological plane, nor does it end in the immanence of the 'soul of the race', but it is tied instead to that higher region to which celestial, solar, and Olympian symbols were referred in antiquity. This is no longer the order of 'nature', but rather that, so to speak, of the 'eternal'.

These references today might seem vague for the reasons we have already indicated. They will be less so if we recall that not only the gentile paternal right but also the very idea of the State and of the *imperium* in the ancient Aryan world had an intimate relation with 'Olympian' symbols, with Rome itself standing in demonstration of this fact. In the 'natural race', the naturalistic element, as a simple community of blood and of bloodline, comes to the foreground, with inevitable collectivist and egalitarian hues: here we find the origin first of the so-called 'natural right' which conceives an equal right for all beings, because it considers all of them to be the children of the great maternal divinity of life. Only by entering into the order of the ideas of 'race of the spirit' does one affirm the paternal right, the idea of personality, the meaning of difference, the ideal of hierarchy, the virile and spiritual concept of the State and of *Imperium*. This stands with respect to the 'natural race' as the masculine principle to the feminine, as 'form' to 'matter', as the solar element to the chthonic-lunar element. From which flows a variety of deductions regarding the relations between one people and another.

Extremely important consequences thus emerge from our apparently subtle distinctions when it comes to the morphology of civilisation and of the political constitutions. But here we wanted also to say something on the relations between race and personality.

It has been objected by many that to the extent to which one emphasises the race, to that same extent one injures the concept of the personality. It is true that those who advance ideas of this kind often confound the personality with the individual, and that they are far from holding to the traditional idea according to which the personality has meaning only in reference to something supernatural. However, it must be recognised that this objection has a certain grounding wherever the concept of the 'race of the spirit' is not introduced. Only on the basis of the 'race of the spirit' is it possible to vindicate the human person in an autonomous and superior sense, as something rising above everything conditioned by the collective, by historical and mundane heredity, without injuring whatever function and value might reside in the same. It is evident that on the plane of the 'race of the soul', too, one might end up conceiving the individual as a transient apparition of the collective bloodline, which might at most survive in its worldly descendants: and we ourselves know of certain extremist racist circles which draw, as consequence of the premise of the inseparable connection between the 'soul' and the 'race', the negation of any theory of the supernatural destination of the personality and of its own super-mundane survival.

This is not the place to analyse problems of the kind, but only to underline that the introduction of the concept of 'race of the spirit' prevents these materialistic deviations, thereby dispelling also the biases which these cause. In a complete doctrine of the race, there is also space for the traditional notion of spiritual and autonomous personality, so long as one remains in that circle of higher humanity, for which alone one might speak of all of this without succumbing to mere daydreaming. We conceive not only a worldly heredity here, but also an overworldly heredity, which acts, so to speak, within the first, in the 'vehicle' of the first. And it is in this way that we might use the doctrine of heredity — one of the cornerstones of first-rank racism — without falling into a depressingly deterministic view.

If we wished to clarify these ideas, we would have to write another dedicated article. An example will come to our aid here. We have had occasion to study, as 'race of the soul', the direct antecedents to a given personage. We have found among his most characteristic traits a kind of inertia, an obtuse attachment not only to consuetude but also to material objects, for which used things, furniture and decorations were conserved in his family to the very last, with a kind of horror regarding every new purchase. In the personality which arose from these antecedents, such inclinations, on the material plane, are not at all visible: there comes to the fore rather on a different plane — that of spiritual vocations — the style of a 'traditional' mind, particularly gifted in illuminating and utilising the heritage of our best past. Here we find an eloquent case of the meeting point and the divergence of two heredities: a spiritual heredity was grafted onto the heredity of the family, so as to 'elevate' it and transfigure it entirely. This is one of the many study cases to which we might refer, which absolutely could not be deeply interpreted however without having recourse to 'race of the spirit'. It is here that the element of 'personality' reveals itself and acts. It is not an arbitrary action. Heredity on the plane of the race of the soul and of the body comes evidently to define a direction and to establish given frontiers. However, an influence of a higher order plays a decisive role *within* those frontiers.

With these brief considerations we hope to have clarified the problem and the *raison d'être* of our tripartite framing of the problem of race. We must guard ourselves against a double danger: we must guard against scientistic and immanentistic formulations on the one hand, and from a badly understood spiritualism and a suspect intellectualism on the other. We daresay that we have laid out for the doctrine of the race a course which lies distant from both of these reefs.

2. ON THE SPIRITUAL PREMISES OF EMPIRE

HE PROBLEM OF EMPIRE, in its highest expression, is that of a supernational organisation, which in its unity does not act in a destructive and levelling way with respect to the ethnic and cultural multiplicity which composes it. Stated in this way, the problem of empire admits of two principal solutions, the legal and the spiritual. According to the first, the empire's unity is that of a simple politico-administrative organisation, of a general law of order, in the most empirical sense of the term. In this case the qualities, the cultures and the traditions specific to the various peoples gathered together by the empire are not injured, for the simple reason that the empire remains indifferent and alien to them. What matters to the empire here are simple politico-administrative organisation and simple juridical sovereignty. It thus behaves with respect to separate peoples as the agnostic State of liberalism behaves with respect to individuals, whom it lets do as they will, so long as the general laws are respected.

In modern times, a characteristic example if empire is that of the English. Some, for example Bryce, have sought to establish in this context an analogy between the English empire and that of Ancient Rome; and even here in Italy we have not lacked in historians who fell into this grave error, on account of their having focused on the juridical and political aspects of the ancient Roman empire, and having neglected, or considered as irrelevant, every presupposition of a higher order, be it spiritual or religious.

It is rather the case that with Rome we find already an imperial organisation of the second kind, an empire corresponding, that is, to the second solution noted above. By this solution, unity is determined by reference to something spiritually higher than that particularism of everything which is, in individual peoples, conditioned by the ethnic or naturalistic element.

In Ancient Rome we find already a reality of this kind, for two reasons. In the first place, for the presence of a single type, a single ideal, corresponding to the *civis romanus*,[1] who was in no way, as some hold, a mere juridical form, but an ethical reality, a human model of supernational validity. In the second place, Rome posited that transcendent point of reference of which we have spoken through the imperial cult. The Roman Pantheon, as is known, contained the symbols of all the faiths and ethnico-spiritual traditions of the peoples subject to Rome, which Rome respected and even protected. But this hospitality and this protection took as their presupposition and their condition a 'fidelity', a *fides*, of a higher order.

Beyond the religious symbols gathered in the Pantheon, the symbol of the emperor ruled over all, conceived as '*nume*', as a divine being: it represented the same transcendent and spiritual unity of the empire itself, because the empire of the Roman tradition was conceived less as a simple human work than as the work of a force from on high. Fidelity to this symbol was the condition. Every faith or particular tradition of the subject peoples, supposing that they had sworn this fidelity in terms of a sacred rite, and did not injure or offend the ethics and the general law of the Romans, was received and respected.

In these terms, Ancient Rome presents us with an example of imperial organisation of perennial and universal value. Indeed, it suffices to set, in the place of those forms which are conditioned by time,

---

1   Latin: 'Roman citizen'. — Trans.

other forms, in order to distance any appearance of anachronism and to realise that whoever today wishes to study anew the problem of a spiritual empire, would not likely be able to find other perspectives from which to begin his work.

Indeed, today, the idea of a supranational organisation based on the affirmation of a particular religious idea, even the Christian, would be considerably more anachronistic. There is no one who can today reasonably imagine of the relevance and the return of an empire in the Spanish mould, the ultra-Catholic and inquisitorial empire of Charles V: but even beyond so extremist, albeit coherent, a form, other vaguer and more 'intellectual' formulae of a supranational unity on a unilaterally religious basis manifest the same defect, in the face of any deep analysis. In an overall portrait of the whole, we cannot forget that there exist a great many religious traditions, which are often of equal dignity and spiritual elevation. If the empire must inflict violence upon these in its attempt to realise a unity defined by the affirmation and the recognition of one alone among all these faiths, then it is clear that it would stand more as an example of sectarianism than of spiritual universalism.

The imperial example which is already foreshadowed by Fascism indicates, moreover, an overcoming of this perspective. Indeed, in the Fascist empire Catholicism is the national religion of the Italian people; but the Fascist empire simultaneously declares itself the defender of Islam, and has recently recognised and declared its respect for the Copts. This signifies nothing, if not that with Fascism the need of a point of reference is affirmed, one which stands far beyond that of any particular religious faith. We say 'beyond' and not 'outside of', because we must not forget that Fascism also has its own ethics, its own spirituality, its own human type, its own aspiration to translate the sense of a permanent and universal reality into the terms of a dominating will. It cannot therefore embrace a merely indifferentistic and agnostic respect, along the lines of the first of the two solutions indicated

above; it must rather be based on the principle of a realisation of a
higher and more 'Roman' order.

Having recognised this, the general problem of the spiritual presuppositions of the empire is that of defining the principle by which
one might attain, simultaneously, the recognition and the overcoming
of every particular religious faith of the nations which are to be organised. This is the fundamental point. Indeed, empire, in the true sense
of the word, can exist only if it is animated by a powerful spiritual
impetus, by a faith, by something which addresses the same spiritual
depths from which religion itself takes life. Without this, there can
never issue anything but a creature of violence — 'imperialism' — and
a mechanical, disanimate superstructure. For this reason it is needful
to capture — if we can put it that way — the same forces which act in
the faiths, without injuring these faiths, but rather integrating them
and carrying them to a higher level. Now, there exists a path to this
end: it is revealed to us by the conception according to which each
spiritual tradition and each particular religion represents nothing but
the varied expression of a single content, which is anterior and superior to each of these specific expressions.

Knowing how to rise to this single and, so to speak, super-tradi-
tional content means also reaching a basis proper for affirming a unity
which does not destroy, but which rather integrates, every particular
faith, and which can be defined an 'imperial' faith, in its reference
precisely to that higher content. To transcend, in its Latin etymology, means 'to overcome by ascending' — and in this word the whole
essence of the problem is contained. Here, we limit ourselves to this
general orientation, which will serve us in a further article as a point
of reference for other considerations, such as might more closely illuminate the view which we have here affirmed.

3. ON CAESAR'S 'REGNUM' AND SPIRITUALITY

P RECISELY BECAUSE the argument today has, as is said, come into in fashion, there are very few works of any real worth among the numerous books dedicated in Italy to the subject of Julius Caesar. Indeed, in such conditions as these, most are led to write on this or like subjects more for reasons of profit and almost even of opportunism than from out of any feeling of spontaneous interest, such as might be sustained by serious preparation and comprehension. Another of the defects of most of the modern works on Caesar proceeds from the application of an exclusively 'humanist' point of view to the subject at hand.

The so-called 'cult of the personality', the concentration of every interest on simply 'human' part of the great figures of the ancient world, almost taking as a principle for their comprehension the type of the 'condottiere' of the Renaissance — all of this constitutes a truly limiting, not to say contaminating, prejudice. And Caesar is among those figures to have suffered most for this, precisely on account of the fact that certain of his traits strike with peculiar force upon the imagination of those who are inclined to view things in the above sense: while other personages, who were superpersonal and, we would like to say, 'fateful', fall into the shadows. The formula to the effect that 'personalities make history' is just as true, if it is brought back to its right scope and counter-posed to a determinism of a lower materialistic or sociological character, as it is dangerous if it is carried beyond those limits, in such a manner as to preclude the penetration of that aspect of the great historical figures by which they appear, if not as instruments, then at least as elements on the plane of a higher order, in a development which — as the development of all greatness — cannot be explained with simply human factors. A consideration of the figure of Julius Caesar which took its bearings by this point of view, detaching itself from the habitual 'humanistic', politico-military and literary evaluation, would be altogether desirable in the new Italian cultural climate.

These reflections came to mind on the occasion of our reading of a new work on Caesar, written by Giovanni Costa. We cannot offer a 'review' of the book here, which would in any case come across as rather banal. So far as direct references to that book go, we will limit ourselves therefore to saying that it is a clear, balanced, compendious exposition, aimed at a wide public, of the life and work of Caesar — an exposition which however appears to be punctuated by a certain, shall we say rationalistic *forma mentis* of the author. He scruples on every page to overcome the limits of so-called 'positive' facts, and to make adequate use of traditions and myths which, though perhaps they be destitute of historical truth in the vulgar sense of the word, for this reason precisely rise to the value of sure witness to meanings of a higher order, and thus alone prove capable of introducing us to the inner, and thus most essential side, of a given reality. In this respect, the above-mentioned work, while it is devoid of rhetorical flourishes, of 'literarinesses' and of ostentatious apologies, and while it appears to us dignified and representative of all thoughtful prudence of a 'scholar', nonetheless does not escape from the aforesaid 'humanism' in the case of Caesar, which at times intertwines with a sceptical vein, which somewhat diminishes its stature.

And yet the book opens with an approach which leads one to believe that the author has set off down the right path, and that Costa has succeeded in grasping that central point which would permit an

ordering of the essential traits of the figure, the action and the function of Caesar, from a referential framework which is not simply
historical, but historical and at the same time superhistorical. Costa
indeed takes his bearings by the speech which an adolescent Caesar
gave on occasion of the obsequies for the wife of Gaius Marius, as the
descendent of the exceedingly ancient, glorious and almost legendary *gens Julia*.[1] Caesar utters on that occasion these fateful words: 'In
my blood is the majesty of the kings, who excell in power amongst
men, and the holiness of the gods, who hold the power of kings in
their hands'. Costa sees in this the appearance of a principle — at
once new and ancient — which sounds already as an alarum in the
agitated, treacherous, disjointed and liberal-tending atmosphere of
Rome in the last century before Christ, almost as if were prelude to
the work of this future dominator. But already in his reference to that
formula — the aspect of simple *imperator*, which in the language of
the time designated a mere military leader — he went beyond, and an
evident and altogether meaningful bond is established with a traditional and primordial order, such as had already incarnated in certain
aspects of the Priscan Rome of the Kings, but which is beyond that
universal, because it can be found in one form or another in a typical
cycle which includes within itself the greatest hierarchico-spiritual
civilisations of the pre-classical world.

This is already the idea of a *sacrum imperium*, of the *regnum*
which is justified as a not merely temporal institution, but one at
the same time sustained and rendered transcendent by a force or an
influence from on high. But Costa was evidently afraid of touching
on this point, fit for an interpretation of a higher kind, given that
we immediately see him intent on diminishing its bearing, first in
his failure to connect this idea pronounced by Caesar with anything
other than presumed 'Hellenico-Asiatic reminiscences', and second in
the abundant incense-burning which he performs for the positivistic

---

1   That is, the 'Julius family' or the 'lineage of Julius', from which Caesar derived
what we would call his 'first name'. — Trans.

prejudices regarding the 'fables', the 'little stories' and the 'diverting adventures' (by which he means the symbolic traditions) regarding the superhistorical origins of Rome. By this route, Costa went the way contrary to that which, in our view, he ought to have gone: namely, that of considering Caesar in the light of a fatal, superpersonal accomplishment of the idea of the Regnum, which at an early moment in the life of the young patrician revealed itself instinctively and we would almost say unconsciously, and at a later moment acted as the objective power of destiny through Caesar's 'humanity' and military action, finally making itself conscious of itself and conscious of the very 'perpetual dictatorship' of the new Roman constitution.

However it is extremely significant that, despite his best intentions, Costa came more or less to this very point. He describes Caesar as a kind of anticlerical positivist *avant la lettre*, who nonetheless through the affirmation of his powerful personality ends up believing in something more than this mere human personality: certainly, not in external divinities or Syrio-Semetic-type 'redeemers', but rather in a mystical, mysterious force of fortune and of victory — *felicitas Caesaris, fortuna Caesaris*[2] — which became slowly evident to him as an occult spirit or subterranean fount of everything which would create itself through him in the visible world. One such force, in its personification as *Venus Victrix* and *Venus Genitrix*,[3] was posited by Caesar in strictest connection with the primordial generative force of his own lineage: which means that it appeared to him in connection with the same principle to which the young Caesar had made reference in his proclamation of the aforementioned *doctrine of the Regnum*, and almost as the concrete efficacy of this principle in Rome and in the world.

Moreover, while Costa discovers a unity of intention and will behind the variety of means and ends which Caesar determined upon

---

2   Latin: 'happiness of Caesar, fortune of Caesar'. — Trans.

3   Latin: 'Venus the Victorious' and 'Venus the Generative', two aspects of the Roman goddess of love. — Trans.

in the various phases of his ascent — a variety which was indeed often contradictory, not to say even Machiavellian and opportunistic,
despite the fact that everything was constantly subordinated to a formula: his own dignity and the dignity of the Roman people — nonetheless here too Costa has recourse to the same motif, which is to say:
the parallelism of the two series, the one being the dominion of the
'person' and the other of a higher principle, from which the element
of the 'person' in a preliminary phase is, so to speak, activated, but in
which it is finally transfigured and given a centre. Costa claims that
Caesar, who 'is not a believer, not only in the sense of the formalis-
tic praxis of the Romans, but even in the wide religious sense which
might be recognisable to the moderns', and who also does away with
pious or speculative hypotheses regarding the immortality of the soul,
nonetheless gave new life, almost through a mere sensation, to the 'ancient primitive [idea] of Roman Fortune' as a cosmic and impersonal
element, 'the single agent, above all in matters of war'; he claims that
this was 'the single conception to which, once it had formed in him,
he remained a tenacious supporter; and this to such an extent that in
the last period of his life he was even overcome with the doubt as to
whether he had so far transfused it into himself and so far confused
it with his own fate that he might really consider himself, as many
believed, 'divine''. He repeats that

in Caesar however this was united with the personal element which we
habitually encounter in all men of genius, since they feel the *daemonium*
burning in them to such an extent that they objectify it and make it the
object of a kind of exaltation from which they draw the necessary energy
and faith requisite to carry out their own work. For this reason, with the
progress of Caesar's fortune in war, the maturation and achievement of this
conception (of the *fortuna Caesaris*) could follow ... like a faith and an
explanation that little by little, it seems, emerged out of Caesar's person and
the events surrounding him

to such an extent that 'both he and his contemporaries saw something
inexplicable in this, in which they believed they saw passing the aura

of the numinous'. But to say all of this means to recognise — albeit with reticence and hesitations, and with the usual limitations and psychologicistic, empericalistic pseudo-explanations which have become *de rigueur* amongst modern historians and 'researchers' — precisely the element of 'fatefulness' indicated above, which we understand as a generic sensation, but one grasped in connection with the very principle of the Regnum — a sensation capable of giving form to a new universal civilisation through Roman power.

Caesar is that man who could say (in reference to a figure who was certainly not of the first rank, namely Cicero) that it is a thing higher in glory to enlarge the boundaries of the spiritual realm, than to be just any given victor and the expander of the material empire — and Caesar is at the same time the man who in his style has about him nothing mystical and vague, whose essentiality and lucidity, more than being 'spiritualistic' or of the literary kind, is that of the scientist or the man of action.

Caesar is that man who nourishes a revolutionary indifference for augurs and sacrifices — and he is that man who at the same time grasps, *through* the affirmation of his personality directly translated into the terms of objective and victorious action and *against* a fatalism of exterior and sacerdotal character, the sensation of a fatalism of higher and immanent character, adumbrated by the force of the origins.

Whoever comprehends a synthesis of these elements approaches the secret of the figure of Caesar, and, through him, that as well of the 'occidental hero' par excellence. In such a 'hero' there is something 'Doric', in the sense of personality, clarity, essentialness, action — but this is not exhausted in the 'humanistic', in the purely profane. Greek civilisation already recognised its heroic ideal, not in the tyrant who draws his power from the dark substance of the demos or from an ephemeral personal prestige, nor in the 'Titanic' and 'Promethean' type, but rather in the type of the victor symbolically allied to the 'Olympians'. Such an ideal might be posited beyond the 'mystical' and the sacerdotal in the limited sense, and might reach, in a manner particular to it, a higher plane, a certain transcendence and fatefulness, through the point in which, according to the formula we have already used, the extreme limit of being a 'personality' fuses altogether with being more than personality.

The principle of *regnum* which through Caesar created for itself, so to speak, the elementary corporeo-political and psychologico-social conditions for its incarnation and universal affirmation, punctuated by the tragic end of the great Emperor, was to be reaffirmed and developed also in a directly spiritual way through an authentic reform of the Roman cult with Caesar Augustus. Here we cannot develop any considerations aimed at establishing the secret ideal continuity that runs between these two figures of Roman times — a continuity which is generally misunderstood precisely because what is alone emphasised in Caesar is ever the aspect of the dictator and of the military leader or the emperor, in a way which deforms our understanding.

That would be however one of the most suggestive subjects for one with a mentality and doctrinal preparation adequate for the treatment of such a matter: it is precisely by virtue of the principle of the *regnum* that the 'eternity' of the Roman Empire would hold good, not in the terms of a glorifying figure of speech, but for its reference to an idea which, instead of historical — which is to say, instead of being the issue of the contingent and perishable — should rather be called 'metaphysical', and, as such, gifted with perennial life and with the dignity of the 'ever and everywhere' in the face of a fundamental meaning of civilisation as virile spirituality.

4. THE ROMAN CONCEPTION OF VICTORY

S ALLUST USES the expression 'extremely religious mortals'[1] to describe the early Romans, and there is a saying by Cicero that ancient Roman civilisation superseded every other people or nation (*omnes gentes nationesque superavimus*)[2] for its sense of the sacred. Analogous testimonies can be found in many variations in many other ancient writers. Against the prejudices of a certain kind of historiography, which insists on evaluating Ancient Rome only from the juridical and political point of view, we hold that the effectively spiritual and sacred content of Ancient Romanness must be brought to the fore, and indeed should be considered the most important element thereof, since it can easily be shown how the political, juridical and ethical forms of Rome in the last analysis took as their basis and common origin precisely a special religious vision, a special kind of human relation to the supersensible world.

Only that this relationship differed considerably from that which was to become paramount in the beliefs that subsequently came to predominate. The Roman, as ancient and traditional man in general, conceived of a meeting and a reciprocal interpenetration between divine forces and human forces. A special sense of history and of time was contained in this, as we ourselves have had occasion to draw to

---

1   *Bellum Catilinae*, 13.
2   *De Haruspicum Responsis*, IX, 19.

our readers' attention, whilst discussing a book by Franz Altheim. The Roman found the locus of divine manifestation, not so much in the space of pure contemplation, detached from the world, nor in the immobile, silent symbols of a *hyperkosmia*, an 'overworld', but rather in time and in history and in everything which unfolds through human action. He thus experienced his history more or less in the terms of a 'sacred history', or at least a 'fateful history': and this was so from the very earliest days of Rome. In his *Life of Romulus*, Plutarch writes that 'Rome would not have succeeded in gaining so much power if it had not had in some way a divine origin, such as might offer to the eyes of men something of the great and inexplicable'.[3]

From here arose the typically Roman conception of an invisible and 'mystical' counterpart to the visible and tangible part of the human world. It is for this reason that every explication of Roman life, be it individual, collective, or political, was accompanied by a rite. And from here, too, came the peculiar conception that the Roman had of the *fatum*: the *fatum* was not for him, as it had been for late Grecian antiquity, a blind power; rather it was the divine order unfolding in the world, to be interpreted and understood by means of an adequate science, in order that the effective directions of human action might be presaged — directions by which human action might attract a force from on high, toward the ends, not only of gaining success, but also of producing a kind of transfiguration and higher justification.

As these ideas were extended in Ancient Rome to every facet of reality, they were also reaffirmed in the domain of military ventures, of battle, of heroism and of victory. From here we see precisely what those scholars miss who consider the Ancient Romans essentially as a race of half barbarians, a race who through the brute force of arms alone imposed themselves on the entire world, taking from other peoples — the Etruscans, the Greeks and the Syriacs — whatever they possessed of true and authentic culture. It is rather the case that Ancient

---

3   *Life of Romulus*, I, 8.

Romanness possessed a particular mystical conception of war and of victory, a conception whose importance has curiously escaped the notice of scholars of Romanness. These last confine themselves to distractedly alluding to the many related and well-documented Roman traditions.

It was an essentially Roman opinion that, if a war was to be won materially, it needed first be won — or at least propitiated — mystically. After the battle of Trasimene, Fabius told the soldiers, 'Your fault was more in having neglected the sacrifices and in having ignored the warnings of the augurs, than in having lacked in courage or ability'.[4] No Roman war was commenced without sacrifices, and a special college of priests — the *fetiales* — was charged with the rites relative to war, which could be considered a 'just war', *iustum bellum*, only insofar as it carried out these rites. As de Coulanges has already had occasion to note, the basis of the military art of the Romans originally consisted in avoiding being forced to fight when the gods were against it — which is to say, when no concordance of human forces and forces from on high could be ascertained through 'fatal' signs.

In this way too the centre of military affairs fell on a plane which was more than merely human — just as both the sacrifice and the heroism of the combatant were considered more than merely human. The Roman conception of victory is of particular importance here.

According to this conception, every victory has a mystical side, in the most objective sense of the term: in the victor, in the leader, in the *imperator* acclaimed on the fields of battle, one had the sense of a sudden manifestation of divine force which transfigured this figure and transcended his humanity. The same warrior's rite during which the *imperator* (in the original sense of the word, not of 'emperor', but of victorious leader) was carried on a special shield, is not without its symbolic counterpart, as can be inferred from Ennius: the shield, which was already sacred in the Capitoline temple of Jove, is

---

4   Livy, *Ad Urbe Condita Libri*, Book XVII, 9. Cf. XXXI, 5; XXXVI, 2; XLII, 2.

equivalent to the *altisonum coeli clupeum*, the celestial sphere, beyond which the man who had triumphed would be lifted by his victory.

Unequivocal and significant confirmations of this ancient Roman conception are offered in the nature of the liturgy and the pomp surrounding a triumph. We speak of 'liturgy' because the character of this ceremony, with which every victor was honoured, was considerably more religious than it was military. The victorious leader here was presented as a kind of manifestation or visible incarnation of the Olympian god himself, from which he drew all of his marks and attributes. The quadriga drawn by white horses corresponded to that of the solar god of the luminous sky, just as the mantle of the triumphant leader, the purple toga embroidered with golden stars, reproduced the heavenly and stellar mantle of Jupiter. The golden crown was as the sceptre held aloft by that same sacred deity. And the winner painted his countenance with minium, precisely as in the cult of the temple of the Olympian god, before whom he then presented himself, solemnly depositing the triumphal laurel of his victory at the feet of the statue of Jove, signifying thereby that Jove was the true author of his victory and that he had won essentially as a divine force, as a force of Jove himself: whence the ritual identification between the two in the ceremony.

Moreover, other considerations arise from the noteworthy circumstance that the paludamentum,[5] which here indicated the triumphant leader, corresponded to that of the ancient Roman kings: it might be reducible to the fact, as Altheim has highlighted, that even before the first definition of the triumphal ceremony of the king, in the Priscan Roman conception, this paludamentum likewise appeared as an image of celestial divinity. The divine order, over which this image presided, is reflected and manifested in the human order, which is centred precisely on the king. In this regard—in this conception

---

5 That is, the cape attached to one shoulder which often accompanied military men of high rank, as is indicated by any number of Ancient Roman statuary portraits of the same. — Trans.

which, as various other first things,[6] was then to re-emerge in the imperial period — Rome bears witness to a tradition of universal bearing, one which is to be found in an entire cycle of great civilisations: in the Indo-Aryan and Aryo-Iranic world, in Ancient Greece, in Ancient Egypt, in the Far East.

But so as not to drift away from our subject, let us mention another characteristic element of the Roman conception of victory. Precisely because it was not considered a merely human fact, the victory of a leader often assumed for the Romans the traits of a *numen*, of an independent divinity, whose mysterious life became the centre of a special system of rites aimed at nourishing it and confirming its invisible presence amongst men.

The best-known example is constituted by the *Victoria Caesaris*. Every victory, it was believed, actuated a new centre of forces, a centre disconnected from the particular individuality of the mortal man who had realised it; or, if you prefer, the victor, through victory, himself became a force in an almost transcendent order, a force not of some victory accomplished at a specific historical moment, but — precisely as the Roman expression had it — of a 'perpetual or perennial' victory. The cult of such entities, which was decreed by the law, was intended to stabilise the presence of this force, so to speak, that it might invisibly join with the force of the race, leading it toward outcomes favoured by '*fortuna*', and thus making of future victories the means for revealing and further reinforcing the energy of the first. And thus it is that in the celebration of the dead Caesar in Rome, confounded with that of his victory and consecrated to the *Victoria Caesaris* of the games, thereby transforming into a significant ritual, Caesar could be considered a 'perpetual victor'.

The cult of Victory, which has been judged prehistoric in its origins, can be called more generally the secret soul of Roman greatness and of Roman faith in its own fated destiny. From the times of Augustine,

---

6   Italian: *come varie altre delle origini*, literally 'like various other origins'. — Trans.

the statue of the goddess Victory had been placed on the altar of the Roman Senate, and it was even a rite that each senator, before taking his place in the chambers, must pass before that altar and burn a sprig of grain before it as incense. The force of Victory thus seemed to preside invisibly over the deliberations of the curia. It was also customary to extend one's hands toward that same image when, at the advent of a new Prince, one swore fidelity, and then again on 3 January of each year, when solemn vows were taken, in the senate, for the health of the emperor and for the prosperity of the empire. Particularly worthy of notice is the fact that this was the longest-lasting Roman cult, existing from the days of so-called 'paganism'; it was the 'pagan' cult which longest resisted Christianity, after the destruction of all the others had been effected.

Other considerations could be made on the Roman notion of the *mors triumphalis*, the 'triumphal death', which presented various characteristics. We might speak of this on another occasion. Here we want only to add something regarding the special aspect of heroic dedication, connected to the Ancient Roman concept of *devotio*. This expresses what might in modern terms be called a 'tragic heroism', but it itself is tied to a sense of the supersensible forces and to a higher, very clear, end goal.

In Ancient Rome, *devotio* did not signify 'devotion' in the modern sense of the meticulous and fearful practice of a religious cult. It was rather a ritual warrior action, in which one made a sacrifice of oneself, consciously dedicating one's own life to the 'nether' powers, whose unleashing, by producing an irresistible power in oneself and panic in one's enemies, would contribute to victory. This was a rite formally decreed by the Roman state as a supernatural weapon to be used in desperate cases, whenever it was believed that the enemy could surely not be overcome with normal forces.

We know from Livy all the details of this tragic rite, and even the solemn, evocative and sacrificial formula that the man who intended to sacrifice himself for victory was to pronounce, repeating after the pontifex, who was dressed in the *praetexta*,[7] with veiled head, his hand poised on his chin and his foot upon a javelin. After which he would hurl himself into the fray, as though conjuring a fatal force, to find death therein.[8] There were patrician Roman families in which this tragic rite was almost a tradition: for instance the line of the Deci practised it in 340 B.C. in the war against the rebelling Latins, then in 295 in the war against the Samnites, and in 79 in the battle of Asculum: almost as if it had been the 'law of their family', as Livy puts it.

As a purely interior attitude, this sacrifice, in its perfect lucidity and willingness, might remind one of what occurs even today in the warfare of Japan: we know of special torpedoes or Japanese aeroplanes that go hurtling with their crew against their target; and here, too, sacrifice, almost always carried out by members of the ancient warrior aristocracy, by the *samurai*, is tied to a rite possessing a mystical aspect. The difference is surely that here one does not aim to the same extent at an action which is something more than merely material, at a true and authentic evocation, as in the ancient Roman theory of *devotio.*

And naturally, the modern and above all Western environment, on account of a thousand causes which have become, shall we say, *constitutional* through the centuries, makes it extremely difficult to draw forces out from behind the curtains, and to give to every gesture, to every sacrifice, to every victory a transfiguring significance, similar to those which we have indicated here. It is nonetheless certain even today, in this wild and unbridled moment, that if one were to feel oneself no longer alone on the fields of battle, if one were to have some presentiment, despite everything, of relations with an order

7 A ceremonial white toga trimmed in purple which distinguished certain royal and priestly functions and functionaries. — Trans.

8 *Ad Urbe Condita Libri*, VIII, 9.

more than merely human and pathways which are not measured by
the values of this visible reality alone — it is certain, I say, that if one
could accomplish all of this, it might become the fountainhead for a
force and an imperviousness, whose effects, on every level, could not
be overestimated.

5. FASCISM AND FREEDOM

A S WE HAVE for some time now underlined the need that the new movements of European reconstruction, toward the end of developing their higher possibilities, should integrate their political ideology with a complex of properly doctrinal principles, it is with some interest that we have skimmed a very recent publication from the Scuola di Mistica Fascista, which appears to take its bearings from this need precisely. This is a book by G. S. Spinetti entitled *Fascismo e libertà*, with the subtitle 'Toward a New Synthesis' (Padova, 1940) Spinetto unhesitatingly affirms — and rightly so — that 'there is no political conception which does not postulate a metaphysics and an ethics, which is to say a conception of being and of the value of the individual and social being' (p. 22); and, departing from this presupposition, he seeks to identify the philosophical synthesis best fit to the political principles of fascism. For him, the Mussolinian doctrine already contains such a synthesis *in ova*. He seeks to explicate it — and precisely in the terms of a conception of life having as its supreme ideal 'self-mastery' and therefore liberty in a higher sense.

His attempt is worthy of attention. We propose here to examine what in it is — from our point of view, which is to say, from the Traditional point of view — sound, and what in it might be in need of further clarification and rectification.

Since the author himself considers his work as a call to arms, which he has sought to bring to term in the shortest possible amount of time (p. 125), one can comprehend the rather hasty character of some its positions, where greater calm and greater preparation would have been desirable.

The habit of political journalism, as well, has surely contributed an influence here which is not wholly favourable, for the peremptory tone which suits it is neither the most persuasive nor the most suitable for questions of doctrine. Thus, to cite but one example, it is altogether reckless to maintain (p. 9) that 'the so-called crisis of the modern world — which has been for some time now the occupation of thinkers and philosophers from every country — was resolved in Italy with the rise of Fascism to power'. This can be maintained only to the extent that one speaks of the political and social domain, and, at most, of the ethical.

But Spinetti intends to carry his considerations further than that. It is evident (for example on p. 6) that he knows the book, which we ourselves have translated, by Guénon, entitled precisely *The Crisis of the Modern World* — in which already there is however quite sufficient material to persuade one of the great many things that are yet to be done, before such a crisis is truly overcome, if only one intends to proceed in this work seriously.

Leaving aside the observations we intend to make here regarding the concept of the State and its higher legitimation, suffice it to observe that we yet lack, to this day, any serious attempt to overcome a concept of 'knowledge' and of 'science', which is laical, profane, anti-Traditional, rationalistic and semi-Judaic, but which unfortunately is the only concept which underpins normal, 'serious' education, here in Italy as much as anywhere abroad.

A second point concerns the importance that Spinetti gives to the idea of the 'new'. Here, too, we perceive the transposition of a political attitude, which is not valid beyond a certain limit. The mania for the 'new' is better left to the futurists and the Marxists, who like to exalt a 'brighter tomorrow'.[1] We should not seek that which is new but that which is normal, because it conforms to principles of perennial validity. It therefore makes little sense to insist on the 'new needs of the spirit', especially when, for example, one would simultaneously like to give an 'honourable burial' to the Middle Ages (p. 5). It goes without saying that there is some confusion here: no one has ever wanted to return to the Middle Ages as a historically conditioned civilisation. It is another matter however to consider the Middle Ages as a 'type', which is as much as to say, as one of the examples of a 'normal' civilisation, adhering to values, to which, in other forms, we will return, should the disorder and the intellectual, social and individual agitations of the latest times ever be overcome.

A third point. Spinetti includes himself in the new generation, and nourishes hopes for it which we would — if only we could — very willingly share. He writes:

> The new generation might seem, to the men of the culture of the last century, a generation of the deluded, of the ignorant and of the superfluous; but it is rather essentially a generation of anticipators and builders, though it does not yet have a mind and a soul adequately tempered for the arduous tasks that it has been called to acquit (p. 12).

In point of fact, on the level of discipline and of temporal and political battles, the new generation has already demonstrated itself to be capable of such tasks. But so far as other matters are concerned, speaking generally we have personally not found anything but disillusionment: it has so far proven to be a very rare occurrence that we might find a 'third dimension' in the new generation. It seems that this generation is lacking even the organ to perceive certain problems at all. One can give it and one can offer it everything necessary for a true creative and 'revolutionary' flight (in the good, which is to say, relative sense) — all

---

1   Italian: *il sol dell'avvenire*, literally 'the sun of the future' or 'the sun of what is to come'. — Trans.

in vain. It simply listens and presses forth as before, as if nothing had happened. We therefore put our hope in the future.

Spinetti, by way of evidence to the contrary, might adduce the reaction of the youth against the 'sophists' and more precisely against Gentilian idealism; Spinetti believes that this has the significance of a battle for a new culture. We are inclined to see things in a somewhat different light. However much reaction here is altogether justified insofar as it is directed above all against the claque of the Gentilians and against their system of greedy monopoly, nonetheless it is certainly not a favourable sign that they took Gentile's philosophy seriously, it being nothing but a caricature of idealism.

If we wish to go about matters seriously, it is from classical idealism that we should take our bearings, examining its fundamental problems, ascertaining its limits, before which it itself stopped up short, almost out of indolence or fear; by surpassing these one would emerge in a doctrine of action, of power and of 'liberty' — almost in the sense of the idea cherished by Spinetti. And here, as proof, we might adduce even a personal case. We ourselves, in a series of books, have brought about just such an overturning of the idealism of the Fichtes, the Schellings and the Hegels of the world in the doctrine of action, of power and of 'autarchy'. These works of ours were published around 1925 and 1926 (see *Teoria dell'Individuo assoluto*, *Fenomenologia dell'Individuo assoluto*, and *L'uomo come potenza*).[2]

The revolt of the 'youth' came no more than eight years afterwards, and it was — in its essence — merely a revolt, a sign of dissatisfaction, an exclusion of the problems of idealism which Gentile had made so banal, and an adoption of vague 'spiritualistic' positions. And from that 'revolt' up to the present day, no forward step. Were we not then correct in our previous judgement on the 'youth'? And, in the interest of relativising certain one-dimensional arguments on certain practical

---

2   *The Theory of the Absolute Individual*, *Phenomenology of the Absolute Individual*,
     and *Man as Power* respectively. None of these early Evolian works has been yet
     translated into English. — Trans.

consequences of idealism, we might remind our readers of the following: the East, in the so-called *Mâhâyâna*, possesses a much more extreme idealism than that of the West. It is however not employed as a 'philosophy' in the professional sense, but as a vision of life, and, moreover, not as a point of arrival, but as a point of departure. This system precisely, in Japan's school of Zen, gives rise to ascetic disciplines and to a heroic formation of the soul, so far as to play a role among that people, even today, in the education of the best patrician youths, who are destined for the military.

This is an example to demonstrate to the 'youths' that if certain of their instinctive reactions are right, something more is needed before they can reach anything truly constructive and solid.

To exhaust our observations here, we would have been pleased to see Spinetti taking up a still more radical stance in his overcoming. Indeed, with respect to the aforementioned reaction, he writes that it 'is not a revolt — thank God — against all philosophers or against philosophy in general'. His problem is to find a *philosophical* system which confirms and develops the Fascist creed. There is a point of ambiguity here, inherent to the word 'philosophy' itself. Already in the last century, when the 'youth' of today were not yet born, a 'youth' of those times, Lachelier, wrote these oft-cited words: 'Modern philosophy is reflection which has come to recognise its own impotence and the necessity of an absolute act departing from within'.

This is precisely the theme which we have developed. We must clear away the epoch of abstract reflection and of speculation — that is, of philosophy in the 'modern' sense — and pass over to the problems of action, of its formation, of its control, of its higher transfiguration.

In truth, the value of Spinetti's book consists precisely in the sense — even if it be in a form which is not altogether clear — that precisely this must occur, if the new fascist civilisation is to have a higher development. But he is not intransigent enough, in our view: he does not despise 'philosophical' helpmeets, wherever the fundamental problem is that of seeking points of reference, not in the domain of that which modern activism has left behind and which is by now merely a matter of 'professors' and 'academics' — namely, the world of speculation — but rather in a domain that the action of today has not yet attained — that is, the world of the supersensible and superrational reality. Or, to say it in a word: in the world of metaphysical reality.

And at this point we can proceed to a direct consideration of the ideas that Spinetti proposes regarding 'liberty'.

* * *

Above all, this is a question of bringing the problem of the exterior world back to human interiority and to conceiving of it as a problem of 'life'. But what is the meaning of 'life'?

We must recognise to Spinetti the merit of making a clear stand against those irrationalistic theories according to which life is immediate spontaneity, instinct, incoercible becoming. To live, for Spinetti, means, in a higher sense, to be man — *vir* and not *homo* — and to actuate this nature of man. To live means to actuate one's very nature — but for man this means, to a certain degree, to act *against* nature, 'to uproot in oneself the rebel spontaneity, the immediate impulse, the irrational instinct'. And so 'it is the battle against oneself which permits a man to live his second nature'. This does not mean renunciation, but rather affirmation. 'Only he who has thrown down his irrational instincts has affirmed his personality and demonstrated that he is truly a man, because only in the complete domain of his own being does the human person progressively enter in the supernatural heaven; only in this way does he comprehend how much of divinity is to be found in that personality; only in this way does he free himself from matter and reach God' (pp. 87–89). And again: 'Whoever identifies human nature with instinct, with immediate impulse, with irrational sentiment, confounds nature with denatured nature and is incapable of defining the concept of liberty, full activation of our nature — which is to say, complete self-mastery' (p. 94).

These views, which Spinotti seems to have reached essentially on a Catholic basis, are perfectly 'in order' from the Traditional point of view, and constitute a valid point of reference. And—let us say it again—given the modern irrationalistic confusions (which are in our mind even more dangerous than the rationalistic ones), it is well that these views should be strongly affirmed and placed into close relation with Fascist spirituality.

Spinetti attempts also to integrate these ideas with an interpretation of the myth of the fall. The 'fall' was caused by the pride of possessing the same power as God, interpreting this power in a materialistic sense. Man unleashed his power of desire and his instincts, and in the name of these things he turned to the dominion of matter and of the external world, without realising that this would fatally denature him, overwhelm him, deprive of him of any power with respect to himself.

As we ourselves have elsewhere written, 'on the pretext of dominating the world, man abandoned the ideal of dominion over himself and became fundamentally passive with respect to himself'. And this is more than a 'myth': in it, the opposition between two ethics is rendered clear—indeed, the opposition between two types of civilisation. Here, one of the fundamental aspects of decadence comes into view, which hides behind the vaunted power of the modern world and its technological conquest of matter. And therefore also: the ideas of liberty as self-mastery—or 'autarchia', in the classical sense.

There follows, in Spinetti's book, the connection of these views on the one hand with the fascist ethic, and on the other with the Fascist conception of the State. The first task does not present any particular difficulties for Spinetti.

With a particularly intelligent choice of Mussolinian citations (p. 46 and following) he demonstrates that the highest ethical ideal of fascism is based on a continual discipline of oneself, on life as inflexibility with respect to oneself, as power of command over oneself first and foremost, as the faculty of yoking one's own individual nature to interests and idealities that transcend it; in short, as disdain for the comfortable life and distance with respect to any purely economic, naturalistic or materialistic concept or ideal of happiness.

The second task — that of establishing the relation between the spiritual ideal of liberty as autarchy and self-mastery and the idea of State — is however rather more difficult, because it is easy to succumb to a confusion of levels which are, in themselves, distinct; it is even easy to effect an inversion of hierarchical relations. Spinetti seeks to get to the bottom of this problem in the final part of his book (p. 99 and following). He proposes to demonstrate how, in the Fascist conception of the State, the individual finds himself, in communal life, not impeded, but even helped toward the ultimate end, namely, mastery of himself. The Fascist State, like the ethical State, constantly places superindividual tasks before the individual, and measures his value on the basis of his capacity for a heroic overcoming, for virile dedication, for mysticism with respect to that transcendent reality which the State itself represents. In this sense, the Fascist State helps the individual to realise himself as a personality as the principle which dominates his lower part. There is thus no contradiction between liberty, personality and the political Fascist idea.

This is all certainly true, but here new problems emerge which Spinetti has not fully examined. To clarify our ideas, let us begin from an extreme: even the brutally tyrannical Bolshevik State could, strictly speaking, align itself with the ideal of self-mastery, and indeed even more so than the Fascist State, because it requires of the individual an absolute subordination, an absolute destruction of the individual 'I' without even the support of myths or of ideals, apart from various materialistic counterfeits. Of the two — the State and the self-mastery of the individual — which is the end and which is the means? The antiliberal authoritarian State helps the individual to master himself. Very well. In this regard — as instrument, as a propitiatory means — it justifies itself before the individual who aspires toward interior liberty and wishes to realise it, not by a strictly aesthetic path, but through disciplines associate to life. There remain, however, two problems.

The first. If the State possessed only this instrumental value, as has been said, the Bolshevik state would be worth every bit as much as the anti-Bolshevik totalitarian state. Once the instrument has been employed and self-mastery attained, the problem remains of the use that the individual must make of his mastered nature, beyond the State and political life. Perhaps he should seek a pure *vita contemplativa*, detached from the *vita activa*, as according to the medieval Guelphic ideal and the Indo-Aryan ethic of the *dharma*?

The second problem. The State must not only justify itself before the individual (in the terms already stated, of its being a catalyst for self-mastery), but also before itself — and precisely on this point arises the true difference between the totalitarian Bolshevic State and totalitarian States of other kinds. It is dangerous to say, with Spinetti (p. 109) that the end of the State is represented by the perfection of society and of the commonweal. This could lead certain persons to materialistic confusions. What is this commonweal? We must guard ourselves from exalting, in the person of a collective, those purely external material, economic, and power values, of the greater number of bathrooms, of radios etc., that are condemned or, at least, put into proper perspective in the individual before the ascetic and heroic values of self-mastery and of true civilisation. The State has need to justify itself with a transcendent idea — transcendent not in the relative sense of superindividual, but in the positive sense, of possessing an effectively supernatural content and mission. Only then will it aid the individual, not only in his discipline, nor in a confused mysticism, of which even the *citoyen* of the 'great' Revolution was capable: it will aid him rather in a conscious and transfiguring flight; it will evoke a force that, departing from an individual ideal of self-mastery, will complete him with the ideal of a 'supernatural' integration of the personality, above all by way of the *vita activa*.

But to seriously get to the bottom of these problems we must come to a doctrine of State, according to which any 'modern' conception, however 'reformed' it might be, can little avail. Toward this end, and to avoid any possible socialising and materialistic deviation in the supreme justification of the idea of the State, we must recover, even if it be in other forms, forms befitting new circumstances, the great ideas about the spiritual State and Empire which were defended by the imperial and Ghibelline Middle Ages. Yet, to us who are truly men of great faith; to us, who believe that a true overcoming of the crisis of the modern world, in all of its aspects, might proceed from Fascism — to us, this seems to indicate, as our ideal heredity, quite another fate than that of a mere 'honourable burial'...

6. THE DEPUTY OF GOD

THE POINT OF INTEREST of this new, dense work on Joan of Arc is found in the fact that, in contrast to almost all other works on the same subject, it does not follow a historico-bibliographical point of view but, essentially, that of a philosophy, not to say a theology, of European history. The human, psychological and national aspects of Joan of Arc are not considered here so much as those traits thanks to which her figure acquires the value of a symbol, and for which her appearance and her destiny indicate a turning point in the history of European Christianity.

The message of Joan of Arc possessed a revolutionary character in her time, by reason of the fact that it affirmed the idea of a chrism which a nation and the head of a nation can receive directly from God, and no longer exclusively through the representatives of the Church or other mediators of the sacred. A new possibility emerged therewith, one which was unknown in the late Medieval Period. Joan of Arc's mission was to announce to the King of the French a kind of 'election' or of divine mandate. The title she gave to this mandate was '*lieutenant de Dieu*' — and this in a context where, since the Guelph revolution of the eleventh and twelfth centuries, the dignity of being a representative of Christ had exclusively been vindicated by the head of the Church alone.

Joan prophesied the advent of a *Saint Royaume de France*[1] — and in preparation for this, the battle with the English and history; for a moment it seems as if history became transparent in its higher meaning, as if history were conforming itself to an eternal, divine decision, announced by the 'voices' that spoke to Joan of Arc and by which she legitimised her mission and, subsequently, her martyrdom itself.

In this respect, Mirgeler clearly brings to light the sense that every true prophecy has always borne, and every true oracle. It is not a question of mere knowledge of the future. The facts preannounced through prophecy or oracle have no standing save as the garments and indices of something indivisible;[2] they are in and of themselves secondary elements, whose true and deep sense reveals itself only afterwards.

> True prophecy reveals what is the essential thing, in the light of a superior dimension, in earthly events, and prefigures this even as a sketch anticipates a work of art.

Thus prophecy indicates essentially a direction. In such cases, a choice is presented to that man who bears the responsibility of giving a form to history; he must say yea or nay to the prefigured direction, which represents that single path by which history may make visible anything transcendent or atemporal. The election or the condemnation of peoples depends on this decision: the degree to which they and their leaders possess the capacity to comply with the transcendence of a given destiny. When the experience produces a negative outcome, when the attempt fails, the two series disassociate from one another: the higher order becomes mere 'history', subject to those contingent factors by which 'history' is determined.

According to Mirgeler, France was given such a possibility upon the appearance of Joan of Arc — the possibility, not only of lifting itself

---

1   French, 'Holy Kingdom of France'. — Trans.

2   In the translator's opinion, Evola's original draft most likely had *invisibile* ('invisible') in the place of *indivisibile* ('indivisible'), as the latter does not appear to make a great deal of immediate sense in the context. — Trans.

up once again in the moment of its extreme danger, but also of attaining to the dignity of a 'Saint Royaume'. But all of this came to naught but a fleeting flash: the possibility that was offered to France, and that might have also possessed a universal significance for the whole of Christian Europe, was lost. The message of the Maid of Orléans was in vain.

Mirgeler rightly observes that, after the defection of Charles VII,[3] France had to follow the decision taken toward the 'absolute state', which constitutes, as the rule of Philip the Fair[4] had already heralded, the precise antithesis of the 'Saint Royaume'. This is the root for the falsification entailed in the nationalistic and chauvinistic exploitation of the figure of Joan of Arc. There is indeed a radical antithesis between the state of affairs in which *raison d'etat* and national pride form the ultimate authority, to such a point that they divinise themselves (this being the direction which issues in modern 'totalitarianism'), and the other state of affairs, in which a people and a leader effectively follow a 'divine' mandate, which implies a kind of catharsis and ascesis, a liberating of oneself from everything which is particularistic and also from every brute will to power.[5]

---

3   Charles VII of France (1403–1461) was king from 1422 till his death, and hence was the reigning monarch during the rise and fall of Joan of Arc, whose military triumphs greatly consolidated his power. — Trans.

4   Philip the Fair, or Philip II of France (1268–1314), was noteworthy in the history of France for the power he granted to legalists and bureaucrats toward the centralisation of his power and for his dissolution of the Knights Templar (and the subsequent arrest and torture of hundreds of the Templars) on the pretext of a complaint brought against them, but in reality quite probably to avoid the enormous debt he had accrued with them. He is sometimes regarded as a 'man ahead of his time' or a very modern ruler; we concur with the observation, though surely not with the evaluation it implies.

5   N.B. that the Italian here is *libidine di potenza*, and not *volontà di potenza*, which would be the common translation of Nietzsche's celebrated (or infamous) idea of *der Wille zur Macht*. *Libidine di potenza* could also be translated as 'thirst for power' or 'hunger for power'; it stems from the same Latin original which gives us our English 'libido'. — Trans.

Mirgeler says that France therefore ever more came to follow the path of a blind '*gloire*', a glory deprived of light: and for this reason, no victory ever availed any Frenchman—not a Louis XIV nor a Napoleon, nor a Clemenceau;[6] nor did it ever result in a positive contribution for a solider European order.

The true France—he says—is revealed when things reach their extreme. In such moments, the the saviour, 'the father of victory', will sometimes appear:[7] but he is no longer a Joan of Arc, he is not even the representative of the healthiest strata of France, which is to say those strata which are existentially Christian despite all corruption and all 'free thought'. Then there are on the other hand figures who entirely pertain to the 'beyond', whose appearance or disappearance, as well as any fleeting energy they might arouse, remain void of any deeper meaning. But nothing better than this could be expected from mass nationalism, whose prototype is offered to Europe precisely by France herself.

6   Louis XIV (1638–1715), the Sun King, was an outwardly resplendent ruler (for a bewildering seventy-two years) of an inwardly frivolous regime which was, by some estimations, already well on its way to the tremendous and catastrophic collapse represented by the French Revolution. George Clemenceau (1841–1929) was Prime Minister of France during World War I, and thus oversaw both the defeat and the subsequent shaming of Germany (he was, for instance, one of the major architects of the scurrilous Treaty of Versailles). The degree to which Napoleon Bonaparte's (1789–1821) in some ways grand attempt on Europe proved finally vain and impossible need not be listed here, so well known are they. — Trans.

7   Quite possibly a deliberate reference to Clemenceau (see previous note), who was known colloquially as 'Father Victory'. — Trans.

7. BEING OF THE RIGHT

RIGHT AND LEFT are designations that refer to a political society which is already in crisis. In Traditional regimes, these designations did not exist, at least as they are presently understood. There could be opposition in Traditional regimes, but not of a revolutionary kind — which is to say, of a kind which calls the whole system into question. This opposition was rather loyalistic and in a certain way functional; thus in England it was possible to speak of 'His Majesty's most loyal opposition'.[1] Things changed after the emergence of the subversive movements of more recent times, and, as is known, the Right and the Left were defined on the basis of the place they respectively occupied in the parliament of the opposing parties.

Depending on the plane which one intends to discuss, the Right takes on different meanings. There is an economic Right based on capitalism, which is not without its legitimacy, only supposing that it does not attempt to make itself master and that its antithesis is understood to be socialism and Marxism.

So far as the political Right goes, it *de rigueur* acquires its full significance if it exists within a monarchy in an organic State — as has been the case above all in central Europe, and partially as well in conservative England.

But one can also lay aside institutional presuppositions, and speak of a Right in terms of a spiritual orientation and a vision of the world.

---

1   The expression is given in English in the original. — Trans.

In this case the Right, apart from standing against democracy and every 'social' myth, signifies a defence of the values of the Tradition as spiritual, aristocratic and warrior values (this last derivatively, and only with reference to a strict military tradition, as occurred for instance in Prussianism). It means moreover nourishing a certain disdain for intellectualism and for the bourgeois fetish of the 'cultivated man'. (A member of an ancient Piedmont family once paradoxically said, 'I divide our world into two classes: the nobility on the one hand and those with a degree on the other'; and Ernst Jünger, in support of this, promoted the antidote to be found in a 'healthy illiteracy'.)

To be of the Right means also to be conservative, but not in the static sense. The obvious presupposition of conservatism is that there is something worthy of being conserved; but this places before us the difficult problem of where such a thing is to be found in Italy's recent past, in the time following its unification: eighteenth-century Italy has certainly not left us an inheritance of higher values to protect, such as might serve as a foundation. Even looking further into the past, none but the most sporadic Right-wing positions are to be encountered in Italy's history; we have been lacking in a formative unitary force such as existed in other nations, which were long ago established by the ancient monarchical traditions of the aristocratic oligarchies.

However, in asserting that the Right should not be characterised by a static conservatism, we intend to say that it must have at bottom certain values and certain ideas, similar to a stable ground, and that these must be given various expressions fit to the development of the times, lest we be left behind, and unable to take up, control and incorporate whatever might come our way amidst changing circumstances. This is the only way in which a man of the Right can conceive of 'progress'; not simple movement ahead, as the left all too often likes to think. Bernanos wittily spoke of a 'flight forward' in this context (*'Où fuyez-vous en avant, imbéciles?'*).[2] 'Progressivism' is a ghost, and

---

2   The citation is French: 'Whither are you fleeing, fools?' It is taken from an essay by French novelist Georges Bernanos (1888–1948) entitled *La France contre*

is alien to every position of the Right. All the more so since, in a general consideration of the course of history, with reference to spiritual values, and not to material values (technological conquests, etc.), the man of the Right is bound to recognise in it a descent, not a progress and a true ascent. The developments of present-day society can do naught but confirm this conviction.

The positions taken up by the Right are necessarily anti-socialist,[3] anti-plebeian and aristocratic; thus, their positive counterpart is to be sought in the affirmation of the ideal State as a structured, organic, hierarchical state, sustained by a principle of authority. So far as this last is concerned, various difficulties emerge with respect to the question of whence such a principle is to draw its foundation and its chrism. It is obvious that such cannot come from below, from the *demos*, which — with apologies to the Mazzinians of yesterday and today — in no way expresses the *vox Dei*.[4] If anything, quite the contrary. Also to be excluded are dictatorial and 'Napoleonic' solutions, which can have

---

les robots (*France Against the Robots*). The original French differs slightly from Evola's reproduction: '*Que fuyez vous donc, imbeciles?*' meaning 'From what are you fleeing, fools?' The response which Bernanos furnishes very much accords however with Evola's argument in the present chapter: 'Alas! You are fleeing from yourselves… One understands nothing of modern civilisation if one does not first admit that it is a universal conspiracy against every kind of interior life.' Bernanos is perhaps best remembered for his novel *Diary of a Country Priest*, which treats of a young but ailing pastor who, assigned to a troubled country parish, struggles against spiritual temptation and faithlessness. Bernanos was a Roman Catholic, a monarchist and an anti-democrat, who nonetheless manifested great intolerance for the politics of his epoch: though he fought in the First World War, he spent the entirety of the Second in self-imposed exile in South America. — Trans.

3   Italian: *antisocietarie*, literally 'anti-societal' or 'anti-corporate'. Obviously neither of these English attempts represents what Evola has in mind here, which is rather opposition to Marxism in its social aspect. — Trans.

4   Reference respectively to the followers of Giuseppe Mazzini and to the Latin expression *Vox populi, vox dei*; 'the voice of the people is the voice of God'. Quite fittingly, it made its historical debut as the title of a Whig tract in 1709, and has since been used in a variety of (generally philo-liberal and philo-democratic) contexts. — Trans.

at best a transitive value, in situations of emergency and in purely contingent and temporary terms.

Once more, we are constrained to refer rather to a dynastic continuity — provided always, of course, in the case of a monarchical regime, that one keeps in view what has been called 'authoritarian constitutionalism', which is to say a power which is not purely representative but nonetheless acts and regulates. This is the 'decisionism' of which de Maistre and Donoso Cortés spoke with reference to decisions constituting the limit-case, including all the responsibility which is connected thereto; this responsibility is to be taken on by a single person when he finds himself standing before the necessity of direct intervention, when the existing order has entered into crisis or new forces have debouched on the political scene.

Let us repeat, however, that this kind of rejection of a 'static conservatism' does not regard principles. For a man of the Right, certain principles always constitute his solid basis, his *terra firma* in the face of transition and contingency; and here, 'counter-revolution' must stand as our clarion watchword. Or if one prefers, one might make reference instead to the only apparently paradoxical formula of a "conservative revolution". This concerns all initiatives that are to be instituted toward the removal of existing negative situations, and which are necessary for a restoration, for an adequate recovery of whatever has intrinsic value and whatever cannot be called into question. In truth, in conditions of crisis and subversion, it can be said that nothing has so revolutionary a character as the very recovery of these values. There is an ancient saying, *usu vetera novant*,[5] and it sheds light on the same context: the renewal which might be realised through the recovery of the 'ancient', which is to say, our immutable Traditional heritage. With this, we believe that the positions of the man of the Right have been sufficiently clarified.

---

5   A Latin phrase which René Guénon found inscribed into the architrave of an old gate in Guénon's native city of Blois. The original phrase read *Usu vetera nova*, 'Use makes old things new'. Evola's modification reads instead 'Old things become new in the use'. — Trans.

8. HIERARCHY AND PERSONALITY

I N THOSE SPECIAL fields of research, so little known to contemporary man, which were once known by the name of psychology of the soul of the races, a number of not altogether irreproachable characteristics are ascribed to the 'Mediterranean man'.

The trait generally indicated in this type is its personalism and love of gestures — a certain extroversion and almost an actor's disposition. This, of course, regards form only; it does not compromise the intrinsic content. Undeniable gifts like heroism, the spirit of sacrifice and so on can also manifest themselves in this form. But there is always the danger of its crumbling, and so the problem of style must be ever borne in mind, especially when one considers the political moment at hand and that ideal which is proper to an elite.

The personalistic accent ought to be sincerely recognised as an unfavourable trait which is rather diffuse in Italy, and it strikes the attention particularly of those who have travelled abroad. Thus, for example, it is difficult to find in our country an instance of the objective, impersonal exercise of power, even on a very profane level. From the customs officer all the way to the city guards you often observe the disagreeable attitude adopted by self-important individuals, of those who believe that their very person, rather than the mere function which has been entrusted to them, is the basis of their authority. Thus, while on the one hand the type in question is often arrogant and excessive, on the other hand he can become altogether accommodating when one knows how to approach him, precisely because he believes himself to be a discrete individual, and above all 'to be someone'.

If we consider certain aspects of the previous period without prejudice, we must recognise that 'hierarchism' formed one of Fascism's negative traits. It was developed on the basis of the very dispositions of the aforementioned human type. We are speaking here of the ostentation of political dignity and of the political party, of an individualistic affirmation connected to the exhibitionism of power, to the love for a certain theatrical scenery, to the ambition to have a certain 'following' in the form of a group devoted uniquely to the person — a following amidst which one might better stand out. This phenomenon, naturally, did not at all possess the sense that the anti-Fascists would now like to attribute to it; and there were also cases of men to whom such a style could be attributed, who overcame this phenomenon altogether and were able to coldly face death in the hour of trial. The trait in question is not for this less real, and it would be well to note it (we repeat: without exaggerating it) because today it, in more than a single case, tends to proliferate once more in certain environments, albeit in the minor key.

Thus we must recognise the neat difference existing between *heirarchism* on the one hand and true *hierarchy* on the other. Impersonality prevails in a true hierarchical system; a man has prestige and authority only on the basis of the function he has assumed, as the symbol of a principle and of an idea; under no circumstances does he use this function to forward his persona.

On another point, *heroism* too gives itself a scenic, exhibitionistico-Romantic form which is not *ipso facto* impaired (indeed, some men attain to heroism only in this form), but which does not correspond to the best style. In its best aspects, Ancient Roman civilisation could be called the 'civilisation of anonymous heroes'. And this can be confirmed in an examination of even certain 'spectacular' aspects of Romanness which might give the contrary impression. It seems that there was nothing so exhibitionist and 'scenic', for example, than the ancient Roman 'triumph' ceremony, because the victorious leader even wore divine insignia. But this detail precisely, in its well-attested and rigorous meaning, tells a contrary tale: it was meant to express that that leader attributed his victory less to himself, to his person, than to a divinity, a super-individual force with which he was identified. This is confirmed in the very conception of the *Fortuna Caesaris.*

The following words are ascribed to Prince Eugene, who spoke them to his officials in a particularly difficult moment (an action against the Turks which was so audacious that, despite the victory he obtained thereby, the prince but barely escaped being called upon to account for himself, in Vienna, for the risk he had caused his troops to run): 'My Lords, you have the right to survive only if you continuously, and even in most dangerous moments, serve as an example: but in such a natural and calm way that no man can reproach you'.

One could not better indicate the style which a true leader possesses, even when his own life is at risk. It is said that among the last words uttered by the Duke of Aosta, the hero of Amba Alagi, were these: 'I would have preferred to die fighting, out there among my men. But perhaps this is vanity. A man should know how to die even in a hospital bed'. There is no true greatness save in an impersonality devoid of vanity, of sentimentalisms, of exhibitionisms and of rhetoric. Only that which is personal in a true, higher sense is liberated and permitted to shine. And wherever such a man must lead or serve as an example, it will be an entirely different kind of bond which so tightly unites the man who commands with the man who obeys — bonds that no longer appeal only to the irrational, emotional part of the human soul, the part which is ever open to suggestion.

Given the low times in which we presently live, given the climate which today predominates of 'democracy', of mobs of low interests, of convolution and of politicantism, the above considerations must be considered rather extemporaneous. Each man can do with them what he will. But despite everything, we are never wrong to posit problems of style, to fix at least theoretically that which was and that which is proper to a higher human type: namely, that type which ought to form the essential framework of a true State, because it alone is fit to incarnate, to assume and to adequately exercise the principle of pure authority.

THE CRISIS OF
MODERN SOCIETY

1. THE CRISIS OF MODERNITY

I N THOSE PEOPLES that are called 'primitive', but which most often represent only the degenerate and ensavaged remains of more ancient races and civilisations, observers have often found their attention drawn to the phenomenon of the '*Männerbunden*'.[1]

In such peoples, the individual, to be considered as a merely natural being, is up to a certain age left to the family and especially to maternal care, under the feminine-maternal sign, beneath which these societies locate everything which has bearing for the material, physical side of existence. But at a given moment a change of state occurs. Special rites, which are called 'rites of passage' and which are often accompanied by a preliminary period of isolation and hard trials, bring about, according to a schema of 'death and rebirth', a new being, which alone can be considered a true man. Indeed, before this, the member of the group, no matter his age, is held to be one of the women and children, indeed even one of the animals. Once he has undergone his transformation, the individual is therefore united to the so-called '*Männerbunden*'. This society, having an initiatic (sacral) and warrior character, has the power of a group. Its right is to be

---

1   Italian: *società di uomini*, literally 'society/societies of men'. I have preferred the German term here because it has clear parallels to the idea that Evola has proposed, and because it is a word which has rightly begun to make headway in the Right. See Andersen, Joakim, *Rising from the Ruins: The Right of the 21st Century* (Arktos, 2018), especially pp. 168–175. — Trans.

differentiated in terms of its responsibility and its functions. It has the
power of command. It has a structure similar to that of an 'Order'.

While in the last century there was a tendency to derive the State
from the institution of the family, a more modern current has rightly
located the origin of sovereignty precisely in the phenomenon of
a '*Männerbunden*'. The scheme which is now indicated effectively
contains the fundamental elements which appropriately define every
order, and specifically every political order, and which do so with
a clarity that one would seek for in vain amidst the crumbling and
degraded theories of our days on the origin of sovereignty. In that
schema, we encounter above all the idea of a virility in an eminent and
spiritual sense, the quality of man as *vir* (as the Romans would say)
and not as simple *homo*.[2] This is connected, as has been seen, to a
'break in level', or a change in state; in its simplest expression, it is the
detachment from the sensible, vegetative, physical state. Then there is
the idea of a specific unity, much different from any other of 'naturalistic' character (as the family, the simple 'people', etc.). Finally, there is
the idea of power as something connected essentially with this higher
plane, so that originally it was recognised as possessing the character
of a force from on high, of a 'sacred power' (*auctoritas*, and with it
imperium, in the ancient Roman idea).

Therefore, we can with good right regard all of these matters as
'constants', that is, basic ideas which, in very different applications, formulations and derivations, appear recurrently in every major political
organisation of the past. On account of the processes of deconsecra-
tion, of rationalisation and of materialisation, which have grown ever
more accentuated in the course of the times, these original meanings
were forced to conceal themselves and to recede. But this remains ever
unchanged: where these meanings have been totally obliterated, so
that they no longer exist even in a transposed and debilitated form,
without any longer even a background of initiatic or sacral character,

2   Latin for 'man' (in the gendered sense) and 'human being' respectively. — Trans.

there no longer exists a true State; every concept has been lost which, in an eminent and traditional sense, makes political reality in its specific dignity and difference with respect to all the other spheres of existence and, in particular, with respect to all that which has an exclusively economic or 'social' character'.

With the epoch of the revolutions, there began, in Europe, a mighty assault against everything which conserved the semblance of a '*Männerbunden*'; this was an assault against the very political principle itself, against the principle of every true sovereignty, proceeding so far as a complete inversion of values and ideals. Indeed, in one form or another the societarian ideologies have reigned for some time now — ideologies which represent simply the anti-State, and also a kind of protest against the virile principle on behalf of all that which, for its connection to the simply physical life of a society, and according to the aforementioned view of the origins, has an analogously 'feminine' and promiscuous character. While for the '*Männerbunden*' honour, battle and dominion are values, for the simple 'society', on the other hand, peace, the economy, material well-being, the naturalistic life of the instincts and of the sentiments, and petty security are values: and, at their limit, hedonism and eudaimonism, as against heroism, rank and aristocracy.

Everyone by now knows in what present-day currents these inverted perspectives most like to swim, through the emergence of strata over which the 'societies of men' should be elevated, and with the demonism proper to every demagoguery. It would already be much if the knowledge of the values here briefly recorded might serve at least to make known, with precision, the true face of these currents, their true significance.

2. AWAKEN, NOBILITY!

E VERYONE HAS HEARD of the recent scandal which concluded with the confinement of two women of the Roman 'aristocracy' and with the 'detention' of various other exemplars of the capital's nobility, who had to be admonished or investigated by the political police. The persons in question had no scruples about inviting a person from an enemy nation and festively and cordially passing the evening and the night with him — to all appearances, even bidding him a sad farewell, since the person in question is not awaiting passage to America.

To whomever has had the opportunity to frequent our so-called 'high society', such a case as this is bound not to shock us so very much. Rather than a sporadic episode, we are dealing rather with a symptom for an entire mentality and an entire style of life. We must recognise this without duplicity: at least three quarters of the 'heraldic' Italian nobility is not up to the standard of our times; it represents — and this is the least that can be said — a neutral and refractory element, extraneous to the values and the ideals in the name of which we fight today.

Certainly, there are exceptions: the names of the great Italian families are once again filling the annals of glory of this war, and there are exponents of the aristocracy who entered into our political hierarchies even without being summoned, with the intention to use the prestige connected to their name and to the grandeur of their titles. But these

are exceptions: they are the sporadic reawakenings of a heredity which
cannot be extinguished in the course of a mere day, not even through
all that the ancient blood has suffered from contaminating crosses.
However, whosoever considers the Italian nobility in its entirety cannot help but recognise to it the aforementioned 'neutral' character,
which is as much as to say, its indifferentism, a more or less ostensive
apoliticality mixed with haughty scepticism and mundane vanity. The
nobility thus comes to represent a sector all its own: it stands *de facto*
outside of the State, and it has ceased to be a political class in any sense
of the word; it constitutes a true vestige because, so far as its ways of
life and its customs are concerned, and despite certain residues of an
artificial exclusivism and leaving aside its more 'brilliant' facets, it is
characterised now by a standard[1] of private and spiritually bourgeois
life.

And in this vain life of the aristocracy, we see the model essentially of the society of the Atlantic nations: a French model, but still
more an Anglo-Saxon one. Mussolini noted this already in 1926:
'These high classes give the example of Frankification, Anglification
and Americanisation'; and not only this, but in snobbishly adopting
the psychology of these peoples, 'they adopt above all their defects'.
'Society', the *monde*[2] of this vestigial heraldic nobility, has nothing
Italian about it; that is already something, but in truth it does not even
have anything which takes its bearings by the best European tradition
of the past. Already the names of the most glorious points of reference
of this mundane-aristocratic life are significant: *bridge, cocktail-party,
golf* or *tennis, poker.*[3] The little figure of the 'gentleman'[4] stands
somewhere between the sportive and the mundane, a mixture of conformistic formalism and of gratuitous hauteur, in internationalistic
key, with means of living that veer comfortably and eternally between

---

1   Evola uses the English word 'standard' here. — Trans.

2   French: 'world'. — Trans.

3   All of these words are given in English, the last of them even misspelled. — Trans.

4   Once more in English. — Trans.

'cruises', 'winter sports', fashionable salons and balls; and this figure of the 'gentleman' represents for the aristocracy in question the ideal, and determines *le bon ton*.[5]

And this has already been going on now for some time: it is not just yesterday that our 'high life'[6] was Anglicised, not to say even Americanised. And given that the doors of many known salons of our high society were generously thrown upon to men and women of America, in which one's belonging to the plutocratic cliques transformed one's Jewish race or one's less-than-transparent past into a small defect in one's overall beauty, something blameworthy only to backward and fanatical minds — given all of this, should it amaze us that in this war the aristocracy and the 'mondain' classes are not at their ease, as they are not able to renege their chosen tradition and to burn the bridges behind them with a *modus essendi* which is essentially taken from nations that today are our enemies? The a-fascism or veiled anti-fascism of these circles, with its internationalistic and philo-Anglo-Saxon nuances, is the natural consequence of their very nature, of the *modus essendi* which characterises them.

We mentioned as well that such a way of being, under another aspect, is simply the bourgeois *modus essendi*. Indeed, what does this secularised heraldic nobility want, in the end? Why will it hear nothing of Fascism or of any authoritarian system? Because it does not wish to be disturbed; it wants to continue its vanity fair, its life of bridge matches, of tea parties and of mundane or sportive hobbies, without bothering itself over politics, without participating in the least in the comprehensive life of the nation. Armed with the most artificial characteristics of a caste — because here, actually, we are dealing with a kind of worldly Masonry, in whose exclusivism but rarely enter concerns like blood, character, or spiritual tradition — this nominal aristocracy represents simply a bastion of the agnostic privatistic and

---

5 French, lit. 'the good tone', from which 'good manners' or 'good etiquette'. — Trans.

6 English in the original. — Trans.

liberal bourgeois ideal. It has nothing whatever of the truly aristocratic, beyond empty titles and a snobbism liable to impress only the
provincial and the 'social climber'.

We could understand a nobility which represents a political opposition, which sought to maintain consistency with one of its proper
traditions — a nobility, for instance, that was anti-Fascist or a-Fascist
because it was violently reactionary, conservative and legitimist, as
was the case to a certain extent with a specific German aristocracy.
But in our case we find nothing of the sort: the nobility of whom we
are speaking is incapable of adducing any justification whatsoever for
its abstentionism, its 'neutrality': it is not the exponent of any particular conception of the state; it is reticent only because it lives and
wishes to continue to live without being disturbed in its vanity fairs,
in the 'brilliant' rhythm of an existence which is, at bottom, strictly
bourgeois. For this reason alone, whenever it shows the first glimmer
of an interest in politics, its sympathies fly toward regimes of a liberal
character: it forgets that it was precisely liberalism which buried the
regimes from which the surviving true aristocracies of Europe could
still draw their prestige, their real power, their dignity...

So it is logical that in the mondain heraldic nobility of Italy, sympathy for 'society' of the French and Anglo-Saxon types should be
associated with an almost unanimous antipathy for the Germanic element, even when we are dealing with the ancient German or Austrian
aristocracy itself. The cause of this aversion is identical to that of
the contrary sympathy. Indeed, it was the Germanic world perhaps
more than any other which conserved the greatest remnants of an
aristocracy which simultaneously represented a party and a political
class and furnished the more precious centres for an authoritarian and
hierarchical state organism. Our aristocracy, in the vast majority of
cases, wishes to hear nothing of all this: it sees something 'barbaric',
something devoid of *bon ton*, something 'Prussian' in the stereotypical
and derogatory sense of the term. There is not enough of the 'mondain' in this aristocracy; there is not sufficient breadth of ideas, no

'refinement', no *esprit*; there is too much 'caste' in the 'obscurantist' sense, which brings it, despite everything, to stand unwillingly before the *mésalliances* with the dollar and with the bloodlines of parvenus and Jews.

Therefore, it is precisely here that we encounter one of the principle causes of our nobility's weakness: this cause — as we have often recalled — is to be found in the fact that the Italian nobility was only in small part a feudal and landed aristocracy, while its greater part was rather a mere court aristocracy, exhausting itself in titles which were accompanied neither by any real power, nor by sufficient goods to be able to decorously lead a certain suitable tenor of life. And the plague of this simply titular aristocracy is alive above all in southern Italy, which pullulates with dukes, princes and marquees, all constrained, by the same system, to every kind of abasement so as to keep themselves in the running — the primary abasement being that constituted by advantageous marriages with foreigners, above all from overseas.[7] To which is added that that smaller portion of our aristocracy which did possess lands, abandoned them: rather than feeling pride in ruling them, as so many little kingdoms, it considered them rather purely as a source of income, to be consumed in the vain life of the cities. Whence came a fatal rhythm of bad administration, in consequence of which, few are the names of the best landed Italian aristocracy that today do not stand upon the delinquent debtors lists of mortgage-lending institutions.

Given this state of affairs, the situation of the Italian nobility — we must confess — is grave: and any symptom of it, like the scandal noted above, is full of significance, because it induces a man to ask himself whether the nobility here alluded to, with its insouciance and its irresponsibility, intends indeed to dig its own grave, as the ancient French aristocracy already did, with equal ecstasy, before the English and liberal model. Those nobles who by accident are still capable of thinking

---

7   Italian: *d'oltre oceano*, 'from across the ocean', where the ocean in question is the Atlantic; Evola is of course alluding in particular to the United States. — Trans.

ought to realise that there are far too many elements today which go
hunting for pretexts and in which the formulae of 'social justice' and
of 'national solidarity', detached from their true content, which would
induce us too to hold to them, transform themselves into disguised
and subversive myths. The 'heraldic' nobility in question must realise
that with the mundane and snobby life that it leads, and with its hidden a-politicality, even should it do nothing imprudent, it will not be
able to last for long. Rather than serving as an example, it serves as a
scandal. It will be replied that scandals arise in other arenas as well.
That should however be only another reason to do differently here
and thus to maintain the high prestige and dignity of an entire class.

The nobility must awaken, or else resign itself to perish, and not
even gloriously: to perish by corrosion and fatal submersion. To
awaken — that means: *to become once more, at any cost, a political
class.* Let our nobility, if it wishes, paraphrase in this respect a well-
known watchword of the Revolution, and say: let us not negate the
State and Fascism, let us conquer them. Neutrality, reluctance, worldly
vanity, tacit sympathies for nations which we today are fighting
against, not so much for their peoples as for their *modus essendi* — all
of this is nothing. And it is also obtuse of the nobility — obtuse not
even as an animal is obtuse so much as a stone — to persist today in
this love with the liberal idea *pro domo sua*,[8] which is to say so as
to continue undisturbed in the 'life of high society' in collusion with
the plutocracy, the cosmopolitan *beau monde*, and finally with the
'social climbers' — unfortunately also in the political sphere — who
long to snatch some title and to boast this or that friendship with the
heraldic nobility. One must rather be persuaded that, on account of a
fatal rhythm of history and a species of immanent justice, liberalism is
only the prelude to a yet more acute phase of subversion, represented
by collectivism, by socialism, by the plebeian element, to which, once

---

8   Latin: 'self-benefiting', lit. 'for one's own home'. — Trans.

the liberal dismantling has been realised, all roads will stand virtually open.

There is only a single safe and sound refuge for the nobility — and this is an authoritarian and hierarchical system. If the nobility cuts itself off, it will have decreed its own end. But on the other hand the nobility will never be able to actively penetrate into this system, not only so as to guarantee its own existence but also to strengthen, energise, and — eventually — even to rectify the system's structures, until such a day as it has demanded of itself the miracle of a reawakening, of a resurrection. As has been said, due to the presence in the Italian aristocracy's past of an entire complex of unfavourable circumstances, this task will be particularly arduous. The times, however, leave no choice. In the new European order there will be no place for any nobility of the type of that purely nominal, anodyne and snobbist sort which we have here indicted; truly, it will be excluded, not from the socialist and tribunalistic point of view, but rather the point of view of whomever truly feels the dignity of the true aristocratic idea. And if in Italy, too, the trial should come to failure, better a swift end than a prolongation wrought of counterfeits and caricatures, of high-sounding titles and names which have validity only as the object of bitter irony.

3. IMPERIAL UNIVERSALISM AND NATIONALISTIC PARTICULARISM

SOME OF THE THINGS that we wrote in our essay 'The Two Faces of Nationalism', to judge by the repercussions that arose therefrom in more than a single place, seem to us worthy of further development. We will carry this development out on the single plane which interests us, that of principles. We will speak candidly in this, and let it be stated that whoever believes that we have been inspired in our considerations merely by the special circumstances of today, such as are present in this or that given country, errs altogether in his estimations.

We will proceed from an analysis of the meaning of the phenomenon 'nationalism' to an analysis of the meaning of the concept 'imperialism'. Moreover, we will determine the relations that stand between one and the other. This further problem, with respect to our prior analysis, presents a greater difficulty. Indeed, the word 'nation', being a new word for a phenomenon which is itself relatively new, has not proved so difficult for us to understand, and it was only a question of comprehending this phenomenon in terms of a more integral historical vision, one conforming to reality itself. The notion of 'empire' on the other hand brings us back to something belonging to an ideal world which is very different than that to which the moderns are accustomed; from this fact one can comprehend how more or less grave

misunderstandings and confusions might be produced in the better
part of those who today take their bearings by such an idea.

We have demonstrated that there are two kinds of nationalisms:
one is a phenomenon of degenerescence because it expresses a *regression of the individual into the collective* (the 'nation') and of intellectuality into vitality (pathos and the 'soul' of the race). The other is a
positive phenomenon, because it expresses the *reaction against yet
vaster forms of collectivisation*, such as, for instance, those offered by
the proletariat internationals or by the pragmatic standardisation on
the economico-social basis (America).

The first (demagogic nationalism) proposes to destroy those qualities proper and specific to individuals, toward the end of promoting
'national' qualities. In the second (aristocratic nationalism) it is rather
a matter of subtracting individuals from that lower state into which
they have fallen, in which each is held to be equal to every other: it
is a question of differentiating them at least so far as that degree in
which feeling oneself to be part of a specific race or nation expresses
a higher value and dignity as compared to feeling oneself to be equal
to all others (egalitarianism and fraternalism, 'humanity' in the communist sense).

Considering the process by which nationalism might have the
sense of a positive phenomenon, we return therefore to the sense of
difference and hierarchy: individuals, becoming themselves, pass
from the plane of materiality, where there can be no true difference,
to that of intellectuality, in which they participate in something that
is non-individual, not because it is sub-individual (collectivism) but
rather because it is *superindividual*: they participate in universality. And then from nationalism we pass over to imperialism — to the
anonymity of great realities which are more than human. Every true
imperialism is universal, and is posited as the positive overcoming of
the nationalistic phase.

Let us attempt to make our position clear. The fundamental point
might seem, to a poorly prepared reader, a mere logical subtlety: it

is the opposition between collectivism and universalism. Collectivism is the aggregation of various things to the point of their intermixing, in which they lose every native characteristic and every autonomy and become an amorphous mass or a uniformity of a single 'type'. Universalism on the other hand means rising from the multiplicity of different things up to a principle standing in a time anterior and superior to their differentiation, which is given only by their sensible reality. In the first case, abolition of difference; in the second, the integration of difference. Universality is a purely spiritual reality: it is reached by rising, through a species of 'ascesis', from sensibility to passionality — the dominion of the particular — to pure intellectuality and, more generally, to a disinterested form of activity. It moreover negates individual realities as little as a physical law negates the particular character of very different phenomena which might have in themselves a common principle.

We have enunciated these ideas in an abstract form in order to maintain their more general meaning. But we can immediately arrive at quite important practical consequences which follow from the distinction between collectivism and universalism. There are certain restricted forms of nationalism which for example tendentiously confound the one thing with the other. They thus extend a legitimate reaction against attempts at internationalisation and the erasure of ethnic differences (legitimate reaction because it is brought against tendencies toward collectivist levelling) to things which have rather a universal meaning and which demand the liberty of the individual in the face of the collectivistic and infraintellectual aspect of nationalism itself. J. Benda has in this matter made numerous very correct observations in his well-known *Trahison des clercs*. We ourselves in the aforementioned essay have indicted the strange demand of certain extremist nationalists, that there should be a *national* science, a *national* philosophy, a *national* art — even a *national* religion.

Now, to desire this kind of nationality means totally failing to realise the universal possibilities present in those phenomena of the spirit: it means limiting these possibilities, transposing them from the plane which is proper to them to a lower plane — an ethnic plane, and no longer a spiritual and intellectual one. We might pose this in the form of a dilemma: a 'national science', insofar as it is 'national', is no longer science, and insofar as it is 'science' it is no longer simply national. And if one wishes only to allude to the fact that a given science has been cultivated particularly by the persons of a given nation, and not to speak so much of the objective results of their work (which has the value of 'science' insofar as it has a value independent of specific persons), it is clear that in this case one halts at the merely episodic and biographical aspect of the question, a thoroughly empirical aspect that no man has the right to impose on any consideration of higher character. *The fact that a given scientist is not from 'our' country certainly does not render his results any falser or less acceptable, if they are exact; and the fact that he is of 'our' country does not make these any truer or more acceptable, if they are false.* While someone could deny the evidence of such a consideration only with the greatest difficult, when it is applied to science, many on the other hand believe that they can deny it when other domains are brought into question — for instance, the domains of speculation, of art, of the supersensible. With this they betray one thing only: that they have no sense whatever[1] for anything which transcends the simply material (i.e. science). They are still incapable of elevating themselves to the point of view of objectivity, of superindividuality.

Once this point has been fixed in place, it is clear that an imperialism is such, when it dominates in virtue of universal values to which a given nation or bloodline is elevated through its power to overcome itself. This is exactly the contrary of the 'morality' of the so-called '*sacred egoism*' of the nations. Without a 'dying and becoming', no nation can aspire to an effective and legitimate imperial mission. No nation can remain closed in its national characteristics to dominate

---

1   Italian: *sono ancora ad uno stato di irrealismo*, literally, 'they are still in a state of unrealism'. — Trans.

the world, or merely another land, on the basis of these. If the imperialistic attempts of modern times have aborted or have brought the nations that have perpetrated them to ruin (the latest example being the central empires), the cause is precisely this contradiction of wanting at one and the same time 'nation' and 'empire'; the cause is the absence at bottom of a true universality.

The attempts of which we have spoken imply moreover a materialistic and barbarian degradation of the very concept of empire. It cannot be otherwise. True dominion comes by rising oneself to that which is superior to that which one wishes to dominate: one cannot have it by remaining on the same level. *A hand as a hand cannot claim to have the power to dominate the other organs of the body.* It can do so only by ceasing to be a hand, making itself into soul — that is by elevating itself to the unitary and immaterial function which is called to unify and to rule the various particularistic corporeal functions. The hypothetical attempt of a hand which wishes to master the body by usurping the functions proper to the soul might clarify the spirit of certain imperialistic ideologies of the nationalistic, materialistic and militaristic kind. Here, the path is not superiority, but the simple violence of a force which is stronger but not for this different in nature to that which they tend to subjugate.

There is surely something strange in the fact that *while in the framework of the life of a civil nation it is thought to be reprehensible to seize the possessions of those who possess more, simply because one has need of them, such comportment between nation and nation seems to be the most natural and most legitimate thing in the world.* Indeed, this is the basis of the aforementioned barbaric concept of imperialism: a poor nation, it is believed, has every right to lay hands on the goods of a richer nation, that it might 'expand' its own life; and the military or diplomatic system in order to arrive at such an end would be the sacred means of imperialists of this kind. Nor is this all: in certain cases a method is even created so that a nation be artificially pressed the necessity of expansion, and thus of 'imperialism'.

An example of this is the demographic method: once overpopulation, the condition of nations that *'do not have enough space'*, has been attained, the necessity of some kind of release is imposed, of an eruption which has to our eyes, moreover, so long as it is reducible entirely to this plane, a character which is not easily distinguished from that of barbaric invasions. The materialism of this latter view becomes clear moreover in the *lack of the sense of quantity and of number in the face of quality*. If a nation does not have a solid basis in a higher culture of quality, all of the expansions created by supernumeration — from phenomena of emigration to military phenomena — will attain one result alone: they will furnish the raw material over which a foreign culture will rule. *The material victors will be the conquered in ideal terms*. The case of Rome and Hellas is not precisely an example here, but it offers a hint for the comprehension of the theses we have just stated; and today we might indicate America, that singular crucible in which masses of immigrants from the most varied ethnic traditions have been almost wholly reduced in the space of two generations to a single type: just as India, for example, has maintained intact its ideal unity notwithstanding the successive rule of stronger but qualitatively inferior races.

Besides this false imperialism, there is another equally false form of the economic type. Certainly, in our day, when almost every activity is conditioned and evaluated in economic terms (in this we can already see the advent of the penultimate of the ancient castes: that of the merchants), there is fertile land for the formation of the illusion that by dominating and monopolising the economic possibilities of a racial group alone might signify 'empire'. But for whomever does not participate in the moral fall characterised in the modern 'standard of living',[2] all of this presents an unquestionably extravagant, not to say ridiculous, face.

---

2   'Standard of living' is in English in the original. — Trans.

The Lords of old left to their wardens and to their freedmen administrative questions. They were concerned essentially with cultivating those superior, 'aristocratic' forms of interest, of life, of action and of dignity, which constituted precisely the essence of the law and of the function of their caste. If someone were suitable to administration and had the will to exercise it, he could do so: the lords were but little interested in being the one to spur the 'economy', so long as there remained the right subordination and the commitment to loyalty of man without the administrative class toward the aristocrat or the Prince. But today things stand quite otherwise. The plutocrats have taken the place of the aristocrats; the administrator and the goldmonger presume to be 'leaders' and do not recognise anyone to whom they themselves must answer — that is, until at a given moment the contingency proper to every material force left to itself and devoid of any principle overwhelms them and puts others (if not even the anonymous masses) in their place.

Within these limits is to be evaluated the danger of such 'imperialism' as the financial Semitic or Masonic international sort. This danger exists and it is real with respect to those who suffer and accept the abasement of every criterion and every idea of power up to the level of mere economy. But on the other hand whoever — whether individual or race — rises a little beyond this plane and puts down solid roots in that realm where things are no longer to be 'bought' or 'sold' — this person will ask himself with wonderment just what it is such 'imperialists' believe they are dominating.

The consideration of these negative aspects introduces us to that of the true and positive conditions for empire. A race awakens to empire when it is capable of throwing itself beyond itself, when it is like a hero, who *would not be such if in his leap he did not conquer the instinct that would keep him bound to the little animal love for his particular life.* It is for this reason that nationalism (in the static and exclusivistic sense) and imperialism are two mutually exclusive terms. An imperial race stands as distant from its own particularities as from those which characterise other races: it does not oppose one particular to another (a nation to another, the law of this to the law of that, etc.), but it opposes the universal to the particular.

That is particular which is subjectivistic, sentimentalistic, 'idealistic' or also utilitarian. That is universal which is pure of all these elements and which can translate itself into the terms of pure objectivity.

In the development both of the individual and of a culture or a race, a decisive phase is attained when one reaches comprehension of the point of view of reality and desires it above every other point of view; before this, it can be said that the spirit does not yet know true virility. If it is sentiments, prides, values, cupidities, hatreds — everything in short which is the 'human' element in the strict sense, or the individual or collective — if these are the things which guide a race, it will necessarily be at the mercy of the contingency proper to those things which have no principle in themselves. But if it, at least in an elite of leaders, succeeds in extracting from all of this the two fundamental elements of life, knowledge and action, then it will be fit for a mission which one might call superior to the empirical and political world.

Universality as knowledge and universality as action: these are the twin foundations of every imperial epoch.

Knowledge is universal when it arrives at the point of giving us the sense of things before whose greatness and eternity all pathos and human tendency disappears: when it introduces in the primordial, in the cosmic, in all that which in the field of the spirit has the same characteristics of purity and of power of oceans, deserts, glaciers. Every true universal tradition has carried in itself this breath of the large, animating with it disinterested forms of activity, awakening the sensibility to values that cannot any longer be measured by any criterion of utility and of passionality, whether individual or collective: introducing through '*living*' a '*more than living*'. This is the type of an invisible empire, which history shows us in the examples for instance of Brahmanic India, Christendom, and Hellenism itself: a unitary culture which rules every 'politically' and economically conditioned reality from within, in a variety, even an independent variety, of peoples or cities.

However, we can imagine a concept of Empire, both visible and invisible, having a material unity beyond its spiritual unity. Such an Empire is realised when, together with universality as knowledge we also find *'universality as action'*. Here, for historical references, we might indicate Ancient China, Rome in part, once again the Middle Ages in the movement of the Crusades on one side and Islamism on the other.

Universalised action is pure action: it is heroism. Thus in the two conditions of impiriality,[3] we find exactly the qualities that defined the two higher castes of antiquity, the wise caste (which does not necessarily indicate a 'priestly' caste) and the warrior caste. We notice at once that the concept of 'heroism' which we mention here is not that of the moderns. In the traditional concept, heroism is an ascesis in the rigorous sense of the term, and the hero is a nature as purified of the 'human elements' as is the ascetic: he participates in the same character of purity of the great forces of things themselves, and he has nothing to do with passionality, with sentimentality and the various movements, ideals or materials of men, whether collective or individual. The specific function of the each of the them: thus war to the warrior held as his end, as well as the path for his spiritual realisation. Thus he fought in a 'pure' way, war itself was a good, heroism was a 'pure' form, and thus a universal form, of activity. The rhetoric of the 'battle for rights', 'territorial claims', sentimental or humanitarian pretexts and so on are altogether and wholly modern things, entirely alien to the traditional concept of heroism.

In the *Bhagavad-gita*, in the Quran, in the Latin concept of *mors triumphalis*, in the Hellenic likening of the hero to the initiate, in

---

3   Italian: *imperialità*, here rendered 'impiriality', the state of being an empire, to be distinguished from *imperialismo*, 'imperialism', with its more specific, and generally negative, connotations. — Trans.

the symbolic Valhalla of the Nordics to which heroes alone were destined, in certain aspects of the 'holy war' known even by Catholic feudalism — in all of this we find, formulated in a variety of ways, the transcendent idea, both supernational and superhuman, of heroism: heroism here is a method of virile ascesis, of the destruction of the lower nature, a path toward immortality and of relating oneself to the eternal. Transfigured by such an atmosphere, action acquires a universal nature: it becomes almost a force from on high, capable of translating the universality of a tradition of spirit even into an earthly body: it is the condition of Empire, its supreme meaning.[4]

Are these but anachronistic and vain disinterments? Perhaps they are. But if so, this would mean only that the current conditions are such as to reduce to a state of pure rhetoric the evocation, dwelt on by many, of ideals and symbols that today have lost their original sense. This does not alter the fact however that in the domain of doctrine we can and must always trace a line of demarcation between concept and concept, and remain cognisant of what would be contradictory. Let us repeat it: when the points of reference are 'national pride', 'irredentist claims', the 'need to expand', etc., we find ourselves amidst the legitimate principles of a strong modern nation, but certainly not amidst those of an empire. Ask yourself if a Roman ever fought for anything of the kind, and if he ever had need to excite himself with passionate rhetoric to attain the miracle of that global conquest, through which the universality of the luminous Greco-Latin civilisation shed its light even to the most distant of lands.

---

4   We have given ample space to the traditional concept of heroism and war in our essays 'Heroic Symbols of the Ancient Roman Tradition' (*Vita Nova*, n. 8, 1929) and 'The Greater and the Lesser Holy War' (in *La Torre*, n. 10, 1930). Regarding this last, whenever we wish to perceive just how far the hypocrisy and impostures of certain irresponsible persons might go, we recall how our defence of the traditional idea, according to which war is waged because it is an integral duty and joy of the warrior caste, and not in order to obtain some plot of land, has time and time again been adduced as if it were an explicit affirmation on our part that... Dalmatia belongs by rights to Yugoslavia (!!!).

We must bring ourselves back to the state of pure forces, of forces which proceed with the same fatality and the same purity and the same inhumanity of the great forces of things themselves. The great conquerors have always felt themselves to be 'children of destiny', the bearers of a force which had to realise itself and to which everything, beginning from their very person, from their very pleasure, from their very tranquillity, had to be bent and sacrificed. In its integral meaning, Empire is something superior, something transcendent: Holy Empire. How then can one associate the myth of empire — as we wrote already several years ago[5] — with this or that 'idealism' or traditionalism (in the limited sense) or sentimentalism or 'utilitarianism'? How can one connect it to the needs of a faction or a nation, not to speak of a mere region, town or country? And yet amongst the moderns it is altogether too frequently the case that one ends up in such absurdities as these.

Whoever re-evokes imperial symbols, whatever land might have given life to his body, must be capable of perceiving all of this. One must know what the 'nation' is and what the 'Empire': what is the limit of the one and of the other. The mind must open itself to all that in man neither commences nor finishes in man: let him comprehend universality as the culmination of the most intense individuality, both as knowledge and as action. And above all it is necessary that, having a sense of the measures to which everything today has been so un-naturally reduced, one knows that there is an entire world one must say 'no' to before the auroral clarity of a possible 'imperial' European epoch might dawn, beyond the world of 'servants' and of 'merchants'.

---

5   Cf. 'Imperialismo e stile realistico' in *Tevere*, 20 January 1929.

ARISTOCRACY

1. THE MEANING OF ARISTOCRACY FOR THE ANTI-BOURGEOIS FRONT

THOSE RESULTS into which the recent and well-known anti-bourgeois polemic, in its more serious aspects, has led us, can more or less be summed up as follows. Bourgeois civilisation and spirit, being as it is incompatible with fascism, must be overcome. There are however two ways of being anti-bourgeois, of desiring the end of the bourgeoisie, and these are not only different, but even antithetical to one another. In the first, the bourgeoisie, along with all of its derivatives — bourgeois ethics, bourgeois culture, plutocracy, capitalism, etc. — must give way to a popular regime of the masses: the 'social' or 'collectivist' era must be affirmed over and above the bourgeois. From the other point of view, the true overcoming of the bourgeois lies instead in aristocracy. A new aristocratic epoch must be affirmed, beyond the bourgeois decadence of Western Civilisation.

It is hardly necessary to note here that only this second conception is acceptable from the fascist point of view and that only in this way can fascism be anti-bourgeois, while not ceasing to be the irreconcilable enemy of communism and of Marxism — movements that also brandish anti-bourgeois attitudes, but naturally in the first of the two senses hereabove mentioned. Nor is this the place to insist on the polemic which we have already various times brought against certain milieus which, under the brand of being anti-bourgeois, attempt to introduce aberrant, counterfeit and 'socialising' interpretations of the Revolution.[1]

THE BOURGEOIS SURROGATES OF ARISTOCRACY

We have thus already had occasion to indicate that a man has no doubt made a false move the moment he takes up the term 'aristocracy of thought'. The superstitious cult of 'thought' is, in reality, one of the traits of *bourgeois* civilisation, which invented this cult and propagated it for obvious polemical reasons. Against the aristocracy of blood and the aristocracy of spirit, and so as to divest these of their authority, bourgeois civilisation, consolidated through the advent of the Third Estate, affirmed the right of 'true' aristocracy, which was supposedly the aristocracy of 'thought'. Now, the anti-intellectualism and the virilism, which are proper to new renovating currents and to fascism, suffice to bring this bourgeois myth to the bar. What is this 'aristocracy of thought'? It can be reduced for the most part to the famous 'intellectuals', to the creators of philosophical theories, to the poets and the literati, which is to say, to those whom Plato rightly wished to banish from his State — a State which was not in the least, as is vulgarly believed, a utopian model, but which reflected what was traditionally always held to be normal in the affairs of ordinary politics. Now, to perceive the total absurdity and anachronism of this view, it is enough to speak aloud the idea that an elite of 'intellectuals' and thinkers should stay in power, though they also might well be, character-wise, cowardly and little more than *petit bourgeois*.

---

1   Where the Italian *Rivoluzione* is obviously meant to refer to the Fascist, and not the French or American, Revolution. When Evola refers to the French Revolution below, he significantly puts the word in the lower case. As for his critique of Fascism, it was certainly one of the major themes of his political philosophy, and can be found primarily in *A Traditionalist Confronts Fascism*, *Fascism Viewed from the Right*, but also in other books, including his last, *Recognitions* (all books available from Arktos). — Trans.

As the fumes of the progressivist and scientistic Enlightenment have begun to clear, we cannot conceive of the 'aristocracy of thought' even in the terms of scientists, inventors, and technicians. All of these are doubtlessly useful elements for a modern society, and it was an excellent thing to give them the means, with the new corporate order which took the place of the preceding demo-parliamentary order, to act more efficaciously in the compages of the new State. But it is also evident that one cannot recognise even to this 'aristocracy' the qualification proper to a ruling class, the creator of a new civilisation beyond the bourgeois. It is much more appropriate to Marxism and Bolshevism than to our Revolution to think that an elite of technicians, aiming at resolving purely material, social and economic problems, will conduct a collectivised humanity, over which they exercise control, toward a new Paradise, to such an extent that they can demand any higher recognition.

Having established in these terms the inconsistency of the formula 'aristocracy of thought', it remains to us to examine the other idea, which refers to a generically authoritarian and dictatorial notion. Already the fact that there exists such a term as 'dictatorship of the proletariat' demonstrates the necessity of clarifying the meaning of the terms 'dictatorship' and 'authoritarianism'. It is one of the merits of Pareto[2] that he demonstrated the inevitability of the phenomenon of elitism, which is to say of a ruling minority. But with this we are still far from being able to speak correctly of 'aristocracy'. Has Pareto

---

2   Vilfredo Pareto (1848–1923) was an Italian political scientist and sociologist, but also an engineer. The Pareto Principle, which states that about 80% of the effects for most events come from about 20% of the causes, was his discovery— a most curious principle with a wide variety of applications. Pareto himself noted, for instance, that in Italy about 20% of the population owned about 80% of the land, and that in a garden about 20% of the pea-pods will contain about 80% of the peas. The idea has been put to valid work in economics, management, science, and sports, and it is entertaining, and often fruitful, to try to put it to use in other fields as well. Julius Evola mentions him often in his work, and devotes a laudatory essay to him in Chapter 30 of *Recognitions*. — Trans.

himself not considered the case in which this elite might be constituted precisely by the bourgeoisie?

But we wish above all to bring something else into relief; namely,
the rapport between the aristocracy and the totalitarian-authoritarian
idea. If one aims with precision to overcome both the bourgeois and
collectivism, one must have very clear ideas regarding the scope, the
sense, the limits and the possibilities for development of the totalitarian-authoritarian idea, specifically in relation to the aristocratic
idea. To what extent can the totalitarian people-leader formula, which
brings liberalism and its irresponsible democratico-bourgeois regime
to an end, serve as a valid cornerstone for the new edifice? To what
extent can it thoroughly resolve the problem with which we began?

THE DOUBLE FACE OF
TOTALITARIANISM

Here it is meet that we enter upon what will seem to be delicate
ground to those who do not possess adequate principles; we must
enter into the field of the relation between the authoritarian idea and
absolutism, between the directing unity of an organic State and the
tribunal of the people. We have already touched upon this argument
in a previous article, where we spoke of the true significance of the
actions undertaken by Philip the Fair of France.

We permit ourselves to take up once more the fundamental idea
by saying that the phenomenon of totalitarianism and of statal concentration has various meanings, indeed contrary meanings, according to the type of regime which preceded it.

Let us suppose, as an initial example, the case in which the pre-existing regime in question is that of a well-articulated society, with social strata and even castes which are clear and distinct, not artificially
so, but from national vocation — not closed or conflictual, but rather
as agents, acting in an orderly concert within a whole hierarchy; let us
suppose moreover that the differentiation and the anti-collectivism of

this society are also expressed through a certain division of power and of sovereignty, with a certain autonomy of functions and of particular rights, over which the central authority reigns, reinforced rather than diminished in its spiritual sovereignty by this partial decentralisation precisely; such a state of affairs can be seen e.g. in the positive aspects of the feudal regime. Now it is evident that if in such a society centralism and totalitarianism were affirmed, these would signify a destruction and a disarticulation, the regression of the organic into the amorphous. To concentrate all powers at the centre in an absolutist fashion is, in such a case, something like to the efforts of a man who wishes to directly refer to his brain every function and activity of the body, and who therefore attains the condition of those inferior organisms who are constituted only by a head and an inarticulate and undifferentiated body.

This precisely is the situation in anti-aristocratic and levelling absolutism, which was methodically pursued, under the impetus of a variety of circumstances, by the Kings of France above all, following upon Philip the Fair. And Guénon has rightly observed that it was not an accident that it was precisely first France to undergo the Jacobin revolution, with the advent of the Third Estate. Indeed, those absolutist Kings, enemies of feudal aristocracy, literally dug their own graves. By centralising, by dissolving and disassembling[3] the State, substituting a bureaucratico-statal superstructure for virile and direct forms of authority, of responsibility and of partial personal sovereignty — by doing all of this, the enemies of aristocracy created a void around themselves, because their vain court aristocracy could signify nothing any longer, and the military aristocracy was by then deprived of any direct connection with the country. The differentiated structure which acted as the medium for the nation as mass was destroyed, detached

---

3   Italian: *disossando e disarticolando*, literally 'deboning' (i.e. extracting all the bones from) and de-articulating (i.e. eliminating all the junctures, pivots, joints etc. of a body) — a vivid metaphor following from the idea of the 'organic state'. — Trans.

from the sovereign and from his sovereignty. At a blow, the revolution easily abolished that superstructure and put power into the hands of the pure mass. *Aristocratic absolutism therefore opens the way to demagoguery and collectivism.* Far from having the character of true *dominium*, it finds its equivalent only in the ancient popular tyrannies and plebeian tribunals, both of which alike are collectivistic forms.

Things stand well otherwise however when the antecedent to the process of authoritarian concentration is not a feudal and organic society, but a 'modern' society, which is to say, a society of dissolution. This is the state of affairs in our own society. Liberalism, democracy, egalitarianism, and internationalism had reduced the nation to the condition of mercurial masses who were on the verge of dispersing in every direction, and of sinking down to the point of that total genuflection represented by socialism and by communism. Before such a state of affairs, the first and most urgent task was obviously that of creating a bulwark, a brake, with all available means, so as to neutralise the tendency toward centrifuge through a centripetal political force. And precisely this is the sense and the positive value of the process of fascist totalitarianising. After having achieved this first task, the next, which immediately presents itself, is to articulate the nation anew, to bring the nation back to itself, to unify it beneath the sign of various myths and symbols and protect it against every disintegrating and dispersive force; this is a matter of shielding it from every form of collectivism and giving life to very clear, hierarchically connected unities, possessing their own persona. Only in this way can it have a structure, an organic reality, capable of persisting in time and armed with its own conservative force — a force that cannot be present in any collective and formless substance, such as is held together only by a given state of mind and by the general structures of the State. *Only then will the Revolution truly have generated a new, completely formed being.*

PRESTIGE AND 'RACE'

At this point, it can be seen that with our last considerations we have only apparently left behind our initial subject — which is to say, the problem of the significance of aristocracy. Indeed, it is evident that one cannot contemplate a new Traditional and organic articulation of the State without setting before oneself the *problem of persons*, in a still higher sense than that implied by the conventional term, or by the nineteenth-century tastes of the 'political ruling class'. And this idea grows clearer yet if only one bears in mind that we are not speaking only of 'political' functions and activities which are more or less connected to the administrative or legislative body of the State. We are rather speaking of the problem of *a personal form of authority*, which issues from the man rather than his office: we are speaking of a prestige and an example which, being common to a given class, needs must form an atmosphere, crystallise a higher style of life, and thus effectively give the 'tone' ' to a new society. We are speaking almost of an *Order*, not in the religious sense, but in the ascetic-warrior sense, and naturally with reference to what this might represent in the world, as in the Ghibelline Middle Ages. Indeed, we have in mind even the most ancient Aryan and Indo-Aryan societies, in which it is known that the elite was not in any way materially organised, nor drew its authority from representing any given tangible power, but still solidly maintained its rank and gave the tone to the corresponding society.

Now, it seems clear enough that it is precisely in these terms that any 'aristocracy' must be conceived, which is invoked against the 'bourgeois' type of society and civilisation. This concerns neither an 'aristocracy of thought', nor the velleities of the 'intellectuals', nor the little popular 'tribunals', such as are aimed at manipulating and enthralling the masses with expedients dictated by the moment: we are speaking rather of an 'aristocracy' which undeniably has many traits in common with the gentile nobility, with the traditional patriciate, and, we almost want to say, with the ancient feudal and warrior-sacral aristocracy of Aryan societies. In this way a new problem emerges: that of examining the *valid elements of 'style'* within this higher aristocracy, as well as determining how to evaluate those who, according to their heraldry, are 'nobles' — for the nobility yet exists in Italy, and indeed fascism has concerned itself with protecting and controlling its titles, and raising new persons to its dignity.

Traditionally, two things above all stand out in the nobility: the value recognised to blood and the subordination of the person to a given lineage and origin. Individualistically or 'humanistically', the single human being has no value here; he is worth something in relation to his blood, to his origins and to his family, whose name, honour and faith he must exalt. In the same way, relevance is given to his heredity and to his origin, to the point of excluding any contaminating intermixing. The relations of this attitude to racism are starkly evident.

For thousands of years racism has been active in the gentile nobility of every people, and even in its highest form, insofar as it has maintained its adherence to the idea of tradition and avoided materialising in the form of a kind of zoology. Before the concept of race was generalised, as it has been in current times, *having race* was always synonymous with aristocracy. The qualities of race always signified the qualities of the elite, and referred not to gifts of genius, of culture or of intellect, but essentially to character and to style of life. They stood in opposition to the quality of the common man because they appeared, to a large degree, innate: either one has the qualities of race or one does not have them. They cannot be created, built, improvised or learned. The aristocrat, in this regard, is the precise contrary of the parvenu, the late-comer, the 'self-made man', who has become that which he was *not*. To the bourgeois ideal of 'culture' and of 'progress' is opposed the aristocratic ideal, which is conservative of tradition and of blood. This is a fundamental point, and is the single true overcoming of all bourgeois and Protestant surrogates for aristocracy.

From the point of view of patrician racism, not only physical qualities but also spiritual elements are transmitted hereditarily — a special moral sensibility, a vision of life, an instinctive faculty of discrimination. All of this is of fundamental importance for new tasks, as well. Here we are speaking of specific gifts which, in the last analysis, derive from superbiological factors of character, factors which are fatally dispersed in the masses. A typical aristocratic trait is the faculty of reacting from out of spiritual motivations, and doing so in as instinctive, direct and organic a way as the common man is capable of doing only with regard to that which closely touches upon his animal or passional life. Moreover — and this is important — in authentic aristocracy the meaning of 'spirituality' has always had little to do with the modern notion: there is the sense here of *sovereignty*, there is contempt for profane things, common things, things up for sale — things such as are born from ability, ingenuity, erudition and even genius — a contempt which is not so distant to that professed by the ascetic himself.

Indeed, we are tempted to express the secret of true noble gifts in this formula: *a superiority with respect to a life which has become natural, a life of pedigree.* This superiority, which has about it something of the ascetic, does not create antitheses within the very being of the aristocratic type; as a second nature, it stands above the inferior human part of his being and calmly permeates it; it translates into imperious dignity, strength, a 'line', a calm and controlled bearing of soul, of word, of gesture. It gives place to a higher human type. By guiding the present theory of race to its logical consequences; by completing it with the consideration of those virile and ascetic values, which play so large a role in fascism; by recognising the fundamental inequality of beings, which is not restricted to the races, but concerns also individuals of one and the same race; by confronting therefore the selective and protective tasks that derive therefrom — by doing all of this, one cannot help but be led back, sooner or later, to this human ideal of the aristocratic tradition. But here the great problem poses itself, of the paths and the basis for practical realisation in these matters.

THE HEBRAISED NOBILITY:
THE PRACTICAL TASK

If heredity is a condition and traditions cannot be invented, it would be logical to seek in existing aristocratic lineages at least a part of the elements necessary for the work of which we have spoken above; in this way, the anti-bourgeois struggle could be brought to its terminus. Unfortunately, there are various difficulties with this solution in Italy. The principal of these is to be found in the fact that the Italian nobility was only minimally a *feudal nobility*. Now, the *relation between title and power* is the inescapable condition of any true aristocracy. It is necessary to have land, over which one can exercise a kind of partial sovereignty, putting to the test one's capacities of prestige, of responsibility, of organisation and of justice; land is required to love, to protect and to transmit, just as the tradition itself of the name and of the blood; such land is the material basis for the decorum and the independence of a family. This has been the state of affairs but little in Italy. Too many titles of nobility have been conferred in the past, light-heartedly by the ruling houses, as the simple ornaments and instruments of a mundane vanity, if not even as signs of corruption; for whoever has a title but no power or wealth, and who is absorbed by the vanity fair of salons and courts, is ever exposed to the temptation to procure for himself every expedient and means to keep to an artificial and conventional style of life. And it is commonly known to what extent this has facilitated the manoeuvres of Jewish infiltration.

At the same time, there has been no way in Italy to systematically employ a specific noble lineage in the role of a true political class, to constantly place before the nobleman functions and clear tasks which are natural to him, in which he may test his real capacities and impede the stagnation, the depression or the decadence of that which blood and tradition have gifted to the individual. And various other circumstances beyond these have brought it about that the present conditions of the aristocracy, even the Italian aristocracy, are something less than ideal.

Let no one at this point mention the exceptions. We are not speaking of exceptions; even a certain portion of the bourgeoisie could assert its exceptions. We are speaking rather of a visible and homogeneous elite, which bears witness in an unequivocal way to the spirit and the level of a civilisation and a society, by representing a tradition in the highest and most spiritual sense of the word. Now, it would be hasty to point to anything that even remotely approaches this within the salons and the milieus of our so-called 'high society', a sphere in which every kind of creature gathers, every kind of 'good name', but, at the same time, snobbism, internationalism and frivolities of every kind. Let us call things by their proper name: if there is any real antithesis to true nobility, it is constituted precisely by this 'worldly' and profane aristocracy, made up as it is by painted matrons and semi-virgins rushing from one tea party to the next, from one flirtation to the next; it is peopled by bridge-players and impeccable executors of the most exotic and ridiculous dances — a true vanity fair with every superficiality, gilded and cosmopolitanised to hide its intellectual vacuity and its spiritual scepticism — even when it opens its doors and invites to its luncheons and its cocktail parties the 'brilliant' literati, the novelist of the moment, the laurelled critic, the journalistic pontificator. Where is that hardness, where is that ascesis of power, where is that contempt for vanity proper to aristocracy, back when it was truly a dominant caste? What has become of that ancient Aryan title of the aristocrats, 'The enemies of gold'? The inbreeding of the international nobility with American girls, as rich as they are stupid and presumptuous, and with the Jewish plutocracy as well, is a well-documented fact and, while it fortunately has not reached among us the dimensions it has in other nations, still, even among us, how many today are not accustomed to confounding superiority with affluence and to welcoming in the parvenu who has learned the fashions of the clique and who, by means of the right connections and even of feminine wiles, has been introduced into 'high society'? And if in certain circles of the so-called 'black nobility'[4] or the like, worldly, cosmopolitan and modernist unscrupulousness has not yet conquered a certain traditionalism, still, in this traditionalism, what really subsists of the true and living traditional spirit, of its strength and its ascetic and heroic intransigence — all of which has nothing to do with conservative conformism, with prejudice, with moralism?

The problem of a new anti-intellectualist, ascetic and heroic aristocracy, almost feudal or barbaric in its hardness and in its refusal to attenuate its forms — an aristocracy not improvised, but legitimating itself with a tradition and with a 'race' — is fundamental. By it alone can bourgeois civilisation be overcome not with newspaper articles, but with deeds; by it alone can we arrive at a qualitative articulation of the State beyond totalitarianism, as has been discussed. But this problem is every bit as fundamental as it is arduous to resolve. To what extent can we seek a reawakening and a reintegration of those qualities which have become latent or degenerate in the surviving nobility? To what extent will it be necessary instead to 'begin anew', to force ourselves to create the germs of a new nobility — one not defined by individual merits or abilities of the secular and bourgeois sort, but by a superior formation of life, which is his to be jealously transmitted to a future posterity?

It is certain at least that we must prevent possible confusions, and must do everything in our power to see to it that the dead be distinguished from the living. The fact that there is a group of people who have the right to carry a noble title only because the Consulta

---

4   Italian, *nobiltà nera*. Reference to the nobility which maintained their faith with the Pope when the Savoys conquered the Papal States in 1870. The term referred to the fact that these nobles kept the doors of their palaces closed, to denote the Pope's self-imposed confinement. The term remained in use even after these events to denote that portion of the Italian nobility which maintained a more or less traditionalist Catholic attitude. In more recent decades, some of them threw their support behind Archbishop Marcel Lefebvre, founder of the anti-Vatican II fraternity, the Society of Saint Pius X. — Trans.

Araldica[5] has recognised it to them, and because they live an 'orderly' life so far as regards bourgeois conventions and the Penal Code, represents, so far as we are concerned, something lethal to prestige, potency and the possibility of the revival of the true aristocracy. We hold that traditional titles, which serve no end if not inflaming private and worldly vanity — which is to say, artificially clearing a path for that vanity — we hold that these titles are incompatible with the realistic spirit of fascism and, at the same time, that they should be the objects of a clear contempt on the part of whoever is truly aristocratic and desires the aristocracy as a potency and as a reality, not as mere smoke and decorations for the Parisian salons. We hold that a revision, a selection of the nominally heraldic nobility is incumbent. If having a bourgeois soul gives one the right to carry an aristocratic title, it is clear that this title is no longer worth anything, that it no longer signifies anything; it is the instrument, not of distinction, but of confusion.

The test to which the surviving nobility could be put, toward the end of discrimination, would be at bottom easy enough. It is a question of *constraining them to not renounce what they are.* As in the traditional civilisations, a title, a power and an office must be once more united indissolubly. Whoever has a title and is a man must be excluded from the empty life of the salons, of tea parties, of fashionable hotels and of the 'high society'; he should be constrained to take up once more that which belonged to his fathers — if his nobility is true — and which he, in the modern world, has cheerfully renounced so as to degrade himself in the worldly life: with his title, he should be constrained to assume a charge and a power, an absolute responsibility, and to do this with the understanding that it must be natural for him to give to an extent that would be exceptional and unnatural for others. Only should he pass this test could his title be confirmed and come to mean anything.

---

5   The 'College of Arms', established in 1869 to advise the newly united Italian government on matters relating to heraldry, nobility etc. — Trans.

It matters not if in this trial by fire many will fail. That will be nothing but a good for the aristocracy. Indeed, this is the unique condition by which the aristocracy will be able to rise again, selected and dominant, offering precious elements for integrating the political hierarchy of the new State with a kind of New Order, whose efficacy is derived from its qualities and its lofty interior bearing. Without the emergence of this Order, it will be difficult to supply its absence with surrogates, and the present confusion will persist: there will be an *aristocracy of the spirit* which is not that of class, not the patrician aristocracy, and there will be a patrician and heraldic aristocracy consisting of the marginal survival of a true aristocracy of isolated individuals, all wavering amidst the fog of the bourgeois imitations of elitism. The hard, Roman construction of the new State, especially if it should be put to the test of a grand new heroic experience, is destined to swiftly rise beyond this fog.

2. CUSTODIAN ARISTOCRACY

NYONE WHO SEEKS, from the point of view of an integrally assumed aristocratic idea, to handle certain books, like that recently published by R. R. Petitto,[1] is sure to find himself in a certain perplexity. Indeed, on the one hand, one cannot help but rejoice to observe that even today there is someone who demonstrates a certain sensibility for the ancient values of monarchy, of fidelity, of honor and of aristocracy; but on the other hand, one must deplore the lack of that solid doctrinal foundation, which alone can justify such values and conduct them to a decided expression.

That 'traditionalism' which Petitto defends in the book just now indicated, and perhaps despite what he himself believes, is above all of an 'empirical', which is to say habitual, type; it lives of nostalgia for an image drawn from the society of yesterday without being aware that this image already constitutes a compromise and a limiting deviation with respect to pure principles. It is also empirical in a second sense: in its dreaming of 'political' demands, in its tending to form that which is today called a 'movement'. Precisely because he does not have in view the aristocratic idea in its — so to speak — supertemporal purity, Petitto does not note the absurdity in thinking that today, in this Western society sustained by the truth of servants and of the

---

1   R. R. Petitto: *Aristocrazia custode*, trans.V. Gatti, Brescia, 1931.

merchants,[2] there remains any effective possibility for a true 'restoration', such as would not merit mockery and being put in a leash.

Today as never before it is necessary to keep oneself intransigently on the crest of the mountain peaks: to create unspannable distances between values of various kinds. Only in this way can we be 'custodians' of the 'tradition'. There is no need for those who keep themselves busy by descending into the marketplace, but there is need for those who have the force and the courage to integrally maintain, unaltered, the tradition of principles, such that this might bear witness to itself on that day that a new cycle of culture finally takes its start from the exhaustion of that 'humanistic' and anarchistic cycle which has unfurled in the West, starting from the Commons and from the Renaissance — if one does not even wish to include in this account the Christian revolution itself, which the medieval feudal and imperial idea sought to reign in.

Already from that which has been mentioned so far, it is apparent that we can follow Petitto, wherever he speaks to us of the most material aspect of the aristocratic idea. Hence the principle that *no State and no society can maintain itself without an elite or aristocracy of families, hereditarily selected and specialised in the core tasks of commanding* — an elite, which has its natural crown in legitimate monarchy, legitimate both in its formal seat and its dynastic right, and in its material aspect of the effective conformity of the monarch as a person to the traditional principles which define his dignity and his function (pp. 118, 16–18). This thesis of Petitto is certainly right. As has already appeared in a distinct form in the defenders of the traditional idea within the new Germany (Everling, Darré, Rosenberg, etc.), the principle of honour and of fidelity takes its place as the true cement of

---

2   We do not use these expressions in the disparaging sense, but in that which they take on when viewed from the vision of the regression of the caste, which we have enlarged in this very same Journal, no. 3 of 1931, under the title *The Two Faces of Nationalism*. [Trans. note: See Chapter 4 of the part on 'The State' in the present volume.]

the political compages. The sense of honour and the pride in serving one's proper prince, above every other advantage and every personal interest, is for Petitto the watermark of true aristocracy, that which makes it fit to cover the highest offices.[3] Fidelity in the place of mere obedience: personal devotion with respect to a lord, about whom it can no longer be said that he 'rules, but does not govern', in the place of passive subordination to institutions or faceless laws.

Save that already here Petitto makes a few false steps, which betray the uncertainty of his ideas. He writes (p. 65), 'Those who fill the highest roles of the State should be those who do not know anything of earning money, and who are rather capable of feeling the joy and the pride in being permitted to serve' — to serve whom? — 'to serve the people, for the honour of serving the people' (the same expression occurs on page 95). In this it is no longer the aristocrat of whom we are speaking, but rather the tribune of the plebe, that root of a large part of the ideas on political governance that have prevailed amongst the moderns. An aristocrat does not serve the 'people', but serves his prince.

Following this, a second false step. Petitto asserts, with good reason, the right of the idea of hereditary gentility, and adds (p. 58), 'The family has not only commonality of blood, but also is as a perpetual body and a perpetual soul. The body consists in the good of the family which each generation receives from its ancestors as a sacred trust, to be conserved religiously, to be expanded and transmitted faithfully to future generations. The soul consists in traditions, that is the ideas of the ancestors, in their sentiments and their customs'. And, further (p. 86), 'Heredity, for the continuity which it assures the social body, is an imitation, and a worthless one without a doubt, of the divine perpetuity'.

Save that, when one makes the objection that the logical consequence of such an idea is the regime of castes, he, rather than at once

---

3   Cf. the article by G. Glaesses: '*Che cosa vogliono gli Elmi d'acciaio?*' in *Antieuropa*, n. 3, 1931.

affirming, with open countenance, this presupposition of all true aristocratic spirit,[4] rather discards it, and says that the consequence thereof is not so much the caste, as it is... professional tradition (p. 86), adding moreover that those 'new men' can be assumed as aristocrats 'who are mobilised by themselves' (p. 9): the which are manifest and contradictory antitraditionalistic concessions to the modern spirit. The professional traditions pertain of course to a healthy ordering of the lower classes, but from the time that the world has begun, have had nothing to do with aristocracy: a Roman would never have confused the *corporationes* and the *collegia* of the artisans with the ranks of the patricians and of the *gentiles* — nor indeed in the Medieval Period could the German *Gilden* and the *Zünften* have raised themselves to the level of or put themselves in contact with the noble class.[5] Moreover, given that it is Petitto himself who writes (p. 47) that 'In normal times, work and austerity, property conserved and grown permit one to enter into the bourgeois; the nobility requires other virtues of a higher order' — he should be the first to recognise his false step. Regarding the second point, that on the breaking of the castes and the election of a new nobility, he might find an attenuating circumstance for himself, given that he is probably ignorant of the entire body of metaphysical presuppositions on which the ancient regime of castes justified itself, in conformity, not to some principle of convention, but to certain laws of the transcendent part of the human being.[6]

The critique Petitto brings against that aristocracy which today in society has been reduced to a graceful and useless bibelot in a salon (p. 23), which is to say to a titled bourgeoisie (p. 32), as well as his

4   Cf. our writings on '*Difesa delle caste*', in *Tevere*, n. 26 and 27, October 1928, and on '*Significato dell'Aristocrazia*', in *Krur*, n. 2, 1929.

5   Cr. H. Waltzing: *Les Corporations professionelles chez les Romains*, Luovain, 1895, Vol. I and II; O. Gierke: *Rechtsgeschichte der deutschen Genossenschaft*, Berlin, 1868, Vol. I.

6   One might refer, for instance, to the doctrine of survival after death and the reincarnation of certain parts of the human being according to the 'law of actions', all of which are professed in India and in Iran, as well as in classicism.

protestation against the fact that by now the rich are considered to stand on the same level as the nobles (p. 39) and against other symptoms of degeneration, though it has not been done with the necessary energy,[7] finds us perfectly acquiescent. Equally just is his idea that the nobility which moves to the city or the court is destined to decadence. 'An extremely grave cause of the decadence of the Italian patriciate was owed to the fact that in many regions here the nobles did not exercise power over true feudal domains and lived instead in the city. An urbane nobility is a contradiction in terms, and in Italy the nobility was precisely such as that, or at least some three quarters of it' (p. 34). But once a thought like this has been taken on, it is necessary to take it to its ultimate conclusions, and say in clear words what economic and political order which would on this basis be necessary, with a return precisely to the Medieval Period, understood in a healthy way;[8] all the more so, given that Petitto once more converges with the feudal idea when he affirms that 'a levelling and hyper-centralising Caesarism is in reality nothing but demagoguery, though it be enthroned, coronated and sceptred' (p. 120). Yet in the book which we are discussing nothing of any of this is to be found, most likely to avoid too clear a contrast with the modes which have come into use in modern times.

Let us pass to the fundamental point. What characterises the aristocratic caste? First premise: 'The differentiation of men on the basis of money is the most insolent of differences, and can create no hierarchy but one built of resentment and hatred' (p. 77). Very well. On the other hand, it is not enough to speak of 'heredity', because heredity can be composed of different things and, in ancient times, not only the aristocratic, but also the other castes were founded on heredity. Heredity of what, however? Petitto makes an important proclamation,

---

7   Cf. on the other hand the courageous statements of the Duke of Lauriano in his writing 'Casta aristocratica e spirito aristocratico', issued by La Torre (n. 8, 1930) and the appreciation it received in the Neues Wiener Journal of 7 February 1931.

8   This kind of problem is amply treated in the work of Darré: Neuadel aus Blut und Boden, Munich, 1930.

which is today fundamental, when he submits that neither intelligence, nor courage, nor culture, nor dexterity alone suffice to define the essence of the aristocrat (pp. 9–10).

But after this, he makes no further steps forward. In reality, he ends up in a rather *secular* concept of aristocracy. Instead of reaching the traditional idea, according to which a 'sacred' quality, and therefore a quality superior to the 'human' domain is incorporated in the aristocrat, so as to define his essence and to justify his authority, he mutates all of this into a quality of character, of morality and of devotion, qualities which evidently continue to be a part of the human sphere. Here it is likely that Petitto does not comprehend this. And it would moreover make for a long discussion, which we have, incidentally, taken up various times and have not introduced for the first time today,[9] precisely toward the end of illuminating the original and effective sense of aristocracy. It will have to suffice presently to say that in the type of the noble 'custodian of morality' and thence of 'religion' (religion in the modern sense), we are not in the least prepared to recognise the true aristocrat. The aristocrat, *in primis et ante omnia*, is the *Lord*, and as such moves more in domains 'beyond good and evil' than in spheres of morality, and, in general, of the laws or customs that are democratically imposed on all.[10] Petitto perhaps has sufficient acquaintance with history in general and with the history of law in particular to know something of this: and given that he is counter to the 'new forms', he will not wish that, to content him, we stop up at a society which is already decadent and anti-aristocratic, which is the

9   Cf. e.g. *Imperialismo Pagano*, Rome, 1928 and '*Gerarchia tradizionale e umanismo moderno*' in nn. 2–3 of *Torre*.

10   With this we do not intend to defend some ill-conceived notion of a Nietzschean 'superman'. If true aristocracy knows nothing of moralism — an essentially plebeian-bourgeois creature — it however did know an ethics, which was its own and proper to it, to which the other classes had no right to refer themselves and which did not have a 'social' fundament, but rather a 'sacred' one. Cf. F. DeE Coulanges: *La Cité Antique*, Paris, 14, 1900, 1. IV, cc. 4–6.

very same which has taken its beginnings in the post-medieval history and after the importation of creeds of Semitic origin.

Regarding the second point, it should be said that Petitto has the air of one who does not know that the Guelph ideal of nobility is an ideal which, from the point of view of principles, effectively represents a compromise, a mixture of contradictory things. On this basis he will understand in what sense we can say that his aristocratic idea is essentially 'laical': it is laical because in it the principle of the 'sacred' is located outside of the aristocracy, in a distinct hierarchy which is supposed to be higher than the gentile class. His 'loyalty' goes to this other hierarchy (p. 39): 'It is only by making itself the protector of the church that the aristocracy is preserved as a class. Its pole star is the church: only guided by the church will it avoid error'. Since things stand in this way, we would like to know what place remains for loyalty to the sovereign. Naturally, there is no contradiction here if the monarch himself is considered in his turn as the first of the church's servants, as the Thomistic and Guelphic theses had him. Save that Petitto, in defending this view, cannot help but adduce examples which are precisely taken from 'new' times. In traditional antiquity, the priestly function and the royal function were one and the same thing, and the patrician cast was simultaneously a sacred caste: indeed, from this came the foundation of its 'legitimate' authority'.[11]

The priest was often only an emanation of primitive regality.[12] Moreover, every true aristocracy takes its sense only from the framework of this kind of conception, which does not culminate in the Guelphic idea of the church, but rather in that of empire, conceived of as a sacred and 'supernatural' institution, of the same authority as

---

11 Cf. De Coulanges, op. cit., e C. Bouglé: *Essai sur le régime des castes*, Paris, 1908. In Servius: *Ad Aen.*, II, 268, we read: '«*Majorum haec erat consuetude ut rex esset etiam sacerdos et pontifex*'».

12 It was such, for example the tradition of the king Numa, who supposedly instituted the *flamen* (Livy, I, 20).

JULIUS EVOLA

the church.[13] For this reason, a Frederick II could say that princes are servants if they recognise the authority of the church, and free men if they recognise that of the emperor: this is the resonating echo — albeit in a world already altered by the Christian vision of life — of the true and universal tradition, known to both Hellas and Rome, as much to Iran and Egypt as China. Only in this case does loyalty to the lord become something more than a purely civic and political, and therefore laical and human, virtue; it is rather — following the medieval expression — *fides*, a participation which we would almost call mystical with the 'sacred' force incarnated by the lords.[14]

If Petitto had the slightest feeling for such horizons as these, he would notice the whole 'bourgeoisie' which has its good and 'black' nobility,[15] faithful to the 'morality' and devoted to the church; and he would recognise also another important thing: that the so-called 'saintliness' is not a quality superior to an aristocracy integrally understood (p. 49) but a quality of a different order altogether. The *Lord* and the *Saint* are not two successive ranks in a single hierarchy, but they are two opposite ideals, belonging, in accordance with their respective spirits, to opposite conceptions of life, however much they might have certain characteristics in common: e.g. a certain ascetic bearing, well-armed and wed to a sense of dominion in the one form, whilst turned toward mystico-devotional dedication in the other.[16] The 'Lord' who makes himself a 'saint' at bottom betrays his own tradition, and the most recent history demonstrates many examples of this to us precisely because in it the aristocracy no longer contained within itself simultaneously a 'sacred' character on the one hand and a political,

13 Cf. J. Bryce: *The Holy Roman Empire*; A. De Stefano: *L'Idea imperiale di Federico II*, Florence, 1927; J. Evola, '*Spiritualità imperiale e autorità religiosa*' in *Vita Nuova*, n. 12, 1929.

14 Cf. More-Davy: *Des clans aux Empyres*, Paris, 1926.

15 Reference to the so-called *nobiltà nera*. See footnote 4 to the chapter 'The Meaning of Aristocracy for the Anti-Bourgeois Front' above. — Trans.

16 Cf. Coudenhove-Kalergi: *Held oder Heiliger*, Vienna, 1927.

moral and military one on the other; it rather possessed only these latter qualities. Even in Rome a consul could not dream of converting himself into a priest, because as consul he already *was* priest, and if he had not had the proper investiture following the rites and the traditional patriciate dignity of his *gens*, he would not have become consul at all. And the *patres* were certainly 'custodians of the faith', but not in the sense of their being dependent on a church or on an external creed which held good as much for the patricians as for the plebeians, *but rather because they incarnated and possessed the mystical force of their* gens.[17]

And if we add that Petitto's assertion to the effect that 'the Catholic premise is at the basis of every conception of order' (p. 15) is rather singular (given that, according to it, India with its castes, China, even the Rome of the Caesars, and so forth, are not permitted to possess any true order!) we do not comment in such a manner in order to throw down some kind of anti-Catholic gauntlet, but only to indicate the limits surrounding the only 'traditionalism' that Petitto gives any demonstration of knowing. To be serious traditionalists, and not mere partisans or dilettantes, we must indeed be 'catholics', but taking this word in its primary sense, given that in Ancient Greek 'catholic' means 'universal'. Which is to say that it is not a matter of holding fast to the habits and the factious exclusivisms of a given historical tradition, but rather of rising to the principles, which stand above every particular historical tradition and, at the same time, stand at their base, in the same way that one and the same meaning can stand behind verbal expressions through the words of various languages. It is a question of taking one's bearings firmly by these principles, recognising in them the primordial and 'non-human' element of every order, quite irrespective of ever particularism and every empirical condition. And in Catholicism in the strict sense, even leaving aside those characteristics for which it is not fit to be the premise for a truly aristocratic

---

17   Cf. René Guénon: *Le symbolisme de la Croix*, Paris, 1931, pp. 9–10.

idea, there are all too many of such limitations and such particular-
isms. From this, too, it will be understood from what point of view we
spoke, when at the beginning of this essay we indicted the 'empiristic'
character of the views defended by Petitto's book.

And if Petitto here were to bring against us the predictable accusation that we have wound up in abstract evocations and that we have
failed to take into account the concrete side of the immediate historical traditions — which is to say, that we have failed to take into account 'reality' — we would reply as it were with a point of order. There
are but two possibilities: either the criterion is precisely the 'concrete',
so-called 'reality', in which case it would be senseless to speak of legitimacy in the first place, and the very same aristocratic ideas held by
Petitto, which come down to him from the generations of the previous
century, can already be accused of not taking into account the 'concrete' revolutionary or constitutional — or federalistic, or syndicalistic,
or corporative, or communistic or plutocratic currents which have *de
facto* 'triumphed' and which ever more dominate in a world in which
little or nothing remains of sensibility for aristocratic values, even in
their ethics and their castes; either this is true, or the criterion is to be
sought in the intimate value of principles, such that if 'concrete reality'
does not follow them, nothing remains to us but to say, 'So much the
worse for it!' — only that then we cannot stop up halfway, as Petitto
does, but we needs must purify the traditions of every empirical and
particularistic trace, and truly rise to the origins, in the sense of the
great primordial traditions, leaving the church and all the rest of it by
the wayside.

So far as we are concerned — and certainly this is not a novelty, nor
is it meant to please anyone — we hold ourselves firmly to the second
alternative, observing in all serenity how much this modern world,
with that accelerating speed proper to falling bodies, ever distances
itself further from every vision of effective hierarchy and aristocratic
spirituality. Petitto's traditionalism seems rather to be of a different
kind, and he is consequently very optimistic: so much so that he fills

the second half of his book with statements, platitudes and speeches regarding a species of curious, and almost 'political', 'movement of nobles'. We do not know what this 'movement' could desire, and with all our good will we would not be able to decide whether or not to take it seriously. Despite all of this, Petitto seems to us to be a sincere person of good faith: and for this there is nothing else to do but to wish him a speedy end to his illusions, hoping that through a broader study of the traditions he might come to comprehend what is the single plane on which it is still possible to be, not a 'custodian aristocracy', but 'custodians of the aristocracy'.

EPILOGUE: REGARDING 'CUSTODIAN ARISTOCRACY'

Someone in the *Bibliografia Fascista* has felt the need to 'comment' on our essay on 'Custodian Aristocracy'. We are not altogether certain what the writer of this comment (reproduced by the Ambrosiano) might have desired to obtain. But the mystifying intention in it is so evident that it merits a few words by way of response.

Essentially, it seems that the terrible accusation has been levelled against us that we 'ignore the efforts of the most recent philosophy', which is to say, Gentilian idealism; this, as well as writing 'magic books' and inviting our readers on voyages toward the 'Oriental mysteries'. The commentator thus pretends not to know that while we have indeed written books on 'magic' (we willingly accept the word) and on Oriental metaphysics in the same sense in which a Tucci or a Formichi might take an interest in such matters, we have at the same time written various other books of pure philosophy, in which, moreover, far from ignoring them, we have spent altogether too much time liquidating the presumptions of the so-called 'idealism'.

The commentator says that we have accused Petitto of 'having wished to write a book on politics without considering India and Iran'. With good reason does he guard then against saying that, beyond India and Iran, we have made reference also to our own classical Roman world, which is found, in this respect, to possess *equivalent* traditional conceptions. Moreover, it must be said that the book does not treat of 'politics', but of the aristocratic idea, which is to us something rather different. And we accused the author of neglecting the spiritual premises of that world to which, in its pure and original sense, the concept of aristocracy belongs: a world, respect to which the 'point of view of idealism' is quite simply the point of view of ignorance itself.

The commentator satisfies himself with that 'history which is what it is, which is explained through its causes and its consequences' — which is to say, precisely as one explains phenomena of matter and the habits of beasts. But let him keep such ideologies to himself and to the few officiants of the cult of a certain kind of 'university' philosophy; the logical consequence of these ideologies, which are of a profane, novel and plebeian character, cannot be aught other than Marxist historical materialism. We have in view one thing and one thing only: the defence of the traditional spirit, which is identical beyond all of its various expressions, be they Oriental or Occidental — and the ideal of a society animated by such a spirit, which is as much as to say the absolute right of pure spirituality over everything human and conditioned. Are these words obscure? The commentator has already well enough indicated where one might go to clarify them; enough is as good as a feast. Let him call us, if he will, anachronists. In point of fact we do not feel that we belong in any way to the 'modern world', which, moreover, we know all too well; but let him be persuaded that if there is any attempt to 'pick the locks of the doors of the centuries', this is precisely the attempt made by his 'historicism' itself; and it is an attempt as vain as it is risible.

3. ON THE ESSENCE AND THE PRESENT FUNCTION OF THE ARISTOCRATIC SPIRIT

1. THERE EXISTS an aristocratic spirit and then there exist its various manifestations, tied to time and to space. These manifestations, as such, have a contingent character, they possess a specific genesis, a development, eventually a corruption and a twilight. The aristocratic spirit however is superior and prior to every one of these. It corresponds to a degree of reality, to a primordial function in the whole. It therefore has a superhistorical, and one can even say metaphysical nature. As such, it persists beyond birth and beyond the decline of the historical aristocracies which incarnate it more or less perfectly in a given period and in the cycle of a given civilisation and a given race.

Like the idea of the *Regnum* and of order, or of tradition, so the aristocratic idea contains in itself its own consecration and legitimation. Already the twilight has fallen within the inner man when there rises the supposition that it is 'history' which creates a *Regnum*, an aristocracy or a tradition, and that these things are justified and have their worth on the basis of contingent factors, or factors of utility or of purely material domination, or of suggestion. History and, in general, all merely human things, can offer at most the *dynamis*, the deep force which forms a *Regnum* and manifests an aristocratic spirit in any given circumstances. But in its deepest essence, this manifestation is enveloped in a mystery: it is the mystery which affirms itself wherever the higher paths meet the lower, wherever correspondences are realised between the highest heights of human ascent and the issuance of influences which are more than human. These points of interference are the fateful moments of history. They are the points in which symbol becomes reality and reality becomes symbol, in which spirit transforms into power and power transfigures into spirit.

2. One of the commonest tactics of the secret forms of global subversion is the substitution of the person for the principle. Wherever one aims at decomposing a traditional order, these forces spy out the moment in which a certain kind of decadence becomes manifest in the historical representatives of the fundamental principles of this same order. This is the most opportune point for subversive action: everything is done so that the process brought against individual persons might extend itself imperceptibly to the principles which these persons represent, so that the principles themselves are afflicted with the same discredit and are therefore thought to be obsolete, in need of substitution by others which are more or less saturated in subversion. This tactic has been long adopted against a certain traditional European aristocracy. The undeniable degenerescence of a part of this aristocracy was the most useful tool possible for an attack against the aristocratic spirit itself: it brought with it, not the request that this decadent aristocracy be shriven of its authority and substituted with another which might be equal to its animating idea, and from which alone it might draw its authority and its *raison d'être*, but rather the disavowal of the idea itself, to the profit of lower forces and ideas.

This was, moreover, naught but an episode in a much broader process of subversion and involution, which it would be well here to briefly recapitulate. Let us recall the four fundamental degrees of the ancient Aryan social hierarchy: the spiritual lords, the warrior aristocracy, the bourgeoisie, and the workers.

The degeneration of the first degree did not bring it about that the unworthy spiritual lords might be substituted by other worthy representatives of the same principle, but it rather became the precious pretext by means of which the second degree, the warrior aristocracy, was brought to usurp and to assume the authority which was legitimate only to the first. Subsequently, the degeneration of a part of the warrior aristocracy did not have as its consequence an uprising aiming at its restoration, but rather a second usurpation, this time operated by the third estate, which substituted itself for the warrior nobility as a bourgeois plutocracy. Finally the degeneracy of the system of the third estate, of the bourgeois and of capitalism, did not lead to a timely elimination of the diseased and parasitic excrescences of this system, but, once again, a process against the principle itself was brought about by it, favouring the attempt at a further usurpation on the part of the fourth estate, of the materialised and proletarised world of the masses (Marxism, Bolshevism).

3. From this brief historical reprisal, it will also be clear that the knowledge of the essence and of the importance of the aristocratic principle is fundamental in the struggle against subversion, and that it is fundamental for a correct orientation above all in times of change, like that in which we presently find Western Civilisation to stand.

Today, our renewing movements have aligned themselves spiritually and materially against bourgeois civilisation and the bourgeois spirit, against the plutocracy, against capitalism. They will the end of the 'bourgeois epoch'. There are however two paths toward the negation of the bourgeoisie and toward bringing the end of the 'bourgeois' epoch which are not only different from one another, but even antithetical. In following the first, the bourgeoisie with all its derivations is overcome so as to give way to the dominion of the masses. From the other point of view, the true overcoming of the bourgeoisie marks the return of an aristocratic idea, which is to say the idea from which, on account on the one hand of the degeneration of a part of its representatives, on the other hand by way of usurpation, the hegemony of the bourgeois and of the idols of the bourgeois — capital, gold, the faceless economy without fatherland — took its place.

This same alternative might clarify a further point of view. Our renewing movements undeniably have certain aspects of 'totalisation' and of socialisation, which are externally similar to those that are proper also to the social Marxist-communist 'ideal'. How much validity does that absurd supposition possess to the effect that, albeit by different roads, our movements pertain to the end of a cycle, to which is proper precisely a regress from that which is differentiated, qualitative, and personal to the anonymity of the collective? To respond to this question we must first clarify that the phenomenon of totalitarianism and of statal concentration has two contrary meanings, depending on the 'direction' and the type of regime of the society which has preceded it. But, in this respect, today the essential testing stone is the new aristocratic idea.

Let us suppose for a moment that the order existing prior to the 'localisation' is that of a well-society articulated — not artificially, but by a natural vocation — in strata, which are not closed and antagonistic, but which are the orderly agents of concert in a hierarchical whole: let us furthermore imagine that the differentiation and the anti-collectivism of such a society are expressed through a certain redistribution of power and of sovereignty, in a certain redistribution of functions and of particular rights, over which however there reigns a central authority, reinforced rather than diminished in its pure, immaterial principle precisely on account of this partial decentralisation. If centralism and totalitarianism are affirmed in such a society, this would signify a destruction and a disarticulation, the regression of the organic into the amorphous. To absolutistically concentrate every power in the centre would be akin, in such a case, to wishing to directly refer every function and every activity of the body to the brain, which amounts to realising the condition of those inferior animals which are constituted only by a head and by an unarticulated and undifferentiated body.

This and nothing else is the sense of anti-aristocratic and levelling absolutism, such as was pursued methodically, under the pressure of various circumstances, by the kings of France above all.

It is no accident that it was precisely in France, through the Jacobin revolution, where there first emerged the demagogy and the advent of the third estate. The absolutistic kings, enemies of the aristocracy, literally dug their own graves. While on the one hand their dignity secularised and lost its original consecration in the centralisation, hollowing[1] and disarticulating the State, setting a bureaucratico-statal superstructure in the place of virile forms, directed by authority, by responsibility and by partial, personal sovereignty, they created a void around themselves, because the vain court aristocracy no longer signified anything, and the military aristocracy was by then devoid of any direct relations with the country. Having destroyed the differential structure which acted as a medium between the function and the sovereign, there remained nothing but the nation as mass, detached from the sovereign and from his secularised sovereignty. With a single blow, the revolution easily swept away that superstructure and placed power into the hands of the pure masses. This is an example of the first, involutive direction of the process of totalitarising the state.

The question is altogether different when the antecedent to the process of authoritarian concentration is not an organic, hierarchical and differentiated order, but rather a society in dissolution, as is the case in the modern epoch. Liberalism, democracy, rationalism, and internationalism had reduced the nations to the state of unstable masses that were about to disperse in every direction and to reach the bottom of the slope, represented by Marxism and Communism. In the face of such a state of affairs, the first and most urgent task was evidently that of creating by all means available a dyke, a break, to neutralise the centrifugal tendency with a centripetal political force. This is precisely the sense which should be ascribed to the process

---

1   Italian: *disossando*, lit. 'deboning'. — Trans.

of totalisation of our movements of renewal. After having acquitted this first task, that which will immediately present itself is the task of newly articulating this nation which has been brought back to itself, unified under the insignia of myths and various symbols: it is a matter of withdrawing it from all forms of collectivism, and giving birth to a stable hierarchical structure, well formed, with clear emphasis given to the principle of the personality and, moreover, of true spiritual authority.

But to recognise this means also to recognise that it is precisely the aristocratic idea, as a direction, which differentiates the two cases: it is this idea on the basis of which currents which belong historically to the end of a cycle are neatly differentiated from other currents which already represent the principle of resurrection and of reconstruction beyond internationalism and the collectivistic collapse.

4. The aristocratic spirit being prior and superior to any single one of its manifestations, a deep comprehension of that spirit is presupposed by the problem of any concrete aristocratic formation. We must in any case bear in mind that, so far as its reconstruction is concerned, we are not dealing with a merely political class, connected more or less to the administrative or legislative body of the State. It is rather a question of a prestige and an example which, connected to a very clear stratum, must be able to form an atmosphere, crystallise a higher style of life, awaken special forms of sensibility, and thus give the tone to a new society. We might think therefore of a kind of Order, according to the virile and ascetic meaning that this term had in the Ghibelline Middle Ages. But it would be better still to recall the most ancient Aryan and Indo-Aryan societies, wherein, as is known, the elite was not in any way materially organised, nor drew its authority from its representing any given tangible power or any given abstract principle, but nonetheless firmly maintained its rank and gave the tone to the corresponding civilisation by means of a direct influence issuing from its essence.

The modern world knows a great many counterfeits of elitism, from which we must distance ourselves. The aristocratic spirit is essentially anti-intellectualistic. In the first place, we must take a clear position against the so-called 'aristocracy of thought'. The superstitious cult of 'thought' belongs typically to the same bourgeois civilisation which we combat; it invented this cult and it diffused it for specific polemical reasons. In order to rid itself of the last remnants of the aristocracy of blood and of spirit, the bourgeois civilisation, after having consolidated itself with the advent of the third estate, invented the right of the 'true' aristocracy, the aristocracy of 'thought', a great many of whose members were the 'noble' princes prepared necromantically by Masonic Enlightenment. The return to a true aristocratic civilisation presupposes the overcoming of this bourgeois myth.

What is this 'aristocracy of thought'? It can be reduced for the most part to the famous 'intellectuals', to the creators of 'philosophies' which are as brilliant as they are arbitrary, to the poets, the literati, the humanists. In short, to those people more or less that Plato, in consideration of the true lords and the true 'sages', rightly wished to banish from his State — which was in no way, as is vulgarly believed, a utopian model, but rather reflected that which traditionally was always held to be normal in political orders. It suffices to merely speak aloud the idea that an elite of intellectuals, of humanists, of thinkers, all of whom might also be in terms of their characters cowards and little more than petty bourgeoisie, should stand at the zenith of a civilisation, in order to perceive how entirely absurd and anachronistic such an idea really is, not only in the face of the problem of the true aristocratic spirit, but even already with respect to the anti-intellectualism and the virilism proper to the current European movements of renewal.

5. Having thinned out the smoke of the progressivist and scientistic Enlightenment, we must also gain some distance from an 'aristocracy of thought' conceived of as being composed of scientists, inventors and technicians. All of these are doubtless useful and indispensable

elements for any society of the modern type, and the new idea of the
State, taking the place of the current demo-parliamentary one, will
certainly affirm the principle of various competencies in the field of
the political element itself. At the same time it is however evident that
not even this scientistic aristocracy can represent the suitable substance for the central nucleus of a new civilisation, beyond the civilisation of the bourgeoisie and collectivism. Indeed, such a thought
is much closer to Marxism and Bolshevism: namely, that an elite of
technicians, intent upon resolving purely material problems, can en-
lighten a collectivised humanity, putting themselves at its service, and
guiding it toward a new paradise, going so far as to demand for their
service a superior degree of recognition.

6. Nor is there even any identity between the aristocratic spirit and
any idea which is generically authoritarian and dictatorial. Already
the very existence today of a term like the 'dictatorship of the proletariat' proves the necessity of specifying what one means by dictatorship and authoritarianism. There have been some who have sought to
demonstrate that the phenomenon of elitism, which is to say a ruling
minority, is a fatal element of history. One author — Pareto — speaks
in this regard of a 'circulation of the elites', with one group of elites
substituting another, each emerging through a technique of dominion
which is more or less analogous to that employed by the last, making use of various ideas which, in this context, are less authentic ideas
than they are *myths*, carefully prepared centres of crystallisation for
suggestive irrational forces.

   In this regard, elitism would appear to be a purely formal concept:
a certain stratum is elite insofar as it is in power, and is able to exercise
a certain influence over power. The normal conception on the other
hand is that a certain stratum should be in power, that it should be
given to it to exercise a determinate influence, precisely insofar as it is
elite, meaning a selected group (*elite* stems from *eligo*)² having in itself

---

2   Latin for 'choose, select'. — Trans.

a superiority, a prestige and an authority which are inseparable from given immutable principles, by a given style of life, by a given essence.

The true aristocratic spirit cannot have any traits in common with Machiavellian and demagogical forms of dominion, as occurred for instance in the ancient popular tyrannies and in the plebeian tribunals. Nor can it take as its basis the theory of the 'overman', if one thinks of this overman only as a power resting on the purely individual and naturalistic qualities of violent and fearful figures. In its deepest principle, the substance of the aristocratic spirit is rather 'Olympian'; we have already said that it derives from a *metaphysical* order.

The basis of the aristocratic type is above all spiritual. The meaning of spirituality here has however little to do with the modern notion of spirituality: it is connected to an innate sense of sovereignty, to a disdain for profane, common, purchasable things, or anything born from ability, ingenuity, erudition or even genius — a disdain which closely resembles that of professed by the ascetic, differentiating itself from it however by its complete absence of pathos and resentment. One might state the essence of the true noble nature in this formula: *superiority over that life which has become nature or race.*

This superiority, which has about it something ascetic, does not serve in the aristocratic type to create antitheses in his being: like a second nature, it calmly stands above the inferior human part and permeates that part with itself; it translates into imperious dignity, in strength, in 'line', in calm and controlled bearing of soul, of word, of gesture. It thus gives birth to a human type, whose calm, intangible strength stands in clear contrast with the strength of the 'Titanic' kind, the Promethean and telluric. If antiquity symbolically attributed a 'celestial', Uranian origin to all the principal lineages, the bearers of the aristocratic spirit, one should perceive in this a clear recognition of this 'Olympian' core of the aristocratic essence. We recall the ancient Aryo-Hellenic conception of the νοῦς, which stood over this essence like a calm and still light. Thus it is that, in the myth, Promethean wile and audacity counted nothing against the Olympian νοῦς: nor could the tragedy of men and even of heroes touch this νοῦς. And whoever participates in it — it was believed — is truly of the royal bloodline, and participates also in the divine community proper to the primordial state. The lineages that are tied to these men constitute of themselves the higher races, the super-races, those that have positively resolved the oscillation between the human condition and the condition of what is more than human, which originally was the preserve of certain terrestrial bloodlines. A reflection of these super-historical meanings is ever preserved wherever in history there has been a realisation of a true aristocratic spirit.

7. Today there is much talk of race, and rightly so. But we must have care that we do not, by way of a generalisation, strip the notion of race of its power and empty it of its higher significance. Throughout history, the idea of race stood always in strict connection with the aristocratic idea, and this connection constantly impeded its materialisation in a kind of zoologism. To *have race* has always been fairly synonymous with aristocracy. The qualities of 'race' have always signified the qualities of the elite. They were opposed to the qualities of the vulgar man because they appeared, to a large degree, essential, innate, connected to higher meanings. To clarify these meanings, it is very important to distinguish between the various aspects of what is generally known as race. The first aspect is the race of the body, the second is the race as soul, the third is race as spirit. We are dealing with three very distinct manifestations of one and the same essence, to which correspond likewise distinct heredities, laws proper to each, given limitations. While in its first degree race is recognised in a given hereditary form of the physical figure, in the second it manifests in a given style of experience, and, in the third, in a given form of tradition.

In the highest form in which it appears, race is connected to a super-biological element, to gifts and forces such that in their purity might be realised and preserved only in an elite, and which in the mass are fatally dispersed. It can thus be said that while race is found in a diffuse manner in all the exponents of a given stock, it is realised in its higher degrees only in a given group, which, within that given stock, presents itself simultaneously as the most immediate substance for an incarnation of the aristocratic spirit. Here lives and is affirmed what we might well call the eternal race: the body of this manifestation is the tradition and the true exponents of the tradition, which represent the inner soul and the metaphysical core of biological race. Biological race, the race of the spirit, are in their turn the Olympian vein of the aristocratic lineage.

Tradition comes from the term *tradere*,[3] which means to transmit. In this regard there seem to be no limits for the content of the concept; anything which has been transmitted can be called tradition. From a higher point of view, matters stand otherwise. Indeed, transmission presupposes continuity, an identity of the contents, which is in its turn inconceivable without a certain overcoming of the temporal condition. There can thus be no talk of tradition in the higher sense wherever this content is not tied to something metaphysical and supertemporal. Tradition can have various forms of expression and of manifestation, conditioned by different circumstances, and these forms can often be mutable, sometimes apparently contradictory. But if this is not to be mere routine, the mechanical transmission of stratified customs, habits and ideas that become ever more opaque and subject to deformation, there must subsist, beyond exterior forms of expression, a deeper and more continuous vein, and men who have full, clear knowledge of this vein. There must be, therefore, *an esoteric of the tradition* which can take nothing for its natural basis of not those elements which are simultaneously the exponents of the aristocratic spirit. Here, at bottom, there is a reciprocal conditionality: tradition serves as the basis for the aristocratic spirit just as it serves as the basis of the tradition, which in its turn expresses the eternal race or the eternity of the race.

---

3   The verb in question is Latin. — Trans.

In this whole the apex and the most interior and subtlest force of a tradition and of the men of a tradition together constitute in a certain way the supernational element of a nation and the over-race of a race. From this there issues the possibility of an understanding and a solidarity under the ensign of the true aristocratic spirit, which the traditional past has always demonstrated in the order of peoples of common origin and which is reflected in certain familiar and racial customs of the previous European aristocracy. It is known that in the raising of animals, 'pure blood' is not always represented by that animal to arise from parents of the same species but might be also the product of a crossbreed between different parents, on the condition, however, the both parents are of identical class and identical purity. The qualities of pure blood on the other hand are dispersed and bastardised if they are crossed with an inferior type, even if it be of the same species. In the intuition of an analogous law from this, working on a higher plane, the system of super-national marriages between various dynasties and various aristocratic European families is carried out — a crossbreeding, that is, according to the principle of quality.

Even if this system has its darker side, nonetheless, at the bottom of it there stands a reflection of a higher truth: the principle of the communality of bloodlines on the basis of the race of spirit; unity and homogeneity through the zeniths, not through promiscuities which are attenuated through the zeniths, but through hierarchical culminations, on the basis of the metaphysical and eternal element potentially contained in each of them and inseparable from the substance of the qualified representatives of the true aristocratic spirit.

8. So far as contemporary racism is concerned, there exists a double possibility of interpretation which is absolutely analogous to that indicated for the phenomenon of totalitarian concentration: and in this case, too, the criterion for judgement is given by the aristocratic spirit.

Some have believed that the contemporary political racism can be considered as a chapter of 'humanism', in the more general sense of the word as a conception of the world and of life, at the centre of which stands essentially man. Beginning from the so-called Renaissance, we have seen the systematic action of the tendency to transfer to man the mystique of the divine, and, incredibly, this has happened all the more so, the more that man ceased to be considered as a privileged being of creation, that he came to be studied no longer on the basis of his origin and his supernatural destination, but rather as one among many natural, and in the end even animal, species. Thus pure anthropology, which in origin signified the science of man in general, in his physical and spiritual completeness, ended up taking on a new meaning: it was no longer the science of man as such, but of man as a being of nature, to whom classification methods could be applied similar to those of zoology and botany: it was a natural science of man. But at the same time the aforementioned tendency to divinise man was at work: it is to be seen already in work in the deist and Enlightenment-Masonic cult of 'humanity', developing so far as the Bolshevic mystique of the collective man and of technological messianism; but, according to the authors just alluded to, it appears also in much different tendencies, such as the tendency to divinise man as a substance of a given nation, of a given lineage, or indeed as a biological reality, as blood and race.

This interpretation, however, works only for certain extremist forms of racism, which, though they have an exclusively 'scientific' character in the modern materialistic and positivistic sense of the term, depart from the scientific field to promote a mysticism *sui generis*. But this is not the case for the whole of racism. Already beginning from de Gobineau its at bottom aristocratic foundation is indeed visible: racism affirmed itself in the modern world as a reaction against the morass of democratic egalitarianism and against the materialistic and antiqualitative climate which, at bottom, is proper to the climate in which scientism itself was incubated: and, by a curious inversion, racism was supposed to borrow various of its arms from this kind of scientism, and to seek in it its pretext. It is quite possible to discriminate and identify in racism the higher tendency just now indicated, understanding by this the principle of revolt against an internationalistic, levelling, rationalistic and plebeian society, and to sense in the return to the idea of race — and above all the idea of the superior race or the over-race — the renewal of a spiritual and aristocratic heritage which we have forgotten or irresponsibly dissipated.

Thus, wherever racism shows traces of its humanistic-materialistic component alone, it very well might occur that, in its extremistic forms, its ideal place falls toward the end of a cycle: having lost the sense of metaphysical reality and of the divine element of man, a certain part of Western civilisation[4] has come to consider man in and of himself — and, subsequently, man as a simple animal species, or, bringing him back to race, to a racial species — as an entirely biological reality; this civilisation thus formed a new mysticism for itself. But wherever racism resists the other component — that aristocratic component which, as we have recalled, exercised a clear influence on the early theoreticians of the 'masculine', 'diurnal' and 'active' races in the general myth of the dominating Aryan, Nordic-Aryan and Aryo-Roman race — whenever this comes to pass, the historical place of racism is very different and might fall at the beginning of a new reconstructive cycle: though it borrows the arms of the modern sciences to defend the race of the body, racism here has the possibility of using these arms against the materialistic, democratic and rationalistic conception proper to the last phases of Western decadence. By affirming, against that conception, the value of the blood, of the tradition, of the race, and intends to re-establish differences and hierarchies, racism can have the meaning of a restoration and a renewal of higher values.

It is the aristocratic spirit, moreover, which conditions this higher possibility of modern racism and, rightly, it is the organic and profound union already mentioned between concepts of race and of

---

4   Italian: *una certa civiltà occidentale*, literally 'a certain Western civilisation'. Evola is clearly not talking about the whole of Western civilisation here, but there is an indication that there are perhaps various 'Western civilisations' which take often contrary or incompatible stands on issues of key importance. — Trans.

degrees of rank within the race, of tradition and of the esoteric of tradition, and, finally, of a virile and spiritual elite, adherent to the ancient Aryan ideal of the Olympian spirit.

9. The fundamental function of a true aristocracy is to give the 'tone' to a civilisation, less through direct action than by means of a 'catalytic' action, which is to say an action exercised by simple presence. This idea must not however result in any dualism, giving birth to the supposition that those who have political power must not be exponents of the aristocracy in question and that, in their turn, those who are exponents of this aristocracy must not have any political power. We must rather consider the function of the representatives of the true aristocratic spirit as also a political function, and clarify it with some brief considerations.

There are far too many people who still today think it to be essential for political qualification that one has a fundamental lack of principles, if not even of character — that one possesses a plasticity and a ductility before the most contingent external circumstances, a realism of low grade. We believe rather that where one cannot find principles and spiritual values, one cannot speak of a true ruling class, not even in the political sense. Now, the part of the new aristocracy of the new State, in this respect, must be that of giving to all the sense of *terra firma*, of an immutable centre, superior to transient affairs and to contingencies, from which it naturally must not however withdraw, but over which it must assert itself so as to bring them back, with the fittest means, to the desired directions. Without this, no faith can be founded in a nation, no educational and formative work in the higher sense can be undertaken: because not even the use of myths suffices for this task, which is to say, of ideas which are not valuable for their intrinsic content so much as for their confused, irrational and subrational power of suggestion.

By way of the participation of the representatives of the true aristocratic spirit in the political ruling class, ethical and spiritual values,

harmonised amongst themselves and well-founded, should therefore
enter into a position of equilibrium with material and social values.
Thus those superior values would come to permeate the entirety of
man, to give an orientation to his activity and to render possible the
formation and the uninterrupted formation of gifts of character and
of 'race', of which the ruling political class should be the first to give
the example. These gifts are loyalty, sincerity, the sentiment of honour,
courage of not only a physical sense, but also intellectual and moral,
the force of decision. But to all of this should be added the tendency to
an authentic style, a lack of vanity, a virile and dignified impersonality.

We would like to introduce this expression: *the ascesis of power.*
These should be the effects of the aristocratic spirit on the ruling political elements. To give the sense of this power, we must make their
distinction from wealth evident. The political power that, by this path,
tends to secure for itself also a spiritual power, must affirm its full
independence from every power which is tied to wealth. It must have,
therefore not wealth, but something more: power over wealth.

Whoever truly has power and is conscious of being worthy of it,
whoever feels himself to be truly superior, also realises that every
kind of vanity and of personalism abase him: these are artificial and
fictitious forms of having worth before oneself and before others,
and he has no need of them. They have nothing to do with an Aryan,
Nordic-Aryan and Romano-Aryan style of life. Thus it is that a new
anti-intellectualistic ruling group might form up, ascetic and heroic,
almost feudal and barbaric in its hardness and insouciance of forms,
silent, compact and impersonal as an Order, but precisely for this reason realising a superior form of personality, one that is not improvised
but which justifies itself with a 'tradition' and with a 'race' experienced
in their deeper and more transcendent values.

The forces of this elite must not lose contact with the various
planes of the national life. Its task will be that in the framework of
various political, national and international problems, the most precise realisation of temporal ends proceeds apace with the adherence to

the fundamental ideas of their respective traditions and with respect to those essential values on which human dignity is founded and the very notion of personality.

It would thus be a question also of an action of inner edification, not dissimilar to that carried out, in civilisations of another nature, by the administrators of a given faith: with this difference, however, that there was in those cases the negation of every one-sided and lacerating dualism. In the modern world there surely prospers a rich throng of political myths, and the word 'mystique' itself is used in the most diverse and peregrine occasions. However, leaving aside cliches, we are living in an epoch in which it is not easy to give to men the sense of the deepest reason for which they work, for which they should set themselves beneath a discipline, for which they generate, for which they strain themselves and for which they often offer themselves up for sacrifice or for a heroic death. In this field our leaders should, by means of word, example, action, and every way possible, offer an example; they should show a path; they should infuse a higher transfiguring meaning into every form of life and of action of the new, anti-bourgeois and anti-collectivistic man.

We recall a view that was classical and Aryan long before it was taken up and in a certain degree altered by the predominant Western faith: there exist two States, the one great and comprehending at once both the human forces and the divine forces — *qua dii atque homines continentur* — and the other in which one is bound to destiny from one's birth. 'There are beings who simultaneously serve the one and the other state, others only the lesser, others only the greater' (Seneca). An ancient Nordic saying has it that 'Let him who is lord be a bridge to us' — that is, a connection between two shores, between two worlds, to comprehend in himself the nature of both. The original, pre-Christian sense of the term *pontifex* is the same: 'maker of bridges' — as meant as well the term which designated, in the ancient Indo-Aryan civilisation, the function that the totality of the spiritual lords bore in themselves.

This function remains the same for every array of men, which in any given point during history goes to incarnate the aristocratic spirit in its high power. This is at the same time an ethical function: the ascesis of power, the testimony to a higher human type. This is also a political function, because it is the duty of the lords to show how holding fast to any given post in the temporal state can assume at the same time the meaning of a holding fast on the front of the inner and transcendent State, for which one might combat in every exterior enemy the same enemy that is to be conquered in oneself, and, finally, for which also the nations, connected by one and the same destiny and by a common origin, might realise in themselves a unity in honour and in fidelity, above every particularistic ambition, every wild will to power and every pitfall lain by the secret forces of global subversion.

In this last aspect we find another reason for which the comprehension of the aristocratic spirit takes on a character of particular currency today — why it, rather than nourishing a flaccid conservatism, incites us to a return to the living tradition, why it does not instill sterile nostalgia for an exhausted past but excites a will which reaches toward a constructive future. From the considerations which we have briefly carried out here, one might even be led to the persuasion that a new manifestation of the aristocratic spirit, in a form fit to our times, in a substance still dynamic and volcanic and agitated by the tragic events of a necessary work of demolition which is yet in course, is a condition for preventing every negative, collectivising and materialising tendency, and for clarifying in an ever more precise way positive tendencies — those for which our movements have without doubt the meaning of a re-ascent, of reconstruction and of reanimation of the highest Aryan-European heritage.

OTHER BOOKS PUBLISHED BY ARKTOS

SRI DHARMA PRAVARTAKA ACHARYA	*The Dharma Manifesto*
JOAKIM ANDERSEN	*Rising from the Ruins: The Right of the 21st Century*
WINSTON C. BANKS	*Excessive Immigration*
ALAIN DE BENOIST	*Beyond Human Rights*
	Carl Schmitt Today
	The Indo-Europeans
	Manifesto for a European Renaissance
	On the Brink of the Abyss
	The Problem of Democracy
	Runes and the Origins of Writing
	View from the Right (vol. 1–3)
ARTHUR MOELLER VAN DEN BRUCK	*Germany's Third Empire*
MATT BATTAGLIOLI	*The Consequences of Equality*
KERRY BOLTON	*Revolution from Above*
	Yockey: A Fascist Odyssey
ISAC BOMAN	*Money Power*
RICARDO DUCHESNE	*Faustian Man in a Multicultural Age*
ALEXANDER DUGIN	*Ethnos and Society*
	Ethnosociology
	Eurasian Mission
	The Fourth Political Theory
	Last War of the World-Island
	Political Platonism
	Putin vs Putin
	The Rise of the Fourth Political Theory
EDWARD DUTTON	*Race Differences in Ethnocentrism*
MARK DYAL	*Hated and Proud*
CLARE ELLIS	*The Blackening of Europe*
KOENRAAD ELST	*Return of the Swastika*
JULIUS EVOLA	*The Bow and the Club*
	Fascism Viewed from the Right
	A Handbook for Right-Wing Youth
	Metaphysics of War
	The Myth of the Blood
	Notes on the Third Reich
	The Path of Cinnabar
	Recognitions
	A Traditionalist Confronts Fascism

OTHER BOOKS PUBLISHED BY ARKTOS

OTHER BOOKS PUBLISHED BY ARKTOS

OTHER BOOKS PUBLISHED BY ARKTOS

Ernst von Salomon	*It Cannot Be Stormed*
	The Outlaws
Piero San Giorgio	*CBRN: Surviving Chemical, Biological, Radiological & Nuclear Events*
	Giuseppe
Sri Sri Ravi Shankar	*Celebrating Silence*
	Know Your Child
	Management Mantras
	Patanjali Yoga Sutras
	Secrets of Relationships
George T. Shaw (ed.)	*A Fair Hearing*
Fenek Solère	*Kraal*
Oswald Spengler	*Man and Technics*
Richard Storey	*The Uniqueness of Western Law*
Tomislav Sunic	*Against Democracy and Equality*
	Homo Americanus
	Postmortem Report
	Titans are in Town
Askr Svarte	*Gods in the Abyss*
Hans-Jürgen Syberberg	*On the Fortunes and Misfortunes of Art in Post-War Germany*
Abir Taha	*Defining Terrorism*
	The Epic of Arya (2nd ed.)
	Nietzsche's Coming God, or the Redemption of the Divine
	Verses of Light
Jean Thiriart	*Europe: An Empire of 400 Million*
Bal Gangadhar Tilak	*The Arctic Home in the Vedas*
Dominique Venner	*For a Positive Critique*
	The Shock of History
Markus Willinger	*A Europe of Nations*
	Generation Identity
Alexander Wolfheze	*Alba Rosa*

Made in the USA
Las Vegas, NV
14 January 2024

84345446R10194